英語にない日本語を伝える
9つのテクニック

増補改訂
第2版

英語で
語る
ニッポン

コスモピア編集部 編

コスモピア

はじめに

　本書は、英語で日本の文化や習慣を世界に発信してみたいというかたがたに使っていただきたい本です。特に膨大な学習を必要とするのではなく、今の自分にできる範囲で、やさしい英語をうまく使って、手軽に発信できるようになる、これが本書のねらいです。

　例えば、あなたが日本に来たばかりの外国人と一緒に和風レストランで食事をしているとしましょう。相手に「（佃煮を指差しながら）これはなんですか？」と聞かれたらすぐに答えられますか？難しいですよね。

　実は私たちもこのような経験を何度もしました。なんとかうまく相手に伝えようといろいろと説明を試みても、説明を終えた後になぜかいつも不安感が残ります。「本当にわかってもらえたかな……」と。では、どうしたら上手く伝えられるのかというのが本書の原点です。

　そこでヒントを得るために、今までに知り合った外国人の先生や、知人の会話を参考に、ネイティブはどのように相手が知らないモノや状態を表現しているのかということに注目してみました。

「言い換える」
「わかりやすいやさしい言葉を使う」
「相手が理解しているか確認しながら話す」

　これです。この3点。「言い換える」というのは、すなわちほかの言葉（＝自分の知っている言葉）で説明するということ。これ

ができれば自然に「わかりやすいやさしい言葉を使う」ことになります。

　本書ではこの「説明する」ための手法に着目し、わかりやすく相手に伝えるためのテクニックを９つに分類しました。ひとつのモノ・コトを説明するのに、９つすべてのテクニックが必要というわけではありません。みなさんが何かを英語で発信しようと思うとき、本書で紹介している９つのテクニックをどれかしら思い出して使っていただけるようになれば幸いです。

　また、本書で紹介している説明文の中からうまい「言い換え」の例や表現方法を吸収して、実際にどんどん流用してみてください。いったん説明をし始めると、それにつなげることばが自然にでてくるかもしれません。

　また相手がいるからこそ成り立つのが会話です。相手が理解できているかどうか、これから説明しようとしているものをどれくらい知っているのか、など相手への投げかけも忘れずに。本書には相手と会話と続けるためのヒントもたくさん掲載していますので、実際に外国人と会話をしている気分で本書を読んでみてください。

　本書が外国のかたがたに日本のことを伝え、コミュニケーションを広げていくお役に立てば幸いです。

2023 年　3 月
コスモピア編集部

目次

第 1 部 ● ニッポンを語るためのテクニック

第 2 部 ● ニッポンを語ってみよう！

🛸 第四章 ● 現代ニッポン

🏆 **第七章● 伝統文化**

📷 第八章 ● 観光地

本書は、第一部『ニッポンを語るためのテクニック』、第二部『ニッポンを語ってみよう！』の2部にわかれています。

第一部では、日本についてのさまざまな事柄を英語で伝えるための9つのテクニックを紹介しています。そして第二部では、この9つのテクニックを使いながら実際の説明の例を取り上げます。第二部は説明だけではなく、豆知識やコミュニケーションに役立つ会話の質問例も紹介していますので、ぜひ参考にしてみてください。

基本ページ

他の単語に言い換えられる単語に * のマークがついています。語彙の学習に役立ちます。

ダウンロード音声（⇒ p.14）に対応するトラック番号です。

各項目を英語で説明している例文

日本語訳

マメ知識
各項目にまつわる雑学や単語についての補足を説明しています。

学校 ▶ Track 16

1年のサイクル

The school year starts in April and ends in March. Usually school entrance ceremonies are held in early April and graduation ceremonies are at the end of March.

学校の学年は4月に始まり3月に終わります。ふつう4月初めに入学式、3月の終わりに卒業式があります。

*school year = academic year

小中高の学期制度

In most cases, elementary, junior high and high school have three class terms. The first term is from April to July, the second is from September to December, and the third is from January to March. In between the terms are vacations. Recently there are more schools that use a two-semester system.

ほとんどの小学校、中学校、高校が3学期制をとっています。1学期は4月から7月、2学期は9月から12月、3学期は1月から3月です。各学期の間には休みがあります。最近は2学期制を採用する学校も増えてきています。

term
期間

two-semester
2学期制

マメ知識
小学校、中学校、高校をまとめて、schools at all three levels と言うこともある。

How long is the summer vacation in your home country? Usually we have about six weeks.
あなたの国では夏休みの長さはどれくらいありますか？　日本ではふつう、だいたい6週間です。

小・中・高の年数

Basically, it's the 6-3-3 system. Six years of elementary school, three years of junior high school, and three years of high school. Elementary and junior high school are compulsory. Since high school is not compulsory, students have to pass an admission exam to enter high school.

基本的には、6-3-3制です。小学校が6年間、中学校が3年間、高校が3年間です。小学校から中学校までは義務教育です。高校は義務教育ではないので、学校に行くためには生徒は入学試験に通る必要があります。

compulsory
義務の、必須の

admission exam
入学試験

102

語注

●基本的な流れ
1：9つのテクニックを知る
2：第二部で取り上げられている項目を読んでみる。
3：説明の例を参考にして自分だったらどのように言い換えるか、どのように説明できるか練習する。

●このほかにも……
日本人として知っておきたい知識や、英語についての補足情報をミニコラムで紹介。

> 🖐 **覚えておきましょう**
>
> 　着物は右の前身頃を体に沿って巻き込み、左前身頃を上からかぶせるように着ます。男女とも同じです。逆さは「左前」と呼ばれ、死者の装束に用います。着物文化に疎い現代人の中には、このルールを知らない人もいます。着付けがわかっている人でも、他人に着せるとなると（例えば外国人の友人に頼まれた場合）、自分に着せるのとは勝手が違いますので、襟を間違って合わせてしまう間違いを犯しがちです。「左前」は単純なミスではありますが、「縁起が悪い」と悪印象を残してしまうものです。人にゆかたや着物を着せるときは、必ず襟の合わせ方を念を入れて確認しましょう。

第一部で紹介している9つのテクニックに関連するアイコンです。
その項目の説明がどのようなテクニックを使っているかの目印にしてください。

🐚 中高一貫制度 〓 ❓

There are many top private schools with unified lower and upper secondary school systems. It's not a major system in public schools yet, but the numbers are gradually increasing. To enter these schools, children in elementary schools need to take an entrance exam. Recently, the students preparing for an entrance exam are increasing, especially in big cities like Tokyo and Osaka.

unified lower and upper secondary school
中高一貫校

　私立の上位校には、中高一貫制のところが多数あります。公立では中高一貫校はあまり多くありませんが、少しずつ増えてきています。中高一貫校に入学するためには、小学校の生徒は入学試験を受けます。最近では、中学入試の準備をする生徒たちが、とくに東京や大阪などの大都市周辺で増えてきています。

外国人が気になっていること、知りたいと思っているであろうこと、また日本人として外国人に教えてあげたい項目をピックアップし、Q&A形式で紹介しています。

Q&A

👤 高校はどのように選ぶのですか？　行きたい高校に行けるのですか？

👩 🗨🗨❓

It depends on what you plan to focus on for the future. Also, your academic performance in junior high school matters. There are several types of high schools, for example general academic high schools, specialized schools targeted for specific jobs in industry, and so on. Of course, schools are usually ranked by academic level.

academic
学校の、学業の

specific
具体的な、専門的な

　将来何に重点的に取り組みたいと考えているかによります。それから中学校での成績も関係してきます。高校にはいくつかのタイプがあります。例えば、普通高校や特定の職種につくための勉強をする専門学校などです。もちろん、それぞれの学校はたいてい学力によってランク付けされています。

会話コミュニケーションに役立つ質問の例や、補足情報についての会話例です。

➕ I've heard that high school is compulsory in some countries. How about your country?
　高校も義務教育に含まれる国があると聞いたのですが、あなたのところはどうですか？

第三章●教育・社会生活

103

11

このページに飛んで外国人の疑問や気になったこと
について説明するための例文をみてみましょう。

チャレンジ

チャレンジページでは自分で、そこに描かれているものを説明してみましょう。
次のページには回答例が掲載されていますが、なるべく自分で言い換えてみよう
と挑戦してみてください。クイズだと思って気軽にトライしてみましょう。

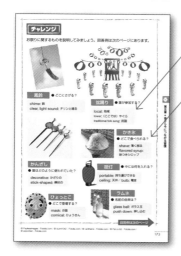

説明に使える用語のヒントです。

説明するときにどんなことに注目
したらよいかのヒントです。

チャレンジの回答例にも、会話コ
ミュニケーションの例があります。
会話を続ける気持ちが大切です！

音声を聞くには

[無料] 音声を聞く方法

音声をスマートフォンやパソコンで、
簡単に聞くことができます。

方法1 ストリーミング再生で聞く場合

面倒な手続きなしにストリーミング再生で聞くことができます。

このサイトに
アクセスするだけ！ **https://bit.ly/gao3q47**

※ストリーミング再生になりますので、通信制限などにご注意ください。
　また、インターネット環境がない状況でのオフライン再生はできません。
※アプリ等を使用して音声を聞きたい場合は、サイトの案内にしたがって
　端末を操作してください。

方法2 パソコンで音声ダウンロードする場合

パソコンで mp3 音声をダウンロードして、スマホなどに取り込む
ことも可能です。
※スマホなどへの取り込み方法はデバイスによって異なります。
※お使いの機種によっては音声を正常に取り込めない場合がございます。

1 下記のサイトにアクセス

https://www.cosmopier.com/download/4864541909

2 パスワードの【S86Y7TG3】を入力する

音声は一括ダウンロード用圧縮ファイル（ZIP 形式）でのご提供です。解凍し
てお使いください。

電子版を使うには

音声ダウンロード不要
ワンクリックで音声再生！

本書購読者は電子版を
無料でご使用いただけます！
音声付きで
本書がそのままスマホでも
読めます。

電子版のダウンロードには
クーポンコードが必要です

詳しい手順は下記をご覧ください。
右下の QR コードからもアクセスが
可能です。

電子版無料引換クーポンコード
8wt4kv

ブラウザベース（HTML5 形式）でご利用
いただけます。

★クラウドサーカス社 ActiBook 電子書籍
　（音声付き）です。

●対応機種
・PC（Windows/Mac）　・iOS（iPhone/iPad）
・Android（タブレット、スマートフォン）

電子版ご利用の手順

❶以下 URL より、本書電子版の商品ページにアクセス
してください。

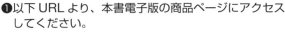
https://www.cosmopier.net/products/detail/1719

❷「カートに入れる」をクリックしてください。

❸「カートへ進む」→「レジに進む」と進み、「ご注文手続き」画面へ。

　※「ご注文手続き」画面に進むには、コスモピア・オンラインショップでの
　　会員登録（無料）・ログインが必要です。

❹「クーポン」欄に、本ページにある電子版無料引換クーポンコードを入力し、
「確認する」をクリックしてください。

❺０円になったのを確認してから、「注文する」をクリックしてください。

❻ ご注文完了後、「マイページ」の「購入した電子書籍・ダウンロード商品の閲覧」
にて、本書電子版を閲覧することができます。

第一部

ニッポンを語るためのテクニック

説明する どういうこと❓

　英語で日本を説明するということは、異なる文化圏 から日本にやって来た外国人に日本を伝えるということです。つまり、外国人に自分の国の伝統や習慣を紹介する、ということ。母語を共有しない人に自国の文化を伝えるとはどういうことか、まずその状況をイメージしてみましょう。

　あなたはイギリスの友人の家にホームステイをしています。朝食に見たことのない食べ物が並べられました。

あなた
What's this?

家の人
It's porridge, a traditional breakfast in Britain. It's a soft food made by boiling oats in milk or water. It's eaten hot. It's a little like *okayu*.

© JJAVA - Fotolia.com

　このように説明してくれるのではないでしょうか。ポーリッジという固有名詞の指しているものが伝わらないため、まずそれが何なのか（この場合は朝食）、そしてそれはあなたが知っている「おかゆ」というものに似ていて、さらにどのように調理されるのかを補足しています。

　つまりお互いの共通認識にはない「ポーリッジ」という言葉を、さまざまなアプローチで説明しているのです。ここでは３つのテクニックが使われました。まず、大きく分類した場合の属性（→ *p*.18）、次に見た目や調理方法の特徴（→ *p*.19）、さらに似ている食べもの提示（→ *p*.20）です。このように、わかりやすい説明にはいくつかのテクニックがあります。このテクニックを頭に入れておくと、難しい専門用語を知らなくても、説明するときに必ず役に立ちます。

ニッポンを語るためのテクニック

パラフレーズ

　パラフレーズとは言いたい単語や表現がうまく思い浮かばないときのための戦略（ストラテジー）です。英語でなんとかコミュニケーションを成立させようするとき、誰もが無意識のうちにこのストラテジーを使っています（もちろん日本語でもこのテクニックは使われています）。日本語では「言い換え」と訳されます。「ポーリッジ」の例で使われていた3つの方法もパラフレーズです。

　パラフレーズにはほかにも以下のようなものがあります。それぞれの内容については、次ページ以降で順にご紹介していきます。

1. ▽ …… 上位概念に置き換える
2. = …… 実態を伝える
3. 🔖 …… 似たものを提示、比較する、具体例を挙げる
   ✖ …… 否定する
4. 📖 …… 日本語の意味を説明する
5. USE …… 用途・使い方・使われ方を説明する
6. 🔧 …… 素材・構成要素を説明する

情報の補足

　また、外国人に日本的なもの・習慣・事情を理解してもらうためには、言い換えるだけではなく、どうしてそうなのかという理由や背景を説明する必要があります。そのような場合は、自分の知っている情報から、重要だと思う要点をピックアップして補足するようにしましょう。

7. ? …… 理由・原因を説明する
8. ✏ …… ルーツ・歴史を説明する

情報の整理

　聞き手が、頭の中で話を理解しやすいように、話の構成にもひと工夫してみましょう。複数の例や動作の手順があるときに使えるテクニックです。

9. 1,2 …… 順番や要点を整理する

では、それぞれのテクニックについて詳しく見てみましょう。

1. 上位概念に置き換える

　これはパラフレーズの基本中の基本です。言いたい単語がすぐにわからないとき、まずその上位にあたる言葉に置き換えます。例えば、「ぶどう」ならフルーツ（fruit）、「草履」なら履き物（footwear）、「総理大臣」なら人（person）という具合です。この上位概念を提示することで、これから説明される対象のイメージがグッとつかみやすくなります。

表現の例

● It's a...　　それは〜です。
Unagi is a fish. A long, thin fish.
ウナギは魚です。細長い魚です。

● (It's a) Japanese...　　日本の〜です。
A *geisha* is a Japanese performer.
芸者は日本の芸人です。

● (It's a) kind of...　　〜のようなものです。／〜の一種です。
Karuta is a kind of card game.
カルタはカードゲームのようなものです。

● (It's) one of...　　〜のひとつです。
Shibuya is one of the popular areas in Tokyo.
渋谷は東京の人気のある場所のひとつです。

2. 実態を伝える

　ある特定の言葉や用語、あるいは動作や概念などあらゆるものをさらにかみ砕いて表現します。これは発想転換ゲームのようなもので、自分の頭の中で日本語として定着している言葉を別の言い方で言い換えていきます。

　例えば「消えるボールペン」の場合、It's an erasable pen. と言うことができます。それは pen であって、さらにどんなことができるかというと erasable（消すことができる）という説明です。

　つまり、説明しようとしているものの特徴を挙げることで、それが何なのかさらに詳しく説明し、ほぼイコール（＝）の状態となるようにすることです。

> 説明しようとしているもの　＝　その特徴を言い換えた説明
> （関係がほぼ等しい）

　もちろんひとつのセンテンスでいくつもの特徴を挙げるのは無理があるので、どんどんセンテンスを足して、イメージを作り上げていきましょう。

説明の例　●お神輿

A *mikoshi* is a portable shrine.

お神輿は移動式神社です。

●畳

Tatami are woven floor mats. They're made from a plant called *igusa*.

「畳」は床に敷くマットです。イグサという植物でできています。

●天狗

Tengu is an imaginary creature with a red face and a long nose.

天狗は赤い顔と長い鼻を持った伝説上の生き物です。

ワンポイント

説明の補足には以下のような関係代名詞もよく使われます。

● A is a B [that / who / which]...　　A は〜する B だ

天狗については以下のようにも言えます。
Tengu is an imaginary creature that has a red face and a long nose.

---

3. 似たものを提示、比較する、具体例を挙げる

　次のテクニックは、そっくりなもの、似ているものを提示することです。そしてさらに、それを比較してどこがどのように違うのか、どんなものがあるのかという例も補足していきます。

　ここでのポイントは「相手がすでに知っていると思われるモノ」を例とすること。もちろん類似を提供するためには、比較できる対象をたくさん知っているほうが有利ですね。日ごろから、相手の国の文化や世界中の文化に目を向けて、似たもの同士をストックしておきましょう。

表現の例

● like... ～のような、～のように ／ look like...　～のように見える

Tsumire are fish meatballs. They look just like other kinds of meatballs.

「つみれ」は魚のミートボールです。見た目もミートボールに似ています。

● ...is similar to... ～に似ている

The rules of *shogi* are similar to the rules of chess.

将棋のルールはチェスのルールに似ています。

● the same as... ～と同じ ／ almost the same as... ほとんど～と同じもの

Shinkeisuijaku is the same card game as Memory.

神経衰弱は Memory と同じカードゲームです。

否定もテクニック

　ここで併せて覚えておきたいのが否定のテクニックです。「AはBではない」という情報を与えることは、類似の例を挙げるのと同じくらいの効果があります。

　例えば「寿司」を外国人に伝えるとき、以下のように伝えるとわかりやすいのです。外国人の中にはお寿司とお刺身が同等のものだと考えている人も少なくありません。

● *Sushi* is not raw fish.
　寿司はお刺身ではありません。

● A *sento* is not the same as an *onsen*.
　銭湯は温泉と同じものではありません。

4. 日本語の意味を説明する

　単純に日本語でそれがどういう意味なのかを伝えるという方法も有効です。日本人でも、漢字を見ればそれがどういうものなのかイメージできることがあります。例えば、漢字が読める中国人は「足湯」が何かをを知らなくても、それが何を意味しているのか理解できるでしょう。英語で伝える場合は、漢字をそのまま提示するわけにはいきませんが、同じ方法で説明することができます。

表現の例

● literally 「文字通りには」

Ashi-yu literally means "foot bath."

足湯とは足のお風呂という意味です。

● ...means... 「(英語で言うと)〜という意味」

Setsubun means "seasonal division."

節分は(英語で言うと)「季節の節目」という意味です。

● refer to... 「〜を指す」

In Japan, "half" refers to someone whose parents have different nationalities.

日本でハーフというのは、両親の国籍が異なる人を指します。

英単語も増やしましょう

　もちろん、説明しようと思っているモノの英語がわかれば、それに越したことはありません。ですから、本書の中では英語に置き換えられる単語も紹介していきます。「これは英語で何て言うんだろう」と気になる言葉があったら、辞書で調べてみましょう。

例

　ちなみに左ページに登場したトランプのカードゲームの名前は次のようなものがあります。

● **Memory / Concentration** 神経衰弱
● **Old Maid** ババ抜き
● **Sevens** 7並べ
● **Cheat / I Doubt It** ダウト

5. 用途、使い方・使われ方を説明する

このテクニックは、普段自分がどのようにそれを使っているか、もしくは利用しているかという体験が生きてきます。というのは、モノだけでなく、お店や交通手段、ゲームの遊び方などにも使えるテクニックだからです。

ひとつ例を挙げましょう。例えば「押し入れ」を説明する場合、押し入れはクローゼットのようなものですが、実際には「洋服を保管する」というよりも、「布団を保管する」という用途のほうが一般的です。説明する対象にもよりますが、そのものの見た目よりも、どのように使われているのかということのほうが重要な場合も多くあります。

表現の例

● for... 〜のために

An *oshiire* is a convenient space for storing *futons* —Japanese bedding.

押し入れは日本の寝具である「ふとん」を入れるのに便利なスペースです。

● ...is used to/for... 〜のために使われる

The *tokonoma* is used to display decorations.

床の間は飾りを置くために使われます。

● to...　〜するための、〜するために

We take a bath not only to get clean, but to relax.

私たちは清潔になるためだけでなく、リラックスするためにもお風呂に入ります。

さらに具体的な例

● はっぴ

Happi is a kind of a jacket. We wear it at festivals.

はっぴはジャケットのようなものです。お祭りのときに着ます。

● 絵馬

Ema is a piece of wood with a picture of a horse. We write our wish on the back and hang it up on a board at a shrine.

絵馬はウマの絵が描かれた木の板です。その後ろに願い事を書いて、お寺の板版に吊るします。

6. 素材・構成要素を説明する

これはテクニックの中で最も単純なものと言えるかもしれません。説明しようとしているものが何から作られているのか、またはどのように作られているのかといった工程を説明します。

このテクニックが最も多く登場するのは第一章「食」(p.33～) の項目です。料理の話題では、必ず材料や調理方法に触れる部分がでてきます。例えば「肉じゃが」を説明するのであれば、使用する具材と調味料、それから「煮る」という調理方法でどんなものかイメージできますね。もちろん「食」以外のテーマでも幅広く流用できるテクニックです。

表現の例 ● made from... ～で作られる

Udon is made from wheat flour.

うどんは小麦粉から作られます。

● made of... ～でできている

A *kokeshi* is a Japanese doll made of wood.

こけしは木でできた日本の人形です。

● made with... (～を使って) 作られる

This cake is made with *kinako* powder.

このケーキはきな粉を使って作られています。

---

made of... / made from... / made with... の違い

上記に挙げた made of... と made from... は似ているようで、実は使い分けがあります。「うどん」には made from... がぴったりですが「こけし」には使いません。なぜか。それは素材が目で見てわかるものと、そうでないものという区別があります。うどんの素材が小麦粉だとは目ではわかりませんが、こけしの素材は木だとわかります。どちらを使ってもネイティブに「～で作られている」という意味では伝わるでしょう。また、made with... は素材にも使えますが「～を使って」というニュアンスが含まれるので、道具などにも使えます。

× *Udon* is made of wheat flour.
× A *kokeshi* is a Japanese doll made from wood.

7. 理由・原因を説明する

　　自分の知らない文化や状況に出会ったとき、誰もが「なぜ？　どうして？」という疑問を抱くでしょう。外国人にとっての日本は「なぜ？　どうして？」の塊です。私たちが外国の文化や習慣に抱く疑問も同じです。

　　もちろん専門的な解説でなくてかまいません。自分の知っている範囲で答えられる、できる限りの情報を盛り込んであげましょう。「日本人はどうしてお辞儀ばかりするの？」というような答えるのに悩ましい質問もあると思います。そのようなときは、個人的な意見や考えも織り交ぜて会話を膨らまし、お互いに意見交換するようにすると会話もさらに弾みます。

表現の例

● ..., because... なぜなら〜

We wear masks because we don't want to spread our cold germs.

マスクを着用するのは、風邪ウイルスをばらまきたくないからです。

● because of... 　〜という理由で、〜なので

We have many hot springs in Japan, because of the volcanoes.

火山があるので、日本には温泉がたくさんあります。

● The reason is... 　その理由は

The number 4 is bad luck in Japan. The reason is that the word for 4, "shi," sounds like the word for death in Japanese.

日本では数字の 4 は縁起が悪ものとされています。理由は、日本語の 4 (shi) の音は、日本語の死を意味する言葉と同じ音だからです。

8. ルーツ・歴史を説明する

伝統的なモノや行事を説明する場合には、時代をさかのぼってその起源を説明することが必要な場合が多くあります。特に観光で日本を訪れる外国人は、歴史的な建築物や伝統的な文化体験に興味のある方が多いはずなので、歴史的な説明を求めていることもあるでしょう。

説明の例　●ラーメン

Ramen is originally from China.

ラーメンはもともと中国から伝わりました。

●大仏

The *daibutsu* in Kamakura was built in the Kamakura period. The year was 1252.

鎌倉の大仏は鎌倉時代に作られました。1252年です。

便利フレーズ

- **was founded in...**
  ～に見つかる
- **is based on...**
  ～に基づいている

- **originated in...**
  ～に起源をもつ、～に生まれた、
- **originally...**
  最初は、もともとは

- **introduced in the (14th century)**
  (14世紀に) にもたらされた
- **in the (Edo) period**
  (江戸) 時代に

今と昔を比較する

歴史的な説明となると、「昔は～だったけれど、今は～になっている」という流れにもなるでしょう。また、ルーツ以外の話題としても、さまざまな種類やジャンルがある中で、一般的な例を持ち出して紹介することが多くあります。そのようなときに使えるフレーズを集めました。これもぜひ覚えておいてください。

例

- **usually**　たいていは
- **generally / in general**　ふつうは、一般的には
- **commonly**　ふつうは
- **typical**　典型的な、よくある
- **traditionally**　昔から、伝統的に
- **nowadays**　今は、最近は
- **It's a custom to...**　～が習慣となっている
- **is considered...**　～と考えられている

9. 順序や要点を整理する

　相手が頭の中で整理しやすいように、話し手が要点を整理しておくことも とても大切です。わかりやすい表現や言い換えがうまくできたとしても、そ れを伝える全体のストーリーと構成がばらばらではいちばん伝えたいことが 明確にならない可能性があります。そうならないように、話し手がしっかり と要点と順番を整理して説明しましょう。

ケース1 順序や要点を整理する

　ゲームの遊び方や、電車の乗り方、銭湯の入り方などは、その行為の順を 追ってストーリーのように伝えます。「最初に」「次に」「最後に」と順序を 整理して話しましょう。

例　コンビニおにぎりの開け方

You can usually find the numbers 1, 2, and 3 on an *onigiri* package.
First, you pull down the strip marked 1.
Next, you pull the corners marked 2 and 3, in that order.
Then, the package will be completely removed.

おにぎりのパッケージに1、2、3と番号が付いているのがわかるはずです。
まず、1番のマークの印のところをひっぱります。
次に2番と3番のマークの角をひっぱります。
すると、すべてのパッケージがきれいにはがれます。

ケース2 要点を絞る

　話す際にすでに要点が把握できている場合は、最初に要点の数を伝えます。

There are two customs you should know about.

覚えておいたほうが良いマナーがふたつあります。

表現の例

- **First**
  まず
- **The first step is**
  最初のステップは
- **Next**
  次に

- **Then**
  それから
- **After that**
  その後は

- **Finally**
  最後に
- **Last(ly)**
  最後に
- **In the end**
  終わりに

チャレンジ

では、ここで説明にチャレンジ。写真を見ながら、それぞれについてテクニックを使って説明してみましょう。

1. 折り鶴

● 折り紙で作る

crane: 鶴
fold: 折る

2. そろばん

● 昔の計算機
● 長方形で玉がついている

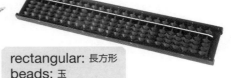

rectangular: 長方形
beads: 玉
calculator: 計算機

3. 夏目漱石

● 19 世紀から 20 世紀に生きていた人
● 作家
● 有名な作品は？

novelist: 小説家

4. インスタントみそ汁の作り方

● まず、味噌と乾燥野菜をお椀に入れる

● 次に、お湯を注ぐ
● ちょっとかき混ぜて、少し待ったら食べられます

open up: 開ける／mix: 混ぜる

5. 絵馬

● 神社やお寺で買える
● どんな風に使う？

wish: 願い事
hang up: かける
（下げておく）

回答例は次のページ

27

1 折り鶴 ▽ 🖍

Orizuru are folded paper cranes. They're usually made with *origam.*
paper.　折り鶴とは、紙で折られた鶴です。ふつう折り紙で作ります。

2 そろばん ▽ = USE

A *soroban* is a traditional kind of calculator. It has a rectangular
frame and rows of sliding beads. You calculate by sliding the beads.

そろばんは昔ながらの計算機です。長方形のフレームの中に動く玉が付いています。その玉
を動かしながら計算をします。　※英語で「そろばん」は abacus。

3 夏目漱石 ▽ 📖

Natsume Soseki is one of the most famous Japanese novelists. He
lived in the 19th and early 20th centuries. Some of his best known
books are *Kokoro*, *Botchan*, and *I Am a Cat*.

夏目漱石は日本の有名な小説家のひとりです。19 世紀から 20 世紀初旬の人で、著書に『こ
ころ』『坊っちゃん』『吾輩は猫である』などがあります。

4 インスタントみそ汁の作り方 [1．2]

To make instant *miso* soup, first you put the *miso* and dried
vegetables into a bowl. Then you add hot water. After mixing them,
wait until the vegetables go back to their normal size, usually about
one minute. Then the soup is ready to eat.

インスタントみそ汁を作るには、まず、みそと乾燥野菜をお椀に入れます。それから熱湯を
注ぎます。混ぜてから、乾燥野菜が通常の大きさになるまで待ちます。おそらく 1 分くらい
ですね。そうしたら食べて大丈夫です。

5 絵馬 ▽ 📄 USE ✏

Ema are wooden boards that you can buy at shrines and temples.
The *kanji* mean "picture" and "horse," but the pictures are not always
horses. You can write a wish on the back of the board and hang it up
in a special place. The reason for the name *ema* is that people used to
offer horses to shrines and temples in ancient times.

絵馬は神社や寺で買う木の板です。漢字は「絵」と「馬」を意味していますが、描かれてい
る絵はさまざまです。板の後ろに願い事を書いて決まった場所に掛けておきます。絵馬とよば
れる理由は、昔の人々はウマを神社やお寺に奉納していたためです。

コミュニケーションを深めるためのコツ

完璧な文法、正しい単語を追及しない

　異なる国、異なる文化圏から日本に来た人たちには「あれは何？」「どうしてそうなるの？」という疑問がたくさんあるでしょう。コミュニケーションの基本は会話です。会話コミュニケーションはテストではありませんから、まずテストで求められるような正しい文法、正しい単語を使おうという意識を捨てるところから始めましょう。自分の知っている単語で、相手に伝えてあげようという意識と、ここまでに説明したテクニックを押さえておけば十分にコミュニケーションは成立します。

オリジナルの情報を入れてあげる

　ひとつの話題から話を広げるために、話題に関連する情報をどんどん提供してあげましょう。自分の国のことだからこそ気がつくお役立ちポイントがたくさんあるはずです。自分の経験から言えることや、ちょっとした雑学でも外国人にとっては新鮮な情報となります。缶ビールと発泡酒の見分け方や、餃子はポン酢につけてもおいしいなど、自分だからこそ教えてあげられる情報を大切にしましょう。

会話をふくらませるための質問を相手にしてみる

　自分の言いたいことだけ言って会話が終わってしまうのは悲しいですよね。話の流れに乗って自分からも相手に質問してみましょう。日本の文化と相手の国の文化との違い、相手の国の行事や習慣など、話の展開方法は無限大です。興味のあることをどんどん聞いて会話を弾ませてください。本書では、例文のところどころに「話を展開させるポイント」として、質問の例を載せています。

相手がそのモノ・ことを知っているか確認する

　説明のレベルは相手の知識によって左右される部分が大きくあります。寿司や着物は英語でも sushi、kimono として知られている言葉ですから、すでにそれを知っている外国人に説明する必要はないかもしれません。また、銭湯を説明するための例として温泉と比較することができますが、これは相手が温泉とは何かを知っていることが前提となります。

　そのようなときは、迷わず自分から聞いてみましょう。「温泉を知っていますか？」とひと言聞いてから説明することで、よりスムーズな会話ができます。

表現の例

● Do you know (about) ... ？　〜を知っていますか？
● Have you ever heard of... ？　〜を聞いたことがありますか？
● Have you ever tried... ？　〜を試したことはありますか？

相手に伝えたいという気持ちを最大限に出すこと

　どうしても言いたい言葉が出てこないときは、何でもありです。言葉以外にもコミュニケーションのツールはあります。大切なのは「伝えたい」という気持ちです。ジェスチャーで表してもいいですし、絵に描いて見せてあげるのもよいでしょう。最近は携帯で簡単にインターネットに接続することができますから、お手上げのときは調べて写真や画像を見せてあげることも可能です。

第二部

ニッポンを語ってみよう！

音声トラック表

第二部「ニッポンを語ってみよう！」の音声は弊社公式サイトよりダウンロードすることができます。ダウンロードの詳しい方法につきましては *p.14*「音声ダウンロードにつきまして」をご覧ください。

Track No.　　内容

Track No.	内容	Track No.	内容	Track No.	内容
1	OPENING		第四章 ● 現代ニッポン	52	その他の感覚
	第一章 ● 食	26	現代を代表する街		第七章 ● 伝統文化
2	食事のマナー	27	現代文化	53	華道
3	寿司	28	芸能・娯楽	54	茶道
4	豆腐・納豆	29	新幹線	55	お茶会の基本マナー
5	調味料・だし	30	割安な旅行手段	56	書道
6	大衆料理	31	現代の生活習慣	57	俳句と短歌
7	大衆料理・おでん	32	現代的な表現	58	百人一首
8	そば・うどん・ラーメン		第五章 ● 昔から今につながる習慣	59	百人一首の遊び方
9	酒・居酒屋	33	国民の祝日カレンダー	60	遊び
10	その他	34	着物と浴衣	61	相撲
	第二章 ● 住まい・生活	35	お花見	62	柔道
11	住宅・家	36	祭り	63	剣道
12	和室・家のつくり	37	祭り（チャレンジ）	64	折り紙
13	家具・室内用品	38	七五三	65	和紙
14	風呂	39	お見合い	66	和太鼓
15	トイレ	40	幸運を呼ぶアイテム	67	舞台芸能
	第三章 ● 教育・社会生活	41	葬儀	68	能
16	学校	42	結婚式	69	狂言
17	学生服	43	お中元とお歳暮	70	文楽
18	学校外での勉強	44	お金を贈る習慣	71	歌舞伎
19	就職活動	45	その他習慣	72	落語
20	会社と人間関係		第六章 ● 価値観・考え方		第八章 ● 観光地
21	ゴミの捨て方	46	時間の感覚	73	寺
22	街の中	47	集団性	74	神社
23	バス・電車	48	謙虚の感覚	75	お寺・神社の参拝の仕方
24	警察・消防・病院	49	お辞儀の習慣	76	大仏
25	文字	50	お礼の感覚	77	温泉
		51	空気を読む	78	有名な場所

第一章 ● 食

食辞典 ❶
日本の代表的な食べ物

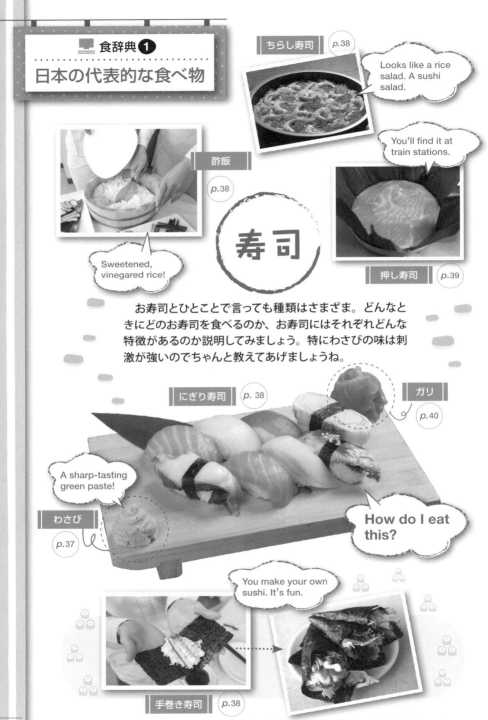

ちらし寿司 *p.*38

Looks like a rice salad. A sushi salad.

You'll find it at train stations.

酢飯 *p.*38

押し寿司 *p.*39

Sweetened, vinegared rice!

寿司

お寿司とひとことで言っても種類はさまざま。どんなときにどのお寿司を食べるのか、お寿司にはそれぞれどんな特徴があるのか説明してみましょう。特にわさびの味は刺激が強いのでちゃんと教えてあげましょうね。

にぎり寿司 *p.* 38

ガリ *p.*40

A sharp-tasting green paste!

わさび *p.*37

How do I eat this?

You make your own sushi. It's fun.

手巻き寿司 *p.*38

大豆ファミリーにはこんなにたくさんの仲間がいます。豆腐、醤油、納豆、みそ、などそれぞれの食品は知っているけれど、原材料がすべて大豆だと知っている外国人は多くないかもしれません。特に枝豆が大豆だということを意外に感じる人が多いようです。

大豆

Momen? *Kinu*? How are they different?

豆腐　*p.*43

I'm from the soybean family too.

枝豆

I'm king of the *neba-neba* foods.

納豆　*p.*43

醤油　*p.*46

The king of Japanese flavorings. I'm from the soybean family.

If you ferment soybeans...

湯葉　*p.*45

A liquid form of tofu.

豆乳　*p.*45

みそ　*p.*46

Yuba is like a sheet of tofu.

食事のマナー

■ いただきます [USE]

We never start eating without saying "*Itadakimasu*." We often say it out loud, but sometimes we just say it in our head or whisper it. *Itadakimasu* is like part of the meal.

食事の前には「いただきます」と言います。声にだして言うこともあれば、頭の中で言うだけだったり、つぶやきながらだったりもします。「いただきます」は食事の一部のようなものです。

「いただきます」を英語に直訳すると、I humbly recieve.。humbly は「謙遜して」という意味があり、謙虚な姿勢を表している

■ ごちそうさま [✍][USE]

"*Gochisosama*" literally means "I have received," so when you say it you're thanking the person who has made the meal for you.

「ごちそうさまでした」は「いただきました」という意味で、食事を作ってくれた人への感謝の気持ちを表します。

➕ **What do you do before and after a meal in your home country?**
あなたの国では食事の前後にどんな習慣がありますか？

■ 食事中のマナー 🔊📖[¹₂]

Firstly, we pick up our bowls when we eat. Secondly, when we eat noodles like *ramen*, we slurp — we make a sound. Slurping your noodles is totally accepted here – in fact it's considered normal.

まず、私たちはお椀を持ちあげて食べます。次に、ラーメンなどの麺類を食べるときは、すする音をたてながら食べます。麺類を食べるときに音をたてるのは、日本では当たり前のこととして受け入れられています。

slurp
音をたてて（ズルズルと）食べる

accept
受け入れる

➕ **You don't make a sound when you eat pasta, do you?**
パスタは音を立てて食べませんよね？

Q&A

 食事中にしてはいけないことはなんですか？

There are three basic etiquette rules when using chopsticks. First, never stick your chopsticks straight up* in your bowl of rice. This reminds Japanese people of funerals, where a pair of chopsticks standing vertically in the rice is placed on an altar. Secondly, don't pass food directly from your chopsticks to another person's chopsticks, because this is also associated with funerals. Lastly, never point at people or things with your chopsticks.

*straight up = vertically
（垂直に、まっすぐに）

altar
（宗教行事で使われる）
祭壇、お供物台

associated with...
〜と関係がある、〜を連想させる

お箸の使い方に3つのエチケットがあります。まず、お箸をご飯に立ててはいけません。お葬式ではご飯にお箸が垂直に立てられたお椀が祭壇に置かれるため、この行為はお葬式を思わせてしまいます。次に、自分のお箸と誰かのお箸で直接食べ物を受け渡ししてはいけません。これもお葬式に関する行為だからです。最後に、お箸で人や物を指してはいけません。

第一章 ● 食

 寿司

▶ Track 03

 わさび

Wasabi is a sharp-tasting* green paste that's used in sushi. It's a grated plant root, similar to horseradish. A little bit of *wasabi* is spread between the rice and the sashimi. The taste is too sharp for some people. If you're one of those people, you can ask for no *wasabi*.

*sharp-tasting = hot
（ツンとする、辛い）

grate
すりつぶす

わさびは辛い緑色のペーストで、寿司に使われています。根菜をすりおろしたもので、セイヨウワサビによく似ています。わさびはご飯と刺身の間に少しだけ入っています。刺激が強すぎると感じる人もいるでしょう。もし刺激的な味が苦手だったら、わさびを抜くようにお願いすることもできます。

英語で Japanese horseradish「日本版セイヨウワサビ」と表現することもできる。

37

🖥 酢飯 （=）🔫

Sumeshi is sweetened, vinegared rice. You add sugar and vinegar to hot rice and mix it. Most kinds of sushi are made with *sumeshi*.

酢飯とは、甘酸っぱい味のご飯です。温かいご飯に砂糖と酢を入れて混ぜます。ほとんどの寿司は酢飯で作られています。

🖥 にぎり寿司 （=）🈁🈂✖

First of all, sushi isn't sashimi. Sashimi is raw fish. The most well known kind of sushi, *nigiri zushi*, is vinegared rice with certain foods like sashimi placed on top of it. You can eat sushi with chopsticks. It's also perfectly OK to eat sushi with your fingers.

まず、寿司は刺身ではありません。刺身とは生の魚のことです。最も有名な寿司、握り寿司はお刺身などを酢飯の上にのせたものです。お箸で寿司を食べてもよいですし、手で寿司をつまんで食べても OK です。

raw fish
生の魚

certain
（特定できるが名前が断定できない）ある、例の

マメ知識

「寿司は刺身ではない」という否定から入るのがポイント。外国人の中には寿司＝刺身だと思っている人も少なくない。

🖥 ちらし寿司 （▽）🈁🔫

Chirashi zushi is a type of sushi. It looks like a rice salad. Vinegared rice is spread out in a dish. Different kinds of seafood and other ingredients are placed on top of the rice. They can be mixed in, too. We often take *chirashi zushi* to a picnic, or eat it on special days like *hinamatsuri* – Girls' Day.

ちらし寿司は寿司の一種です。ご飯で作られたサラダのように見えるかもしれません。お皿に酢飯を平たくよそいます。その上に魚介類やほかの食材をのせます。混ぜても OK です。ちらし寿司はピクニックに持っていくこともあれば、女の子の日であるひな祭りのような特別な日に食べたりします。

ingredient
材料

🖥 手巻き寿司 （=）🔫

Temaki zushi is hand-rolled sushi. You put dried laver seaweed, vinegared rice, and sashimi out on the table separately. You can make your own *temaki zushi* by rolling up the rice and sashimi in the seaweed. It's often served at house parties.

dried laver seaweed
海苔

手巻き寿司は手で巻く寿司です。海苔、酢飯、刺身をテーブルの上に分けて用意しておきます。海苔の上にご飯と刺身をのせて、自分でそれを巻いて手巻き寿司を作ります。ホームパーティによく出されます。

📺 押し寿司

Oshizushi means pressed sushi. A small wooden box is used to press the sushi into certain shapes. *Oshizushi* is usually sold at train stations and souvenir shops in rural areas.

押し寿司は「プレスした寿司」という意味です。小さな木の箱に寿司を入れて適切な形に型をとります。地方の駅やお土産物屋でいろいろな押し寿司が売られていますよ。

マメ知識
バッテラ（mackerel）、鱒寿司（trout）が有名。

第一章 ● 食

rural
田舎の

➕ **Do you have sushi in your home country? What is it like?**
あなたの国でも寿司を食べますか？　それはどんなものですか？

📺 恵方巻

Eho-maki is a kind of big sushi roll that looks almost the same as a normal sushi roll. Originally, eating *eho-maki* was part of a ritual in the Kansai area on *setsubun*. People eat an *eho-maki* roll which contains seven ingredients symbolizing the Seven Gods of Fortune, facing in the lucky direction of the year.

ritual
行事

「恵方巻」は太巻き寿司の一種で、通常の巻き寿司とほとんど同じように見えます。もともと恵方巻を食べるのは、関西で節分の行事の一環としてでした。長い恵方巻には7種類の具材が使われており、それらは七福神を象徴しています。人々はそれを、その年の縁起の良い方角を向いて食べるのです。

➕ *Eho-maki* is quite big, but it is said that you have to eat it without cutting it into slices.
恵方巻って本当に太いんです、でも切り分けず一本そのまま食べるのが正しいと言われています。

■ ガリ (=) (USE)

Gari is a side dish of pickled ginger eaten with sushi. At sushi restaurants it's usually in a little box on the table. When you buy pre-packaged sushi, there's often some *gari* in the package.

ガリは寿司に合うショウガの漬物です。寿司屋では、たいていテーブルの上の小さな入れものにガリが用意してあります。外でパックされた寿司を買うとガリも一緒に入っています。

Q&A

  回転寿司のシステムを教えてください。

When you go to a *kaiten-zushi* restaurant, you sit either at a counter or in a booth. There is a conveyor belt running around the restaurant with plates of sushi on it, and you just take the type of sushi you want. Meanwhile, you can make green tea with the tea powder and hot water provided at your table.

booth
ボックス席、ブース

meanwhile
その間に。ここでは「食事をしている間に」という意味。

マメ知識

「回転しながらものを運ぶベルト」という意味では、rotating conveyor belt がベスト。conveyor は「搬送装置」。

回転寿司に行くと、まず、カウンターの席かボックス席に案内されます。お寿司の皿をのせて回転しているベルトがあり、そこから食べたいお寿司をとります。食事中は、テーブルに用意されているお湯と粉末のお茶で緑茶を作ることができます。

 覚えておきましょう

イタリック表記の意味

英語にとって外来語にあたる言葉はイタリックで書く、というルールがあります。ですから、この本で紹介している日本の言葉はイタリックで表記しています。しかし、もともとは日本語だけれども、英語圏でも標準的に使用されている sushi や tofu のような言葉は、英語の一部と見なされ、イタリックではなく標準の文字で表記されるようになりました。

Q&A

（回転ずし屋にて、タッチパネルを見ながら）これはなんですか？

It's a touch screen panel for placing an order. When you don't see what you want on the conveyor belt, you can order from it. After a minute or two, you'll see your order on the conveyor belt with an "ordered" card on it. Don't forget to take your order from the belt!

注文用のタッチパネルですよ。食べたいものが回転ベルトの上にないときは、パネルから注文できます。1、2分後には、注文した寿司が「注文」カードを添えられてベルトの上に流れてきます。注文した料理をとり忘れないように！

マメ知識

タッチパネルは和製英語。touch panel でも通じますが、正確には touch screen panel と言います。

➕ Be careful not to take an "ordered" dish. If you do, you'll be stealing someone else's order!

自分の注文した料理ではない皿をとらないように注意！　だれかの注文を横どりしていることになっちゃいますよ。

●寿司ネタの名称

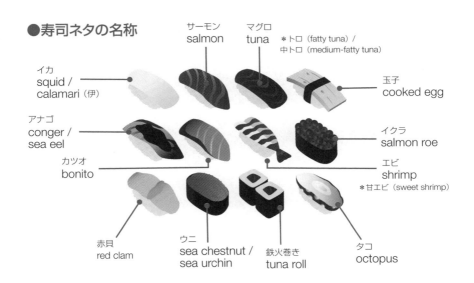

サーモン salmon

マグロ tuna　＊トロ（fatty tuna）/ 中トロ（medium-fatty tuna）

イカ squid / calamari（伊）

玉子 cooked egg

アナゴ conger / sea eel

イクラ salmon roe

カツオ bonito

エビ shrimp　＊甘エビ（sweet shrimp）

赤貝 red clam

ウニ sea chestnut / sea urchin

鉄火巻き tuna roll

タコ octopus

🖥 皿のしくみ USE

The plates are different colors according to price. Most of the dishes are between 100 and 500 yen. Usually there are two pieces of sushi on one plate. Besides sushi, some plates also have things like French fries and desserts.

皿はそれぞれ別の色をしていて、色によって値段が決まっています。ほとんどの寿司は 100 円から 500 円の間です。たいていひとつの皿にはふたつの寿司がのっています。寿司だけでなく、フライドポテトやデザートがのっている皿もありますよ。

🖥 会計 1.2

When you are done with your meal, you call the server*. They count the number of plates and calculate the total cost. To pay, call out to the waiter or press the button on the touch panel that says "*kaikei*" to call the waiter. The waiter will count the plates and settle the bill.

*server =
wait staff
（お店の人）

食事を終えたら、お店の人を呼びましょう。お店の人が皿を数えて、料金を計算してくれます。支払いの際は、店員さんに声をかけて呼ぶか、タッチパネル上の「会計」と書かれたボタンを押して呼びます。店員さんが皿の数を数え、料金を清算してくれます。

➕ If you find a hole at the side of the table, that's where you put your finished plates. The number of plates is automatically counted.

テーブルの横に穴をがあったら、それは食べ終わったお皿を入れる場所です。お皿の数が自動的にカウントされるんです。

👆 覚えておきましょう

海苔の名前

英語では、海苔、わかめ、昆布、もずくなどの海藻類の総称として seaweed が使われます。寿司で使う seaweed と言えば、たいていの人が海苔だとイメージすることができますが、海苔の種類もさまざまです。

（一般的な）海苔 : dried laver seaweed	焼き海苔 : roasted laver
干し海苔 : dried laver	青海苔 : green laver
海苔の佃煮 : laver in boiled-down soy sauce	

豆腐・納豆

🖥豆腐 =

Tofu is soybean curd. It's white, and it's usually cut into a block. We use tofu in many ways. It's very nutritious. Sometimes soybeans are called the "meat of the field."

curd
（凝乳状の）凝固物

nutritious
栄養価の高い

豆腐は大豆から作られる凝固物です。白くて四角くブロック状にカットされています。豆腐の調理方法はさまざまです。大豆は栄養価が高く、「畑の肉」と呼ばれることもあります。

> ➕ Have you ever eaten tofu? How did you eat it?
> 豆腐を食べたことはありますか？　どんな風に食べましたか？

🖥冷ややっこ・湯豆腐 USE

The easiest way to eat tofu is cold. The dish called *hiyayakko* is cold tofu with soy sauce, a little bit of sliced green onion and grated ginger on top. On the other hand, if you boil the tofu, the name of the dish is *yudofu*.

grated ginger
おろしショウガ

いちばん簡単な豆腐の食べ方は、冷たいまま食べることです。冷ややっこという食べ物で、醤油、刻んだ長ネギ、おろしショウガをのせて食べます。また、温めて食べる場合は、湯豆腐と言います。

🖥納豆 =

Natto is fermented soybeans. It has a unique smell and a sticky texture. Stirring *natto* not only makes the smell stronger, but it also makes the texture more sticky. This kind of texture is called *neba neba* in Japanese. Even though *natto* is very nutritious, many foreigners and some Japanese find it unappetizing.

ferment
発酵する（させる）

texture
質感

unappetizing
まずそうな、食欲をそそらない

納豆は発酵させた大豆です。独特な匂いとねばねばした食感をもっています。かき混ぜるとその匂いはさらに強くなるだけでなく、粘り気も増します。このような粘り気のあるものを日本語で「ねばねば」と呼びます。納豆は栄養価がとても高いのですが、多くの外国人と一部の日本人にはあまり好まれないようです。

第一章 ● 食

Q&A

 絹ごし豆腐と木綿豆腐の違いはなんですか？

The ingredients are the same, but the amount of water is different. *Kinu goshi dofu* — which is "silken tofu" in English — is very soft and smooth. *Momen dofu*, which literally means "cotton tofu," is firmer than *kinu goshi dofu*. When you make *momen dofu*, you drain some of the water out after adding the *nigari*. When you make *kinu goshi dofu*, you don't drain out any water.

silken
絹の、シルクの

firm
堅い、引き締まった

drain
流す、水気をとる

材料は同じですが、水の量が異なります。絹ごし豆腐——英語にすると「シルク豆腐」——は、とてもやわらかくてなめらかです。木綿豆腐——直訳すると「コットン豆腐」——は、絹ごし豆腐よりもしっかりとしています。木綿豆腐を作るには、ニガリを入れた後に（豆乳に含まれている）水分をいくらか取り除きます。絹ごし豆腐を作るときには、水をとり除きません。

 マメ知識

ニガリを厳密に表現するには coagulant「凝固材」を使うとよい。

🖥水戸納豆 ⊜

Mito City in Ibaraki Prefecture, located to the north of Tokyo, is well known for *natto*. You'll find *natto* labeled "Mito Natto" in the supermarket. Some people think Mito Natto is the name of all natto made in Mito, but in fact, it's a brand. Mito Natto is made from small soybeans.

東京の北にある茨城県の水戸市は、納豆で有名です。スーパーなどでも、水戸納豆と書かれている納豆を見かけるでしょう。水戸納豆を水戸で作られた納豆だと思っている人もいるのですが、実際は「水戸納豆」はブランドの名前です。水戸納豆は小粒の豆から作られています。

➕ Actually, there are many Japanese who don't like *natto*. How about you?
実際には、納豆が嫌いな日本人もたくさんいるんですよ。あなたはどうですか？

■ 湯葉 USE

Yuba is like a sheet of tofu. When you heat soy milk, a film forms on the top — just like when you heat milk. That sheet* is *yuba*. There are many ways to use *yuba* in cooking. You can wrap food in it, eat it raw with soy sauce, or use it as an ingredient in soup and other things. It is known as a traditional food of Kyoto.

form
形づくる、形成する

***sheet = film**
（薄い膜）

湯葉はシート状の豆腐みたいなものです。豆乳を熱すると、上に膜状のものができます。牛乳を熱するときと同じような感じです。その薄膜が湯葉です。湯葉はさまざまな料理に使われます。食べものを包んだり、醤油をつけて生のままで食べたり、汁ものの具などとしても使われます。京都の伝統的な料理でもあります。

調味料・だし

▶ Track 05

■ 日本食の調味料

There are two basic kinds of Japanese flavorings. One is *dashi*, or stock. The other is the five basic seasonings: sugar, salt, vinegar, soy sauce and *miso*.

flavoring
調味料、香辛料

stock
スープやソースの素になるもの。外国ではブイヨンが一般的。

日本の調味料には大きくわけて 2 タイプあります。ひとつはダシと呼ばれる煮出し汁です。もうひとつは 5 つの基本調味料で、砂糖、塩、酢、醤油、みそがあります。

■ だし ≡

Dashi is a simple broth* made from dried kombu (kelp), *katsuobushi* (shavings of dried bonito), or *niboshi* (dried sardines).

***broth = stock**
（ブロス。肉・魚・野菜などを煮出したスープのこと）

kelp
昆布

だしはシンプルな煮出し汁で、乾燥した昆布（kelp）やかつお節――乾燥したかつおを削ったもの――、または煮干し（dried sardine）――乾燥したいわし――からつくられます。

🖥 さ、し、す、せ、そ 🈁🈁

To remember the five essential Japanese seasonings, use the *sa-shi-su-se-so* rule. This is the *sa* row of the Japanese phonetic alphabet. *Sa* for *satoh* (sugar), *shi* for *shio* (salt), *su* for *su* (vinegar), *se* for *shoyu* (soy sauce), and *so* for *miso* (fermented soy paste).

phonetic alphabet
音標文字

日本の5つの基本調味料を覚えるには、「さしすせそ」を使いましょう。これは日本語のひらがな表（音標文字）の「さ」行です。「さ」は砂糖、「し」は塩、「す」は酢、「せ」は醤油、「そ」はみそを表しています。

➕ Did you find the non-matching word? It's *se* for *shoyu*. In the old days, *shoyu* was called "*seuyu*."

音が合っていない言葉に気がつきましたか。醤油の「せ」です。昔は、醤油は「せうゆ」と呼ばれていたのです。

🖥 みそ ＝🈁🈁

Miso is a paste made from fermented soybeans, along with other ingredients like rice or wheat. *Miso* is used in a lot of other things besides *miso* soup. It's often used in sauces, glazes, marinades and dressings.

glaze
煮出し汁、つや煮

marinade
マリネード（マリネの漬け汁）

みそは発酵させた大豆や、米や麦から作られるペーストです。みそはみそ汁以外にもたくさんのものに使われています。ソースや、煮物、マリネ、ドレッシングなどにも使われます。

🖥 みりん ▽＝ USE

Mirin is a type of Japanese rice wine. It's mainly used in cooking. It has a lower alcohol content than regular sake, and it's lightly sweetened. It's used to flavor foods and give a gloss* to the surface of foods.

*****gloss = sheen**
（光沢、艶）

みりんは米から作られる酒で、主に料理に使われます。日本酒よりもアルコール分が少なく、ほんのり甘みがあります。料理の味付けや、食べものの表面に照りや艶を出すために使われます。

麹 (こうじ) ▽ USE

Koji is a kind of mold that grows on the surface of wheat and in rice bran. It's used as a starter for the fermentation process. *Koji* is used to make *miso*, soy sauce, sake and other things.

mold
かび、菌

rice bran
米ぬか

starter
スタート係

fermentation
発酵

麹は麦や米ぬかの表面に繁殖する菌の一種です。発酵のプロセスのスタート係です。麹は、みそ、醤油、酒などを作るのに使われます。

➕ Have you ever heard of *amazake*? It's a thick, sweet, whitish alcoholic drink. It's made from rice fermented with *koji*. You should try it sometime!

甘酒って聞いたことありますか？　ドロリとしていて、甘くて白いお酒です。これも麹で発酵させたお米から作られています。いつか試してみてくださいね。

塩麹 ▽ USE

Shio koji is a kind of seasoning made with *koji*. Salt and water are added to *koji* to ferment it. It looks like a white sauce made of melted rice. Until recently people used it mainly for making *tsukemono* — Japanese pickles — but recently it's become quite popular in other dishes.

マメ知識
肉や魚を塩麹に漬けるとうまみが増すと言われている。

塩麹は、麹からつくられた一種の調味料です。塩と水を麹にまぜて発酵させます。見た目は、お米がとけてソースになったような感じです。少し前まで、主に漬物──日本版ピクルス──を作るときに使われていたのですが、最近になってそれ以外の料理でとても人気が出てきました。

うまみ ＝

Umami is called the fifth basic taste. The other four are sweet, salty, bitter and sour. Some people translate *umami* as "savory." *Umami* occurs naturally in many foods, like seaweed, *shiitake* mushrooms, meat and Parmesan cheese. It enhances the flavor of other foods.

savory
いい味、いい風味

enhance
高める、強化する

マメ知識
5つの味をまとめて5基本味と言う。

うまみは5番目の味と言われています。ほかの4つの味は、甘味、塩味、苦味、酸味です。うまみを「savory」と訳す人もいます。うまみは海草類、シイタケ、肉、パルメザンチーズなど、さまざまな食品に自然に含まれる味で、ほかの食材の味を引き出します。

食辞典 ❷
大衆料理

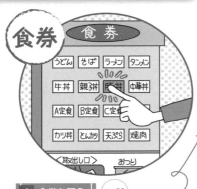

2 席に着く *(p. 60)*

Are most of the fast food restaurants counter-style?

1 食券を買う *(p. 60)*

How do I order?

　最近の日本の代表的なファーストフードと言えば、牛丼、ラーメン、天丼などのチェーン店が頭に浮かびます。券売機のしくみやお店の雰囲気、どのようなチェーン店があるのかなどの情報を加えながら話せると楽しいですね。

Is this *zarusoba* or *morisoba*?

そば
うどん

もりそば、ざるそば *(p. 59)*

You can eat it hot

or stir-fried.

天ぷらうどん

冷たいうどん *(p. 59)*

or cold,

焼きうどん *(p. 59)*

お祭りや縁日などで路上に並んでいるさまざまな屋台。その中には外国人にとって珍しい料理がたくさん並んでいます。お好み焼きやたこ焼きなど日本独特の屋台料理をあなただったらどのように説明しますか？

屋台

A Japanese snack?

お好み焼き　p. 56

たこ焼き　p. 56

It's a kind of thick pancake.

A Japanese-style hotcake or waffle.

たい焼き　p. 56

石焼きいも　p. 61

What are those toppings?

Where can I buy *ishiyaki imo*?

ソース焼きそば

p. 58

大衆料理

▶ Track 06

💻 おでん

Oden is a hot-pot type of dish. Many different kinds of foods are simmered in broth. There are usually dumplings, fish meatballs, fried *tofu*, a hard gelatin-like food called *konnyaku*, a type of seaweed called *konbu*, boiled eggs, and *daikon* radish. *Karashi*, which is hot Japanese mustard, goes well with *oden*.

おでんは、温かい鍋料理の一種です。さまざまな具材をだし汁で煮込みます。ダンプリングや、魚の肉団子、厚揚げ、コンニャクというゼラチンのような食べもの、海藻の仲間である昆布、ゆで玉子、ダイコンなどがあります。からし——辛い和製マスタード——はおでんにとてもよく合います。

pot
調理用の鍋

simmer
煮る

broth
ブロス ※肉、魚、野菜などを煮だしたスープ

gelatin
ゼラチン

 おでんはどこで食べられますか？

Generally speaking, *oden* is a winter dish, like *nabe*. In winter you can find *oden* in most convenience stores. You just pick whatever ingredients you want from the pot and put them in your plastic container. Then you pay the cashier.

おでんは鍋と同じように、一般的に冬に食べるものです。冬になるとコンビニにもおでんがあります。おでんの鍋から自分の欲しい具材をとって、容器に入れます。そして、レジで会計をします。

 覚えておきましょう

ダンプリングって何？

小麦粉を練って丸めた団子のことです。ゆでてシチューやスープに加えたり、肉、野菜、果物などを包んで蒸しあげたり、様々な料食べ方があります。日本のすいとんや中国の餃子、イタリアのニョッキなども英語では dumpling と言います。

50

チャレンジ

おでんの具を説明してみましょう。回答例は次のページにあります。

ちくわ

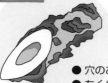

- 穴のあいた棒のような形
- ちくわは漢字で「竹輪」

ちくわぶ

- 材料は小麦粉と水
- 棒の形にして蒸したもの

がんもどき

- 豆腐にヤマイモなどをまぜた揚げ物
- 表面はこんがり

はんぺん

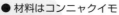

- 魚のソーセージ
- ちくわよりも軽くてソフト

こんにゃく

- 材料はコンニャクイモ
- おでんの汁がしみこむ

しらたき

- 糸状こんにゃく
- すき焼きにも使う

ダイコン

- ニンジンに似た野菜
- 生で食べると辛い

つみれ

- 魚の肉団子
- つくねという食べ物もある

回答例は次のページ

おでんの回答例

► Track 07

🖥 ちくわ

Chikuwa is like a fish sausage. It's shaped like a stick with a hole in the middle. It's white, and the outside is brown from cooking. *Chikuwa* means "bamboo ring." The name comes from its shape, which looks like bamboo.

> ちくわは魚のソーセージのようなものです。穴のあいた棒状の形をしています。色は白いのですが、回りは火であぶってあるため一部茶色いこげめがついています。ちくわというのは、「竹の輪」という意味です。形が竹に似ていることに由来しています。

from cooking
料理の過程によって

> **マメ知識**
> 茶色く焦げている様子は browned を使っても表現できるが、焦げ過ぎている印象を与えることもあるので、cooking の方がより適切。

🖥 ちくわぶ

Chikuwabu is a long white dumpling. You make it by mixing wheat flour and water and steaming it in a stick shape.

> ちくわぶは白くて長細いダンプリングです。小麦粉と水を混ぜて、棒の形にして蒸したものです。

🖥 はんぺん [USE]

Hanpen is a kind of fish sausage, too. It has the same ingredients as *chikuwa* plus yams, and is a different shape. It's lighter and softer than *chikuwa*. The original shape is squarish, but usually it's cut into triangle shapes for *oden*.

> はんぺんも魚のソーセージの一種です。ちくわと同じ材料にヤマイモを加えたもので、形が異なります。ちくわよりも軽くてソフトです。本来の形は四角いのですが、おでんに入れるときは三角形にし切られることが多いです。

squarish
ほぼ四角の

🖥 がんもどき

Ganmodoki is tofu mixed with grated yams and other vegetables, and fried in a round shape. It's browned on the outside and very tasty.

52

がんもどきは、豆腐にすり下ろしたヤマイモとほかの野菜を混ぜ、丸い形にして揚げたものです。表面がこんがり焦げてしていてとてもおいしいです。

■ こんにゃく

Konnyaku is a food made from the "*konnyaku* potato." Its texture is similar to a firm jelly. *Konnyaku* has almost no flavor, but it absorbs the flavor of the *oden* broth. *Konnyaku* is known as a healthy, low-calorie food.

こんにゃくはコンニャクイモから作られる食べ物です。こんにゃくは堅いゼリーのようなものです。味はほとんどないのですが、おでんの汁の味がしみこみます。低カロリー食品として知られています。

■ しらたき

Shirataki is noodle-type *konnyaku*. You'll find it in *sukiyaki*, too.

麺状のこんにゃくです。すき焼きにも入っています。

■ ダイコン

Daikon is a kind of vegetable. A whole *daikon* looks like a huge white carrot. If you eat *daikon* raw, it tastes a little sharp. But when you cook it, it has a mild taste.

ダイコンは野菜の一種です。1本の形は大きな白いニンジンに似ています。生で食べると少々辛いかもしれませんが、調理するとやわらかい味になります。

■ つみれ

Tsumire are fish meatballs. Meatballs made of chicken are called *tsukune*, which are also common in *oden*. You can put vegetables and mushrooms in the meatballs, too.

つみれは魚の肉団子です。鶏肉から作られる肉団子はつくねと言います。つくねもおでんによく入っています。キノコや野菜を混ぜてつくねを作ることもできます。

absorb
吸収する

マメ知識

こんにゃく芋は英語で、konjac plant と言う。

第一章 ● 食

53

🖥️鍋 (=)(🧺)

Nabe is Japanese-style hot-pot cooking. It is popular in autumn and winter. You put things like vegetables, meat or fish in a pot with some kind of stock or soup. You can put in whatever you like. The pot is usually placed on a gas burner on the table. At the end, when only the soup is left, you can put rice, *mochi* (rice cakes), *udon* noodles, or even ramen into the soup. It tastes great!

鍋は日本風のポット料理（鍋料理）です。秋と冬によく食べます。野菜、肉、魚などを鍋に入れてダシ汁かスープで煮ます。何でも好きなものを入れます。テーブルの上にガスコンロを用意して、その上に鍋を置きます。最後に、汁だけが残った状態になったら、ご飯、もち、うどん、もしくはラーメンなどを入れます。これがとてもおいしいのです。

➕ **Do you have food like *nabe* in your country? French pot-au-feu is a little like *nabe*, isn't it?**

あなたの国にもこんな鍋料理はありますか？　フランスのポトフは鍋にちょっと似ていると思いませんか？

🖥️鍋の味付け (=)(USE)

The most basic kind of soup for *nabe* is a simple *dashi*, or stock. As the vegetables, meat and fish cook in the stock, their *umami* flavor comes out and mixes with the soup. When the ingredients are ready to eat, you take some out and flavor them with sauces like *ponzu* or creamy sesame sauce.

鍋のスープで最も基本的なものは、だし汁をそのまま使ったものです。野菜、肉、魚を入れて煮込むと、うまみが汁に溶け込みます。具材に火が通ったら、それを取り出してポン酢やごまだれをつけて食べます。

マメ知識

ポン酢（醤油）は citrus-based vinegar とも言えます。

🖥️鍋の素スープ (🎴)

The flavor of *nabe* depends on what type of soup is used. When you cook *nabe* at home, you can buy a variety of prepared soups at the supermarket — *miso* or soy sauce-based, soy milk-based, *kimchi*-based, curry-based, and so on.

鍋の味は、どのスープを使うかによって決まります。家庭で鍋をするときには、味付けされたさまざまなスープをスーパーで買うことができます。みそ味、醤油味、豆乳味、韓国キムチ味、カレー味などです。

🔵 **What would you suggest for a *nabe* soup if you were to make *nabe* in your home country?**

あなたの国で鍋料理をするなら、スープを何味にしたいと思いますか？

🖥 すき焼き ⊟ 🎤

Sukiyaki is a soy sauce-based dish containing meat, *naganeg*i onion, tofu and *shirataki* noodles cooked in a *sukiyaki* pot*. You can eat it in a restaurant or at home. Usually high-quality beef is used for *sukiyaki*, so it is generally considered an expensive dish. If you dip the ingredients in raw egg, the taste is milder.

***sukiyaki pot** = **griddle**
（円形の）鉄板

すき焼きは肉、長ネギ、豆腐、しらたきをすき焼き鍋で調理する醤油ベースの料理です。外でも家庭でも食べられます。すき焼きにはたいてい質の良い肉を使うので、高級料理と見なされています。具材を生卵に浸してから食べると、味がまろやかになります。

🖥 しゃぶしゃぶ ▽ 🎤

Shabu-shabu is a type of hot-pot dish. You swish a slice of meat in boiling *dashi* soup — it's like having it swim in the soup. You also eat the vegetables in the soup whenever they're ready. You dip them in *ponzu* or creamy sesame sauce.

swish
サッと動かす

しゃぶしゃぶは鍋料理の一種です。ひと切れの肉を沸騰しただし汁の中に入れて、泳がせるように動かします。だし汁の中の野菜は、火が通ったらいつでも食べられます。具はポン酢やごまだれにつけて食べます。

🔵 **The name *Shabu-shabu* came from the swishing action. Is there any food name that came from a cooking or eating action in your country?**

しゃぶしゃぶという名前はサッと動かすような動きからきています。あなたの国にも、動きに由来するような料理の名前はありますか？

■ たい焼き 🍢🍡🍵

Taiyaki is a fish-shaped waffle with sweet red bean paste inside. *Tai* is a type of fish called "sea bream" in English. *Yaki* means "grilled." *Taiyaki* tastes best when it's eaten hot, and it goes well with green tea.

たい焼きは魚の形をしたワッフルで、中に小豆のペースト（あん）が入っています。「タイ」は、英語でシー・ブリームと呼ばれる魚です。「焼き」は「グリルした」という意味です。たい焼きは温かいうちに食べるとおいしく、緑茶によく合います。

マメ知識

あんは red bean jam と言われることもあるが、paste のほうが正確なイメージ。

■ たこ焼き 🍵🐙🥢

Takoyaki are a baked round food. They are made with a dough of wheat flour and water. They have chopped octopus inside. They're about the size of golf balls. They're usually sold in servings of six or eight. *Takoyaki* are generally eaten as a snack. They are famous as a specialty of Osaka, but you can eat them all over Japan.

dough
生地

specialty
名物

たこ焼きは、小麦粉と水を混ぜた生地を焼いて作る丸い食べ物です。中にタコのぶつ切りが入っています。ゴルフボールくらいの大きさです。普通は6個か8個のセットで売られていて、一般的におやつ感覚で食べるものです。たこ焼きは大阪の名物ですが、日本全国どこでも食べることができます。

➕ Don't eat *takoyaki* all at once, because they're really hot on the inside and you might burn your tongue!

たこ焼きをいきなり口に入れないように。中がとても熱いので舌を火傷しちゃうかもしれないよ。

■ お好み焼き 🍢🍡

Okonomiyaki is a kind of thick pancake, but it isn't sweet. It has cabbage and other things inside it. The word "*okonomi*" means "what you like." "*Yaki*" means "grilled" or "cooked." The most common ingredients are shrimp, squid, octopus and pork. *Okonomiyaki* is served with a special sauce, mayonnaise, and seasonings like *aonori* (seaweed powder) and *katsuobushi*.

マメ知識

かつお節は dried bonito flakes などと言う。

お好み焼きは厚いパンケーキのようなものですが、甘くありません。キャベツなどの具が入っています。「お好み」とは「あなたが好きなもの」という意味です。「焼き」は「グリルされた」もしくは「調理された」という意味です。具材として一般的なのは、エビ、イカ、タコ、豚肉などです。お好み焼きには、専用のソース、マヨネーズ、青海苔、かつお節をかけて食べます。

もんじゃ焼き

Monjayaki is similar to *okonomiyaki*, but the batter's texture* is more watery and it doesn't have egg in it. *Monjayaki* came from Tokyo, while *okonomiyaki* came from Osaka.

> *batter's texture=
> **liquid dough**
> （生地）

もんじゃ焼きはお好み焼きに似ていますが、生地が水っぽくなっていて、卵が入っていません。もんじゃ焼きは東京の発祥で、お好み焼きは大阪発祥の食べ物です。

Q&A

お好み焼き屋について教えてください。

In an *okonomiyaki* restaurant, there is a hot iron griddle called a *teppan* in the center of the table, and the food is cooked in front of you. In some restaurants you order the ingredients, then mix and cook them yourself. It's fun to create your own *okonomiyaki*.

griddle
鉄板

お好み焼き屋では、テーブルの中央に鉄板という鉄製の焼もの用の板があり、料理は目の前で作られます。自分で具材を注文して、それをまぜて、自分で焼くことができるお店もあります。自分好みのお好み焼きを作ることができるので、楽しいですよ。

■ ソース焼きそば ⬛ 🔧

Sosu yakisoba is a type of fried noodles cooked with cabbage, onions, carrots, pork and a special sauce. *Yakisoba* is usually served with *aonori* (green nori seaweed), *beni shoga* (red pickled ginger) and *katsuobushi* (dried bonito flakes). You can also put mayonnaise on top.

ソース焼きそばは、キャベツ、タマネギ、ニンジン、豚肉と専用のソースを一緒に炒めた麺料理です。青海苔、紅しょうが、かつお節をかけて食べます。お好みでマヨネーズをかけたりもします。

そば・うどん・ラーメン ▶ Track 08

■ そば ▽ USE

Soba is a kind of Japanese noodles. They are made from *soba* (buckwheat) powder, flour and water. You can eat them hot or cold.

そばは日本の麺の一種です。そば粉、小麦粉、水から作られています。温かくしても、冷たくしても食べられます。

■ 温かいそば ⬛ 🥢 USE

Hot *soba* is served in a bowl with soup. You can add various kinds of toppings, like *wakame* (a type of seaweed), raw egg, sliced *naganegi* onion, mushrooms and so on.

温かいそばは、どんぶりにスープに入れられて出されます。ワカメ、生卵、刻んだナガネギ、キノコなどさまざまな具材をトッピングすることができます。

➕ We eat hot *soba* on New Year's Eve. Do you eat something special on New Year's Eve?

日本人は大晦日に温かいそばを食べます。あなたの国では大晦日に何か特別なものを食べますか？

🖥 冷たいそば ＝

Cold *soba* is called *zarusoba* or *morisoba*. *Zarusoba* is *soba* washed in cold water and served on a bamboo mat called a *zaru*. It's topped with *nori*. A special dipping sauce is used for cold *soba*. *Morisoba* is almost the same, but it doesn't have seaweed on top.

マメ知識

英語にも「ざる」という単語があります。英語では sieve。

冷たいそばは、ざるそばもしくはもりそばと呼ばれています。ざるそばは冷たい水で洗った後に、竹製のざるに盛られて出されます。上には海苔がトッピングされています。冷たいそばには、つけて食べる特製のつゆがついています。もりそばはほとんど同じものですが、海苔のトッピングがありません。

🖥 そば湯 ＝

Sobayu is the water that *soba* has been boiled in. After you finish eating the cold *soba*, you can add some *sobayu* to the remaining dipping sauce and drink it.

そば湯とはそばのゆで汁です。冷たいそばを食べ終えた後、そば湯を残ったつゆに入れて飲むことができます。

➕ Do you have any allergies? Some people are allergic to *soba*. You should make sure that it's OK for you to have *soba*.

何かアレルギーはお持ちですか？　そばアレルギーの人もいるので、そばを食べても大丈夫かどうかしっかり確認したほうがいいですよ。

🖥 うどん ＝ 🈁 USE

Udon is noodles made from wheat flour, salt and water. The noodles are usually thicker than *soba*. The way of eating it is almost the same as *soba*, but there are other ways, too. For example, there is stir-fried *udon* called *yaki udon*.

うどんは、小麦粉、塩、水から作られる麺です。うどんはたいてい、そばよりも太いです。うどんの食べ方はそばとほとんど変わりませんが、ほかの食べ方もあります。例えば、うどんを炒めた焼きうどんなどがあります。

💻立ち食いそば・うどん

Tachigui means to eat standing up. You'll find *tachigui soba* and *udon* places in or near train stations. In these places the noodles are already boiled, so the service is really fast.

立ち食いというのは、立ったまま食べるという意味です。立ち食いそば屋を駅の中や駅の近くで見かけるでしょう。ここでは、麺はゆであがった状態で用意されているので、料理を出すのがとても速いです。

💻ラーメン

Ramen is one of the most popular dishes in Japan. It's originally from China, but it developed as a Japanese dish. The noodles can be thick or thin, and the soup can be made with various ingredients such as pork bone or dried sardines.

dried sardine
煮干し

ラーメンは日本の人気料理のひとつです。もともと中国から伝わりましたが、日本の料理として発展しました。麺には太いものも細いものもあり、スープは豚骨や煮干しなどさまざまな食材から作られます。

➕ *Ramen* has a lot of fanatical* fans. There are many fans overseas, too. Are there any *ramen* shops in your country?
ラーメンには熱狂的なファンがたくさんいます。海外にも多くのファンがいます。あなたの国にはラーメン屋がありますか？

*fanatical = maniac
（熱狂的な）

💻食券

In Japan, many chain restaurants have a ticket vending machine at the entrance. When you go in, you choose what you want and buy a ticket for that dish, then give the ticket to the person at the counter. This system speeds up the service.

日本では、多くのチェーン店レストランが店の入り口に販売機を設置しています。店に入ったら、何を食べるかを決めてから、チケットを買います。それから、そのチケットをカウンターの人に渡します。こうすることで、サービスが速くなるのです。

🖥️ 牛丼

Gyudon is rice topped with grilled beef that is flavored with soy sauce and sugar. *Gyu* means "beef" and *don* is from *donburi*, which is a big rice bowl.

牛丼は、醤油と砂糖で味付けされた牛肉をご飯の上にのせたものです。*gyu* が「beef」という意味で、*don* は「どんぶり」という大きなご飯茶碗の名前に由来しています。

🖥️ 石焼きいも ⊜

Ishiyaki-imo are sweet potatoes baked in a special oven. They're usually sold from special trucks in the winter. The trucks have speakers with a recorded voice singing "*Ishiyaki-imo*." You can also get *ishiyaki-imo* at supermarkets in the wintertime.

石焼きいもは、特別な釜で焼くサツマイモです。冬になるとよく専用のトラックで売られます。トラックには「石焼きいも」と歌うような録音された声が流れるスピーカーがついています。冬はスーパーでも買うことができます。

> ➕ You can buy baked sweet potatoes from carts or stands, like pretzels.
> 石焼いもは、プレッツェルのように屋台で買うことができます。

Q&A

 牛丼屋のような形式のファストフードはほかにどのようなものがありますか。

Besides *gyudon* restaurants, there are *tachigui soba* shops (where customers eat standing up), *udon* shops, curry restaurants, *tendon* shops (*tendon* is rice topped with assorted *tempura*), and even fast food sushi restaurants. And of course, there are lots of fast food burger shops!

牛丼屋のほかに、立ち食いそば・うどん、カレー屋、天丼屋、それから寿司のファストフードだってありますよ。もちろん、たくさんのハンバーガーショップもあります。

マメ知識

立ち食いそば屋は standing noodle shop や *soba* stand などと言える。

食辞典 ③
居酒屋・酒

日本の居酒屋は、屋台でもない、バーでもない、レストランでもない日本独特の飲み屋と言えるでしょう。さまざまな料理を注文し、小皿に取り分けて食べられるという特徴をぜひ伝えましょう。外国人にもきっと気にいってもらえるはずです。

居酒屋

焼き鳥

Grilled chicken on sticks

取り皿 *p.69*

We can put whatever we want on here

揚げもの

Fried food

キュウリのたたき

Pounded cucumber

はまぐり

Clams.

Wow, we can barbecue on the table!

厚焼き玉子

A thick omelet.

お刺身

Raw fish.

酒

明治神宮の入り口にある日本酒樽

麹
こうじ

What is sake made from?

What is *koji*?

Are they all sake?

ホッピー *p.67*

It looks like beer. How is it different?

● さまざまな酒の入れ物 ●

焼酎

How is it different from sake?

とっくり

A special sake bottle.

お猪口
ちょこ

A small sake cup.

ちろり

A glass wine pitcher.

冷酒

How do you drink it?

升

A wooden box for sake.

酒・居酒屋

▶ Track 09

■ 日本酒 ▽ ☰

Nihonshu is a type of traditional Japanese liquor. It's made from fermented rice. In English *nihonshu* is called sake, but in Japanese sake means any kind of alcoholic drink. *Nihonshu* is often called "rice wine" in English, but it isn't really wine because the production process is different. *Nihonshu* tastes best when it's just made. It doesn't improve with age, as wine does.

日本酒は伝統的な日本の酒です。発酵させた米から作られます。英語でsake というと日本酒を意味しますが、日本語で酒はさまざまなアルコール飲料を意味します。日本酒は英語で「米のワイン」と呼ばれることがありますが、正確にはワインではありません。製造過程が異なるからです。日本酒は新鮮なものほどおいしいとされています。ワインのように年を重ねるごとに熟成することはありません。

➕ There are different types of *nihonshu* made for each season. It's interesting to discover unique flavors for different seasons.
日本酒はそれぞれの季節によって異なる種類のものがあります。季節ごとのユニークな味を発見するのも楽しいですよ。

■ 日本酒の種類 ¹⁄₂

There are many kinds of *nihonshu*. The taste differs depending on the ingredients and how it's made.

日本酒には多くの種類があります。原材料と製造過程によって味もさまざまです。

■ 吟醸酒 ☰ 🔖

Ginjo-shu is made with rice, rice *koji*, water and brewing alcohol. The grains of rice have to be polished down to 60% or less of their original weight. *Ginjo-shu* has a light, fruity or flowery taste.

brew
醸造する

grain
（穀物の）粒、穀物

polish
精米する、磨く

64

吟醸酒は、米、米麹、水、醸造用アルコールから作られます。米粒は本来の重量の 60% 以下になるまで精米されます。吟醸酒は軽い、フルーツや花のような風味を持っています。

💻 大吟醸酒

It's very similar to *ginjo-shu*. The difference is how much the rice is polished. If the rice is polished down to 50% or less of its original weight, it's called *daiginjo-shu*.

大吟醸酒は吟醸酒とよく似ています。違いは米の精米具合です。お米が本来の重量の 50% 以下まで精米されたものである場合、大吟醸酒と呼ばれます。

💻 純米酒

Traditionally, *junmai-shu* is made from rice polished down to 70% or less of its original weight. However, this is no longer a requirement. Rice *koji* and water are also used in making *junmai-shu*. Unlike *ginjo-shu*, alcohol is not added. *Junmai-shu* often has a stronger* taste than other types of *nihonshu*.

もともと純米酒は、お米の精米歩合が 70% 以下のもので作られたものとされていました。しかし、現在ではその規定はなくなっています。純米酒には、米麹と水も使われます。吟醸酒とは違い、アルコールは入れません。純米酒は、ほかの日本酒よりも強い風味を持っている傾向があります。

💻 本醸造酒

Honjozo-shu is similar to *junmai-shu*. It's also made from rice polished down to 70% or less. But unlike *junmai-shu*, small amounts of alcohol are added in the production process. *Honjozo-shu* is known for its mild, crisp flavor.

本醸造酒は純米酒に似ています。これも 70% 以下の重量になるまで精米されたお米で作られます。しかし、純米酒とは違い、製造過程の中で少量のアルコールが足されます。本醸造酒は、マイルドでスッキリとした味わいで知られています。

tend to...
〜する傾向がある

***stronger =
bolder**
（力強い、はっきりした）

日本酒の分類

Categories of Nihonshu 種類	Ingredients 原材料	Rice Polishing Ratio 精米歩合
Daiginjo-shu 大吟醸酒	Rice, rice *koji*, brewing alcohol	50% or less
Ginjo-shu 吟醸酒	Rice, rice *koji*, brewing alcohol	60% or less
Junmai-shu 純米酒	Rice, rice *koji*	—
Honjozo-shu 本醸造酒	Rice, rice *koji*, brewing alcohol	70% or less

出典　日本酒造組合中央会　ＨＰ
https://www.japansake.or.jp/sake/know/what/02_02.html

燗酒と冷酒

You can drink *nihonshu* either hot or cold. Hot *nihonshu* is called *kanzake*, and cold *nihonshu* is called *reishu*. *Nihonshu* can also be served warm or at room temperature. So it can be enjoyed at a wide range of temperatures. The suitable temperatures are from about 5 to 55 degrees Celsius.

日本酒は熱くしても、冷たいままでも飲むことができます。熱い日本酒を燗酒といい、冷たい日本酒を冷酒と言います。また、日本酒は、ぬるい状態や常温で出されることもあります。つまり、日本酒は幅広い温度で楽しむことができるのです。適温は5度から55度です。

マメ知識
degrees Celsius=℃

地酒

Jizake is locally brewed *nihonshu*. It's usually made in rural areas. Each *jizake* has a unique flavor, because it is made in a local brewery with an original production

rural
田舎の

brewery
醸造所

method. A local brewery is called a *kura* in Japanese.

地酒とは、それぞれの土地で醸造される日本酒のことです。田舎のほうでよく作られています。それぞれの地酒にオリジナルの製造法があるため、ユニークな味を持っています。地元の醸造所は日本語で蔵と言います。

焼酎

People often say that *shochu* is similar to vodka. It's a clear distilled liquor. It can be made from various ingredients which contain natural sugar, like sweet potatoes, rice and wheat. *Shochu* originally comes from Kyushu, the southern island of Japan, but it's produced in other parts of Japan, too.

distill
蒸留する

焼酎はウォッカに似ているとよく言われます。焼酎は透明な蒸留酒です。焼酎はサツマイモ、米、麦など天然の糖を含んださまざまな原材料から作られます。焼酎は、もともとは九州――日本の南方にある島――が発祥地ですが、日本のいたるところで作られています。

焼酎の楽しみ方

There are various ways to drink *shochu*. You can drink it straight, with ice*, mixed with hot water, in a cocktail with things like oolong tea or fruit juice, or with *umeboshi* (pickled plum).

*with ice = on
the rocks
(オンザロックで)

焼酎の飲み方はさまざまです。ストレート、オンザロック、お湯割り、また、ウーロン茶やフルーツジュースで割っても飲めますし、梅干しを入れて飲むこともできます。

ホッピー

Hoppy is a low-alcohol drink that tastes like beer. When you order a Hoppy, a glass or mug of *shochu* is brought along with a bottle of Hoppy. People mix *shochu* with Hoppy, and the taste is like a light beer.

ホッピーは、ビールのような味の低アルコール飲料です。ホッピーを注文すると、グラスかジョッキに注がれた焼酎と、ホッピーのボトルが出されます。焼酎とホッピーを混ぜて飲むと、軽めのビールのような味がします。

Q&A

焼酎と日本酒はどう違うの？

The main difference is the production process. *Nihonshu* is brewed, and *shochu* is distilled. Also, *nihonshu* is always made from rice, while *shochu* can be made from a variety of ingredients. *Nihonshu* has a fruitier taste than *shochu*.

最も大きな違いは製造工程です。日本酒は醸造され、焼酎は蒸留されます。また、日本酒は必ず米から作られますが、焼酎はさまざまな原材料で作られます。日本酒のほうが焼酎よりもフルーティな味がします。

■ハイボール

Highball in Japanese is similar in meaning to the English word. It's a mixed drink with an alcoholic base, like whiskey, and a mixer like soda or tea. Examples are a gin and tonic and an oolong tea highball (*uron-hai*). The origin of the word "highball" is not known for sure. Some say it came about because the drinks are served in tall glasses.

日本語の「ハイボール」は、英語の highball と同じような意味です。これはウイスキーなどのアルコールをベースにして、炭酸水やお茶などをミックスした飲み物です。例としては、ジントニックやウーロン茶ハイボール（ウーロンハイ）があります。「ハイボール」という語の確かな語源はわかっていません。この飲み物が高さのある（tall）グラスに入れて提供されることに由来していると言う人もいます。

■発泡酒

Happo-shu looks and tastes like beer, but technically it isn't beer. To be labeled beer, a drink has to have a certain amount of malt, and *happo-shu* has less than that amount. That's why it's cheaper than regular beer.

technically
厳密には、技術的には

malt
モルト、麦芽

発泡酒は見た目も味もビールに似ていますが、厳密にはビールではありま

68

せん。ビールとされるには、一定量のモルトを含んでいる必要がありますが、発泡酒のモルトは規定量を満たしていません。そのため、普通のビールよりも価格が安くなっています。

居酒屋

An *izakaya* is a type of bar-restaurant. Most *izakayas* have a casual and friendly atmosphere. The dishes are usually placed in the middle of the table and everyone shares them, using small individual plates.

居酒屋はバーとレストランが一緒になったようなものです。ほとんどの居酒屋は、カジュアルで親しみやすい雰囲気です。料理はテーブルの中央に置かれ、それを個別の小皿に分けあって食べるのが一般的です。

お通し・つきだし

Otoshi, also known as *tsukidashi*, is a small appetizer. It is served when you sit down at an *izakaya*. There is usually a charge of 300 to 500 yen for the *otoshi*. It's a little like a table charge. This is standard practice in Japan, so don't be surprised when you see it on your bill.

appetizer
前菜

practice
習慣、慣例

お通し、もしくはつきだしとは、居酒屋で席に着くと自動的に出される小皿料理のことです。たいてい300円～500円くらいの料金がお通し代として加算されます。テーブルチャージにちょっと似ています。日本では当たり前と捉えられる習慣なので、そう心得ておきましょう。

Q&A

 ビールと発泡酒はどのように見分ければよいのでしょうか？

You can easily distinguish them by checking the price. Real beer usually costs around 200 to 300 yen for a 350-milliliter can. If you're looking at a can that costs around 140 yen, it's *happo-shu*!

値段を見れば簡単に見分けることができます。本物のビールであれば、350mlの缶で200円～300円くらいの値段が普通です。同じ容量の缶で140円だったら、それは発泡酒です！

おせち料理、もち、漬物

おせち料理

お正月に欠かせないおせち料理。重箱の中に並んでいるさまざまな料理には、それぞれの見た目や料理の名前にちなんだ願いや意味が込められています。外国人と新年のテーブルを囲む際の話題になりますので、覚えておきましょう。

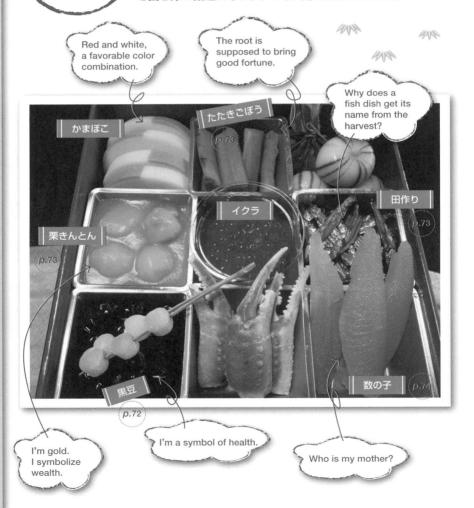

Red and white, a favorable color combination.

The root is supposed to bring good fortune.

Why does a fish dish get its name from the harvest?

かまぼこ

たたきごぼう
p.73

田作り
p.73

イクラ

栗きんとん
p.73

数の子
p.74

黒豆
p.72

I'm gold. I symbolize wealth.

I'm a symbol of health.

Who is my mother?

もち

もちは正月だけでなく1年中大活躍です。お正月はお雑煮や鏡もちにして、普段は海苔と醤油、きな粉もちなどで食べます。

Mochi soup for New Year's Day.

お雑煮　p.74

大福

Rice cakes!

もち　p.75

Mochi and red bean paste make good sweets.

漬物

ごはんによく合う漬物たち。

Japanese pickles

しば漬け　p 75

梅干し　p.75

たくあん　p.75

How do I make *tsukudani*?

What should I put on *ochazuke*?

お茶漬け

p.78

佃煮　p.75

その他

▶ Track 10

🖥 おせち料理 ⬛ [USE]

Osechi ryori is a special kind of food for the New Year. It's prepared ahead of time and served to people who come to visit over the three-day New Year holiday. As a result, most *osechi* dishes are foods that keep for several days. Traditionally, *osechi* is served in *jubako*, which are three-tiered or five-tiered boxes. A lot of *osechi* foods have symbolic meaning.

ahead of time
前もって

tiered
段、層になった

おせち料理は新年のための特別な料理です。新年の三が日の休みに訪れる客のために、前もって用意されます。そのため、おせち料理のほとんどは数日間保存が利きます。伝統的には、重箱と呼ばれる三段か五段の箱で供されます。それぞれの料理は象徴的な意味をもっています。

🖥 現代のおせち料理

In the past, everyone made *osechi* dishes at home. But nowadays you can get *osechi* at department stores or supermarkets. Many people still make some *osechi* dishes themselves. But they tend to buy the really labor-intensive* dishes at stores.

昔は、おせち料理は家庭で作るものでした。しかし最近は、デパートやスーパーでおせち料理を買うことができます。家庭でおせちを作る方もたくさんいますが、本当に手間のかかるものは店で買うことも多くなりました。

> マメ知識
>
> In the past..., but nowadays... (昔は〜だったけれど、今は〜) のフレーズはセットで覚えておくと便利。In the past の部分はTraditionally でも OK.。

*labor-intensive
= time consuming
(時間のかかる、手間のかかる)

➕ Why don't you make your own *osechi*? Recently, there are many kinds of *osechi*, like Italian, French and so on. You just need to place the foods in a *jubako* box.
自分のおせちを作ってみたらどうでしょう？　最近はイタリアンやフレンチなどのおせち料理もあります。料理を重箱に入れてみればいいんですよ。

🖥 黒豆 ▽ ⬛

Kuromame are simmered sweet black beans. Black beans are a kind of soybean. They symbolize health.

黒豆は黒大豆を甘く似たものです。黒大豆は大豆の一種です。健康を象徴しています。

🖥 栗きんとん 🔊

Kurikinton is a sweet paste made with chestnuts and sweet potatoes. The gold color is a symbol of wealth.

栗きんとんは、サツマイモとクリから作られたペースト状の食べ物です。黄金色をしていることから、富の象徴とされています。

chestnut
クリ

🖥 たたきごぼう ⬅ 🔊

Gobo is a long, thin root vegetable. The root symbolizes stability. And the split ends of the root are supposed to multiply good fortune. *Tataki gobo* is *gobo* that is pounded and then simmered with sesame and other flavorings.

ゴボウは細長い根菜です。根は安定の象徴です。枝分かれしている先端は幸運を増殖させると考えられています。たたきごぼうは、たたいた後にゴマやその他の調味料で煮たごぼう料理です。

stability
安定、持続

multiply
繁殖する

fortune
運

pound
バンバンたたく

🖥 紅白なます ⬅ 🔊

Kohaku namasu is a kind of marinated food made of carrot and *daikon* with vinegar. Red and white is a favorable* color combination.

紅白なますはニンジンとダイコンを甘酢でマリネにした食べものです。紅白は、縁起の良い配色です。

*favorable =
auspicious
（縁起の良い）

➕ What is a favorable color in your home country?
あなたの国で縁起がよいとされている色は何色ですか？

🖥 田作り ▽ ⬅

Tazukuri is *teriyaki*-flavored dried anchovies, which symbolize a bountiful harvest. An anchovy is a kind of sardine. Sardines used to be used as fertilizer.

田作りは照り焼き風味の乾燥カタクチイワシで、豊作の象徴です。カタクチイワシはイワシの一種です。イワシは昔、肥料として使われていました。

anchovy
カタクチイワシ、アンチョビ

bountiful 豊富な

sardine イワシ

fertilizer 肥料

■れんこん ▽

Renkon is a kind of root vegetable called lotus root in English. The lotus is a symbol of Buddhism.

レンコンは根菜の一種で、英語では lotus root（ハスの根）と呼ばれています。ハスは仏教の象徴です。

lotus
ハス、レンコン

■数の子 ▽ ＝

Kazunoko is herring eggs, a symbol of family fertility. Each clump of *kazunoko* consists of hundreds of tiny eggs. They're crunchy and a little salty.

数の子はニシンの卵で、家族の豊饒の象徴です。ひと塊の数の子は数百もの小さな卵の集合体です。プチプチしていてちょっとしょっぱい味です。

herring
ニシン

fertility
繁殖力

clump
群れ、集団

crunchy
プチプチした、歯ごたえのよい

➕ *Ikura*, salmon eggs, are often found in *osechi ryori,* too. They have the same symbolism as *kazunoko*.

サケの卵であるイクラがおせち料理に入っていることもあります。意味は数の子と同じです。

■お雑煮 ▽ 🎎

Ozoni is a kind of soup with rice cakes in it. It's eaten as the first meal of the New Year. There are a lot of different types of *ozoni*. How you cook depends on the family and region. The most basic ingredients are a green leafy vegetable, like spinach, and *mochi* (rice cakes). Some people put in sliced *kamaboko* (fish cake), carrots, *shiitake* mushrooms, or even chicken.

お雑煮はもちの入ったスープです。お正月に食べます。家族の好みや地域によって、さまざまなタイプのお雑煮があります。基本的な具材は、ホウレンソウのような緑葉野菜、かまぼこ、もちです。ニンジン、シイタケ、さらには鶏肉や魚を入れる人もいます。

green leafy vegetable
緑黄色野菜

マメ知識

ここで言う cake はケーキではなく、何かの生地を固形にした状態のもののこと。cake にもさまざまな意味がある。

もち (=) (USE)

Mochi is rice cakes made from a special type of sticky rice called *mochigome*. *Mochigome* is stickier than regular white rice. *Mochi* can be used in cooking or in sweets. The simplest way to eat *mochi* is to grill it and dip it in soy sauce or *kinako* powder.

もちは、もち米と呼ばれる粘り気のある特別な米で作った固形状のものです。もち米は一般の米よりも粘り気があります。もちは料理やお菓子などに使われます。いちばん簡単なもちの食べ方は、焼いて醤油かきな粉をつけて食べるものです。

漬物 (▽)(=)(✂)

Tsukemono is Japanese-style pickles. Unlike Western pickles, Japanese pickles are not marinated in distilled vinegar. The vegetables are usually pickled in salt or *koji*.

漬物は日本版のピクルスです。西洋のピクルスとは異なり、蒸留酢でマリネにされるものではありません。塩や麹を使って野菜を漬けるのが一般的です。

distilled vinegar
蒸留酢

pickle
塩漬け・酢漬けにする

代表的な漬物 (👄👅)

Some of the most popular kinds of *tsukemono* are *umeboshi* (pickled plum), *takuan* (pickled *daikon* radish), *beni shoga* (pickled red ginger), and *shibazuke* (pickled eggplant).

最も代表的な漬物の中には、梅干し、たくあん、紅ショウガ（赤い色をしたショウガを漬けたもの）、しば漬け（ナスを漬けたもの）があります。

eggplant
ナス

佃煮 (=)(📢)

Tsukudani is food simmered in mainly soy sauce, sugar and *mirin*. It doesn't have a watery sauce. *Tsukudani* is known as a preserved food because it can be stored for a long time. It goes very well with white rice.

佃煮とは、主として醤油や砂糖、みりんで味付けされた煮物です。汁はありません。佃煮は保存期間が長いため保存食として知られています。白いご飯とよく合います。

🖥 懐石料理

Kaiseki ryori is traditional multi-course Japanese cuisine. Menus change according to the season, since seasonal ingredients are used. *Kaiseki ryori* is typically served at specialized restaurants and Japanese-style inns (*ryokan*). The dishes are beautifully arranged. The visual aspect of *kaiseki* is as important as the taste.

multi-course
コース料理

aspect
見た目、外観

懐石料理は伝統的な日本のコース料理です。メニューは季節に応じて変わり、季節の素材が使われます。懐石料理は一般的に、専門料理店か旅館と呼ばれる日本式の宿で出されます。懐石料理は美しく盛りつけられます。味と同等に見た目が重視されるのです。

🖥 精進料理

Shojin ryori is very similar to *kaiseki ryori*, but it's completely vegetarian. It was introduced to Japan along with Buddhism about 1,500 years ago. Preparing meals is a part of the training for Zen monks, and eating meat is discouraged in Buddhism.

vegetarian
菜食主義の、ベジタリアン

Zen monk
禅僧

discourage
やる気をなくさせる、(〜
するのを) 止められる

精進料理は懐石料理にとても似ていますが、完全に菜食主義です。約1500年前に仏教とともに日本に伝えられました。食事の用意は禅僧の修行の一環であり、仏教では肉を食べることは禁じられています。

Q&A

精進料理ではどんなものを食べるのですか？

The main ingredients are vegetables and soybeans. The dishes change according to the season. For example, sprouts are used in spring, leafy vegetables in summer, fruits and nuts in autumn and root vegetables in winter.

sprout
モヤシ

leafy vegetable
葉もの野菜

root vegetable
根菜

主な食材は野菜と大豆です。料理は季節ごとにかわります。例えば、春はモヤシ、夏は葉もの野菜、秋は果物やナッツ類、冬には根菜がよく使われます。

Q&A

 ベジタリアンです。日本での食事で注意するべきことは何ですか？

The concept of vegetarianism has started to spread in Japan, but not as much as in the U.S. or Europe. Being a vegetarian in Japan can be difficult, because meat and fish stock are used in all kinds of dishes. If you want to make sure, you should ask the waiter before you order.

　日本でも菜食主義という考え方は広まりつつありますが、アメリカやヨーロッパほどではありません。日本でベジタリアンになるのはなかなか難しいかもしれません。魚や肉のだしがさまざまな料理に使われています。確認するには、ウエイターに料理の材料を質問するようにしましょう。

お茶

　Ocha is commonly known as green tea in English. Green tea was originally brought to Japan from China. It is the most popular drink in Japan and is consumed all year round, regardless of the season. It can be enjoyed hot or cold. The tea served at chanoyu, or tea ceremonies, is called *matcha*, which is powdered green tea. Other types of tea are also drunk in Japan, such as *hojicha*, *mugicha*, and *genmaicha*.

　英語では、ふつう green tea と言えば緑茶を指します。緑茶はもともと中国から日本に伝えられました。季節に関係なく常に飲まれている最も定番の飲み物です。熱くしても冷たくしても飲めます。茶の湯で出されるお茶は抹茶と呼ばれるもので、緑茶を粉末にしたものが使われます。日本では他にも、ほうじ茶、麦茶、玄米茶といった種類のお茶が飲まれています。

🖥 お茶漬け ▽📖🔊

Ochazuke is a traditional light meal in Japan. It's a little like rice soup. It's made by pouring green tea over cooked rice. You can add a variety of toppings, such as *tsukemono*, *tsukudani* (seafood, meat or seaweed simmered in soy sauce), grilled salmon, *wasabi* or *nori*.

お茶漬けは昔からある日本の軽食です。米のスープのようなものです。炊いたご飯の上に緑茶を注いで作ります。トッピングとして、漬物、佃煮（魚や肉を醤油で煮詰めたもの）、焼ザケ、ワサビや海苔を載せたりします。

🖥 メロンパン ▽🔊

Meron-pan is a type of sweet bread. It looks a little like a cantaloupe, although *meron-pan* isn't necessarily melon-flavored. A typical *meron-pan* is made from soft dough covered with a relatively thick, uneven layer of crispy cookie dough. *Meron-pan* is available not only in bakeries, but also in convenience stores and drugstores in Japan.

cantaloupe
メロン

dough
生地

relatively
比較的、割合に

uneven
凸凹した、平らでない

「メロンパン」は甘いパンの一種で、外見がネットメロンに似ています。しかし、必ずしもメロンの風味があるわけではありません。典型的なメロンパンは、柔らかい生地で出来ており、表面が比較的厚く凹凸のある、サクサクしたクッキー生地で覆われています。日本では、メロンパンはパン屋だけでなくコンビニやドラッグストアでも売られています。

🖥 コンビニ・コーヒー USE

You can buy fresh-brewed coffee in most convenience stores. To distinguish it from coffee from a café, we call it "*konbini* coffee." Generally, a coffee machine is located to the side of the cash register for self-service. If you ask for hot coffee, you are given a paper cup. If you ask for iced coffee, you are given a plastic cup filled with ice. You just put the cup on the coffee machine and press the button for whatever drink you asked for.

distinguish...
from...
〜と〜を区別する、〜と〜を見分ける

マメ知識

cashier はレジにいる人、つまりレジ係を指す。レジそのものを指す場合は、cash register。

多くのコンビニでは淹れたてのコーヒーを買うことができます。カフェなどのコーヒーと区別するために、「コンビニ・コーヒー」という言い方をよくします。たいてい、レジの近くにコーヒーマシンが置いてあり、セルフサービスで使います。ホットコーヒーを注文すると紙コップが手渡され、アイスコーヒーを注文すると氷が入ったプラスチックのカップが渡されます。コーヒーマシンにカップをセットし、注文した飲み物のボタンを押します。

💻 セルフレジ 1-2

Many convenience stores have self-checkout systems. Payment can be made by both card and cash. Payment by two-dimensional barcode is also supported. The display can appear in either Japanese, English, Chinese or Korean.

多くのコンビニエンスストアでは、セルフレジが設けられています。支払いはカードと現金両方で行えます。二次元バーコードでの支払いにも対応しています。表示は日本語・英語・中国語・韓国語から選ぶことができます。

© yuuki/stock.adobe.com

Q&A

 トンカツにかけるソースは醤油とはどうちがうのですか？

Tonkatsu sauce looks like soy sauce, but it's very different. *Tonkatsu* sauce is thicker than soy sauce and has a spicier flavor. The most famous brand of *tonkatsu* sauce is Bull-Dog. It says "Vegetable and Fruit Sauce" on the label. As you know, fruits like pineapple complement* pork quite well.

トンカツソースは、見た目は醤油に似ていますが、まったく異なるものです。トンカツソースは醤油よりも濃厚で、スパイシーな味がします。トンカツソースの最も有名なブランドはブルドックです。そのラベルには、「野菜とフルーツのソース」と書かれています。ご存じのように、パイナップルのようなフルーツは豚肉をとてもうまく引き立たせるのです。

*complement
引き立たせる ＝
enhance
（強める）

トンカツは Japanese-style deep-fried breaded pork。

【味と食感】

● 食べ物にまつわる用語と表現です。●

おいしい

- It's very good.
- It tastes good.
- It's tasty.
- Delicious!
- Excellent!
- It's yummy! (子ども向け)

味がしない

- It has no taste.
- It's tasteless.
- It's bland.

まずい

- It's not good.
- It's terrible.

【味・食感】

- It's sweet. 甘い
- It's hot/spicy. 辛い、ピリっとする
- It's super-hot. 激辛、とても辛い
- It has a sharp taste. /It's pungent. (ツンとする) 辛い
- It's salty. しょっぱい、塩辛い
- It's sour. すっぱい
- It's bitter. 苦い

- It's oily. 油っぽい
- It's strong. / It has a strong taste. (味が) 濃い、(お茶などが) 渋い
- It's weak. / It has a weak taste. (味が) 薄い
- It's light. あっさりしている
- It's heavy. こってりしている
- It's rich. 濃い、濃厚だ
- It's creamy. クリーミーだ
- It's delicate. 繊細だ
- It's fruity. フルーティーだ
- It's powdery. 粉っぽい
- It's watery. 水っぽい
- It's mild. まろやかだ
- It's tender. (肉などが) やわらかい / (反) tough 堅い
- It's crunchy. パリっとしている
- It's crispy. カリっとしている、パリパリしている
- It's chewy. かみごたえがある
- It's juicy. 汁けがある、ジュワーとしている
- It has a smooth flavor. (飲み物などが) まろやかだ
- It has a fresh flavor. (飲み物などが) すっきりしている

第二章 ● 住まい・生活

日本の住居

外国人と住居の話をするときに勘違いされやすい言葉 No.1 はマンション。海外でマンションと言うと超豪華ルームがイメージされてしまいます。日本のマンションはどんなところだと説明できるでしょうか。そして、アパートはどうでしょうか。

マンション　*p.84*

Wow, you live in a mansion? You must be rich!

アパート　*p.84*

How are mansions and apartments different?

玄関　*p.84*

This is the *genkan*, isn't it? The space to take off shoes.

Slippers? Can I wear them on *tatami*, too?

和室

床の間　*p.87*
What can I put in here?

仏壇　*p.91*
Wow, you have a shrine in the house!

障子　*p.86*
What kind of paper is this?

こたつ　*p.89*
Is that a *futon* on the table?

押し入れ　*p.86*
Great space for *futons*!

日本の古風な住宅には日本独特の住居様式がたくさんつまっています。和室は、ただ家具を配置するだけの部屋ではなく、部屋そのものにすでにさまざまな機能が備わっているのが特徴です。また、縁側も日本オリジナルのベランダと言えるでしょう。

雨戸　*p.88*
A shutter for the windows, right?

縁側　*p.87*
Is it like a veranda?

蚊取り線香　*p.92*
Spiral incense! What is it for?

縁側

住宅・家 ▶ Track 11

🏠 住宅のタイプ

Basically there are two main types of homes: private houses* and apartments. The word "mansion" has different meanings in Japanese and English. In Japan, a *mansion* is a modern apartment or condo. In English a *mansion* is a big, luxurious house.

> 基本的に、住宅のタイプはふたつあります。一戸建てと集合住宅です。「マンション」は日本語と英語では意味が違います。日本では、現代的なアパート、もしくは分譲アパートを指しますが、英語では広くて豪華な住宅を指します。

* **private house = detached house**
（戸建て住宅、独立住宅）

apartment
アパート（集合住宅の一区画）
※日本の「アパート」ではない。

condo
分譲アパート
（condominium のくだけた言い方）

🏠 日本の賃貸事情

When searching for a rental apartment, the first place to look is a "property information portal websites," where multiple real estate companies have registered their properties. You can find your desired property based on a variety of criteria such as rent, floor plan, indoor facilities, and information on the surrounding area. Recently, there has been an increase in the number of "concept rentals," apartments that are specialized for a particular lifestyle, such as gaming.

> 賃貸を探す場合、複数の不動産会社が物件を登録している「物件情報のポータル web サイト」を最初に利用します。賃料や間取り、室内設備や周辺地域の情報など、様々な条件をもとに希望の物件を見つけることが出来ます。最近ではゲーミングマンションなど、特定の生活スタイルに特化した「コンセプト賃貸」も増えています。

🏠 おじゃまします・どうぞ

If you're a guest, when you enter a home you say "*ojamashimasu*." It literally means "I will disturb you." Of course, it doesn't really mean that. *Ojamashimasu* is just a polite, respectful greeting when you're visiting someone's house. If you're the host, you say "*dozo*." It means "Please come in."

84

客として、誰かの家に上がるときには「おじゃまします」と言います。言葉の意味は「私はあなたの邪魔をします」です。もちろん本当に邪魔するという意味ではありません。誰かの家を訪問する際のていねいなあいさつです。もし、あなたが客を迎える側であれば、「どうぞ」と言います。これは「どうぞ、お入りください」という意味です。

🏠玄関——靴を脱ぐ

Before you go inside the house, you need to take off your shoes at the entrance. You may be offered a pair of slippers to wear in the house.

家に上がるときには、玄関で靴を脱がなくてはなりません。室内用の履きものとしてスリッパを勧められるかもしれません。

和室・家のつくり

▶ Track 12

🏠畳

Tatami are built-in floor mats. They're covered with woven plants called *igusa*. *Igusa* give the mats a soft, smooth surface. A *tatami* room is usually a multi-purpose room. It can be used for sleeping, eating, entertaining visitors, or almost anything.

built-in
内蔵式の、組み込みの

畳は部屋に最初から組み込まれているマットです。イグサと呼ばれる植物を編んだもので覆われているので、このマットはソフトで表面がすべすべしています。畳の部屋はたいてい多目的室として使われます。寝室、食卓、応接室など、どんな部屋にもなります。

Q&A

 畳の部屋にスリッパで入るのは NG ですか？

You should take off your slippers before going into a *tatami* mat room, because *tatami* can easily be damaged.

畳の部屋に入るときには、スリッパは脱ぎましょう。畳は傷つきやすいものです。

🏠 寸法としての畳 🈁 USE

The size of a room is measured by the number of *tatami* mats, even if the room doesn't actually have tatami. One *tatami* is just big enough for one adult to lie down on. Common Japanese room sizes are four and a half, six, and eight mats.

measure
測定する、寸法をとる

部屋の広さは畳の枚数で測られます。その部屋に実際には畳がなくてもです。1畳はだいたい大人ひとりが横になれるくらいの大きさです。日本の部屋の広さは4畳半、6畳、8畳が一般的です。

🏠 ふすま ▽ USE 🎤

Fusuma are a kind of door in Japanese rooms. They're covered with *washi* paper. Each door is a little larger than a *tatami* mat. Sometimes *fusuma* are used as a kind of movable wall, like a partition. You connect or divide rooms by opening or closing the *fusuma*.

ふすまとは和室にある扉のようなものです。和紙で覆われています。1枚のふすまは畳よりも少し大きいくらいです。ふすまはパーティションのように移動することができる壁としても使われています。ふすまを開け閉めすることでふた部屋をひと部屋にしたり、ひと部屋をふた部屋にすることができます。

➕ Guess what we do when *fusuma* get a hole in them. We cover them with cherry blossom-shaped paper.

ふすまに穴が開いてしまったときどうすると思います？　桜のような花の形に切った紙をあてて穴をふさいだりするんです。

🏠 押し入れ ▽ ＝ USE

An *oshiire* is a Japanese-style closet. It has two sliding doors, called *fusuma*. An *oshiire* is a convenient space for storing *futon* — Japanese bedding.

押し入れは日本式のクローゼットです。ふすまといわれる2枚のスライド式の戸がついています。押し入れは日本の寝具である布団をしまうのに便利なスペースです。

🏠 障子 ▽ 🈁 USE 🎤

Shoji are sliding screens or doors. A *shoji* can be a wall, door, or window. It's made of a wooden frame covered with *washi* paper. In traditional homes, *shoji* are used to separate the living spaces from the outer hallways. Since the *washi* paper is very thin, it takes in light but still hides the inside of the room from outside view.

障子はスライド式のスクリーン、もしくは扉です。障子は壁や扉、窓として機能します。木の枠に和紙が張られたものでできています。伝統的な家では、障子は廊下と居室を仕切るものとして使われています。和紙はとても薄い紙なので、外からの光を取り入れますが、外からは家の中が見えません。

🏠 床の間 〓 ✖ USE

A *tokonoma* is a special space in a *tatami* room where you can place something decorative. It's not a piece of furniture, like a cabinet; it's actually built into the room. You can hang a painting on the wall of the *tokonoma*, or put a flower arrangement in it.

床の間は畳の部屋に備わっている特別なスペースで、装飾品などを置くことができます。戸棚のような家具ではなく、部屋の一部として備わっているものです。床の間の壁に絵をかけたり、床の間に生け花を飾ることができます。

decorative
装飾の

英語で床の間のようなスペースを alcove（壁のくぼみ）と言う。

➕ There's no rule about what to put in *tokonoma*. What would you put in it?
床の間には何を置いてもいいんです。あなただったら何を置きますか？

🏠 あぐら 〓 🔲🔲

If *seiza* is difficult, men can sit cross-legged. But for women, sitting cross-legged is generally considered inappropriate. Women can sit with both legs off to one side.

正座が難しい場合、男性はあぐらをかいて座ります。しかし女性があぐらをかくことは、ふつう行儀が悪いこととされています。女性は両足をどちらか片方にずらして座るとよいです。

cross-legged
あぐらをかいて、足を組んだ

➕ Are your feet OK? Are they falling asleep?
足は大丈夫ですか？　しびれていませんか？

fall asleep
（足が）しびれる
※「眠りに落ちる」も fall asleep

🏠 縁側 〓 USE

The *engawa* is a narrow hallway. It's in between the inner rooms and the outside, facing the yard. It's higher than the ground outside and works well as a bench.

縁側は狭い通路です。家の内部と家の外の間にあり、庭に面しています。地面からは少し高い位置にあり、ベンチとして使うのにちょうどよいです。

Q&A

  和室で正座をしないとマナーが悪いと思われてしまいますか？

It isn't considered bad manners. Even though Japanese are taught to sit on their legs — in other words, do *seiza* — in *tatami* rooms, there are many people who can't sit on their legs because the position is uncomfortable or even painful. So it's not a strict rule anymore. Make yourself at home.

sit on one's legs
正座をする

make oneself at home
くつろぐ

行儀が悪いとは思われないですよ。日本人は、畳の部屋では折った足の上に座るように、つまり正座するようにと教わりますが、心地よくなかったり痛いということで、正座ができない人もいます。ですから、もはや厳格なルールではありませんよ。くつろいでください。

 雨戸

Amado literally means "rain door." An *amado* is a window cover — it's like a shutter. It also protects the house from cold, strong winds.

work well as...
〜に使うとうまくいく、〜にちょうどよい

雨戸は、文字通りには「雨のドア」という意味です。雨戸は窓を覆うもので、シャッターのようなものです。寒さや強風から家を守る役目もあります。

➕ It works great against typhoons. Do you get typhoons in your home country?

台風のときに活躍します。あなたの国では台風が来ますか？

 軒

The *noki* is the lower part of the roof. It keeps the rain from dripping on the outer wall.

英語にも「軒」に値する言葉 eave（軒、ひさし）がある

軒とは屋根の下側の部分です。雨が直接壁にしたたり落ちないように壁を守っています。

家具・室内用品

🏠 こたつ 〔=〕〔USE〕

A *kotasu* is a low table covered by a *futon**, with an electric heater attached underneath. When you sit at the table, you cover your lap with the *futon* and the heater keeps you warm.

こたつは布団で覆われた低いテーブルで、電気ヒーターがテーブルの下についています。そのテーブルに座るとき、ひざを布団で覆うと温かくしていることができます。

*futon =
comforter
（掛け布団）

attached
（小さなものが大きなものに）ついている、付着する

underneath
下の、下部の

🏠 掘りごたつ 〔🔊〕〔USE〕

A *horigotatsu* is the same as a *kotatsu*, but it has a hole underneath—a space to put your legs in. It's more comfortable for a lot of people, because it's like you're sitting on a chair.

掘りごたつはこたつと同じようなものですが、下に足を入れられる穴が開いています。椅子に座っているのと同じような感覚なので、掘りごたつのほうが居心地がよいと思う人が多いでしょう。

🏠 布団 〔🔊〕〔USE〕

A *futon* is traditional Japanese bedding. Basically, a *futon* is a thick mat. In general, *futons* are used on the floor or *tatami*, but recently *futons* are sometimes placed on top of Western-style beds.

布団は日本の伝統的な寝具です。基本的には分厚いマットです。布団は床や畳の上に敷くのがふつうですが、最近は洋式ベッドの（ベッドフレームの）上に敷くこともあります。

bedding
寝具

> ➕ **Which do you like better, a *futon* or a bed? Why?**
> 布団とベッドのどちらが好きですか？　なぜですか？

第二章 ● 住まい・生活

Q&A

 布団はどのようにメンテナンスするのですか？

 USE ?

When the weather is sunny and dry, we hang *futons* outside to air them out. Sunshine makes *futons* softer and keeps them fresh-smelling. Sometimes we beat the *futons* to get the dust out.

get the dust out
ほこりを払う

　天気がよくてカラッとしている日には、布団を外に干して空気にあてます。太陽の光で布団がふわふわになって新鮮なにおいがします。ほこりをはらうために布団をたたいたりします。

➕（相手がベッドを使っている場合）
How do you take care of the mattress of your bed?
ベッドのマットのメンテナンスって、どうしているんですか？

布団の使用マナー　USE 1₊2

Futon should be put away in *oshiire* after waking up in the morning and taken out right before going to sleep. It certainly is an effective way to use limited space. Unless you are sick, you should not leave your futon out all day.

　布団は朝起きたら押し入れにしまい、夜寝る直前になってまた敷くというのがルールです。ベッドが置かれているはずのスペースが丸ごと空くのですから、限られた空間の有効利用としては大変効果的です。病気ではない限り、布団を一日中敷きっぱなしというのはいけません。

のれん　＝ USE

A *noren* is a decorative curtain that hangs at the entrance. It usually has a slit in it to walk through. It doesn't go all the way down to the ground. You often see *noren* at the entrance of Japanese restaurants and stores. When the *noren* is hanging out in front, that means the shop is open.

　のれんは入り口にかける装飾用のカーテンです。通るときに邪魔にならないように切れ目が入っていて、床まで届くような長さはありません。和食のお店などの入り口でのれんを見かけることがあるでしょう。のれんが表に出ていたら、お店は営業中という意味です。

🏠 仏壇

A *butsudan* is like a very small Buddhist shrine that people have in the house. It might look like a closet when the front door is closed. The purpose of the *butsudan* is to remember our ancestors and relatives who are no longer living. We can pray there anytime we want to.

仏壇は、個人宅に置かれる小型のお寺のようなものです。正面の扉が閉じているとクローゼットのように見えるかもしれません。仏壇は亡くなった先祖や親類を心にいつも残しておくためのものです。お祈りはいつでもできます。

➕ **Do you have something similar to a *butsudan* in your home?**
あなたの家には仏壇のようなものはありますか？

🏠 お祈り

Before praying, we light incense and ring a bell. Then we put our hands together and pray that our ancestors' souls will rest in peace. It makes us feel like they're always with us. Sometimes we put food or drinks in front of the *butsudan*.

rest in peace
（霊などが）休まる

お祈りの前に、線香に火をつけて、鈴を鳴らします。それから、手を合わせて、先祖が安らかに眠れるようにと祈りをささげます。そうすることで、先祖が常に私たちの近くにいるように感じられるのです。仏壇に食べ物や飲み物を置くこともあります。

➕ **Would you like to try? Our ancestors will be glad if you pray for them.**
お祈りしてみますか？　お祈りしてくださると、先祖もきっと喜びます。

🏠 線香

Senko is a type of stick-shaped incense that is often used in Buddhist ceremonies. The custom of burning *senko* started when Buddhism was introduced to Japan. Incense used for relaxation is usually called *ko*.

incense
香

線香は、仏教の儀式で使われるスティック状の香です。線香を炊くという習慣は仏教とともに中国から伝わりました。リラックスのために使われているお香は（線香ではなく）「香」と呼ばれます。

🏠 蚊取り線香 （=）(USE)

Katori-senko is used to keep mosquitoes away. It's a spiral-shaped stick of slow-burning incense. Typically, one *katori-senko* burns for about 12 hours.

蚊取り線香は蚊を寄せ付けないためのものです。うずまき状の香でゆっくり燃えます。12 時間くらい燃え続けます。

風呂

▶ Track 14

🏠 風呂の入り方 （1，2）

In a typical home bathroom, there's a bathtub and an area for washing yourself. First you rinse or wash your body outside the bath, and then you get into the tub. You wash yourself first so the bath water doesn't get dirty. If there's no shower for washing, you can use a bucket to scoop out water from the tub and pour it over you.

典型的な家庭の風呂場は、浴槽と体を洗う場所があります。まず、浴槽の外で体をすすぐか洗った後浴槽に入ります。浴槽の水が汚れないように、最初に体を洗います。シャワーがついていない場合は、桶を使って浴槽のお湯をすくって体にかけます。

🏠 お風呂のルール 1 （?）

Usually the bath water is changed once a day. Everyone uses the same bath water, so don't drain out the water after your bath. And be sure to wash your body in the washing area, not in the tub!

ふつう浴槽のお湯は 1 日 1 回しか新しいものに換えません。みんなで同じお湯を使うので、自分がお風呂に入った後にお湯を抜かないようにしてください。それから、体は洗い場で洗うようにしましょう。浴槽の中で洗ってはいけません！

spiral
うずまき

英語にも蚊取り線香を表すことばがある。mosquito coil で「蚊取り線香」。

蚊取り線香には天然殺虫剤が含まれている。天然殺虫剤は英語でnatural insecticide。

rinse は動詞になると「洗い流す、すすぐ」の意味。日本語の「リンス」とは使い方が違う。

➕ **When do you usually take a bath or shower? In the morning or at night?**
普段はいつお風呂に入ったり、シャワーを浴びたりしますか？ 朝、夜どちらに入りますか？

🏠 お風呂のルール2 [1₋2]

After you wash your body, make sure you rinse off the soap completely. Then get in the tub and soak in the hot water. When you're finished, put the cover on the tub so the water doesn't get cold. It's important to have consideration for the next person who uses the tub.

体を洗ったら、せっけんをしっかり流してから、お湯につかりましょう。お湯が冷めないように、お風呂からあがるときには、浴槽にふたをします。次にお風呂を使う人が、気持ちよく使えるようにする心遣いが必要です。

🏠 銭湯 USE

A *sento* is a public bathhouse. *Sento* are mainly used by people in the neighborhood, but anybody can use them. *Sen* means "fee," and *to* means "hot water."

銭湯は、公衆風呂です。銭湯は主に近所の人たちが使いますが、でも誰でも入ることができます。*sen* が「料金」で、*to* が「お湯」を意味しています。

> ➕ Would you like to go to a *sento*? You should bring at least a bath towel, soap, shampoo and conditioner.
>
> 銭湯に行ってみますか？　少なくともバスタオル、せっけん、シャンプー、リンスは持っていったほうがいいです。

Q&A

 日本人はなんで朝ではなく、夜にお風呂に入る人が多いのですか？

 ❓

One reason is that we take a bath not just to get clean, but to relax. After a long day of work, it feels really good to soak in a hot bath. But these days a lot of younger people who are busy with work or school take a shower in the morning instead, so they can sleep longer.

ひとつには、風呂に入るのがきれいになるためだけではなく、リラックスのためだからです。長時間働いたあと、熱いお風呂に体を浸すととても気持ちがいいものです。しかし近ごろは、仕事や学校で忙しい最近の若い人たちの中には、朝シャワーを浴びる人も大勢います。そうすれば、睡眠時間が長くとれるからです。

🏠 銭湯の起源 ?🖊️

There were basically no private houses with baths until the middle of the 20th century. But even then, many people used *sento*. The *sento* was also a place to see your neighbors and talk.

20世紀半ば前まで、ふつうの住宅には基本的にお風呂がありませんでした。しかし、当時から多くの人が銭湯を利用していました。銭湯は、近所の人と会い話をする交流の場でもありました。

🏠 スーパー銭湯 ≡🎴

A *super sento* is a high-class public bathhouse featuring several different types of bathing facilities like open-air baths, saunas, Jacuzzis and so forth.

「スーパー銭湯」は高級な公衆浴場で、露天風呂、サウナ、ジャグジーなど違ったタイプの入浴設備をいくつも備えている点が特徴です。

Q&A

 銭湯ではどのようにお風呂に入ればよいのですか？

First you check your shoes into a little locker and pay the admission fee. The men's bath and ladies' bath are separate. Next you go to a changing room, take off your clothes and put a towel and your clothes in a basket. Then you can enter the bathing room.

まず、靴を小さなロッカーに預けて、入場料を払います。男性と女性の浴場は分かれています。次に、脱衣所に行って服を脱ぎ、脱いだ服とバスタオルをかごに入れます。それから、浴場に入ることができます。

admission fee
入場料

check には「確認する」以外の意味がいくつかある。ここでは「（荷物を）預ける」という意味。

🏠銭湯のマナー [USE]

The manners are basically the same as at home. Make sure to rinse your body before getting into the tub. It is considered impolite to put a towel inside the tub. And before coming out of the bath area, rinse your body in the shower.

銭湯でのマナーも基本的には家のお風呂と同じです。体をしっかりお湯で洗ってから湯船の中に入ります。湯船の中にタオルを入れるのは行儀が悪いとされています。お風呂から上がるときにはシャワーで体をゆすぎましょう。

🏠ゆず湯

There are special baths called *yuzuyu*. *Yuzu* is a type of citrus fruit. People put a lot of *yuzu* into the hot bath water, which gives it a citrus scent. We prepare this kind of bath on the shortest day of the year, called *toji*. Traditionally, this custom is to keep good health.

ゆず湯という特別なお風呂があります。ゆずは柑橘系の果物です。浴槽の中にゆずを入れると、柑橘系の香りがします。冬至と呼ばれる1年で最も日が短い日に、ゆず湯にします。昔からこの習慣は健康を保つためのものだと言われています。

マメ知識
冬至は英語で winter solstice、夏至は summer solstice。

🏠菖蒲湯（ショウブ湯） [=] [USE]

On May 5th, Children's Day, there's a custom of taking a special bath called *shobuyu*. *Shobu* is a kind of plant with long green leaves and a special aroma. Traditionally, people believed the aroma had the power to drive away evil. Nowadays, people put the leaves in the tub to wish for children to stay healthy over the summer.

5月5日の子どもの日には、菖蒲湯という特別なお風呂に入る習慣があります。菖蒲は長い葉を持つ植物で、独特の香りをもっています。昔はこの香りに邪気を払う特別な力があると考えられていました。今では、子どもが夏を健康に過ごせるようにと願って菖蒲をお風呂に入れます。

マメ知識
菖蒲の葉とあやめの葉がよく似ていることから、あやめの葉を入れたあやめ湯というものもある。

➕ Is there anything you would want to put in the tub and bathe in?
湯船に入れて入ってみたいものはありますか？

トイレ

▶ Track 15

🏠 和式トイレ ⊜🖉

In some public places, you might see *washiki* toilets. *Washiki* means "Japanese-style." A *washiki* toilet doesn't have a seat. Basically, it's a hole in the floor covered with porcelain. People squat over the toilet to use it.

porcelain
陶器

squat over
かがむ、しゃがむ

公共の場所では和式トイレがあるところもあります。和式とは「日本スタイル」という意味です。和式トイレには便座がありません。基本的には、床にあいた穴の上に陶器が置いてあるものです。その上にまたがって使います。

🏠 トイレと風呂は別 ⊜❓

In a typical Japanese house, the bath and the toilet are in separate rooms. But lately there are more bathrooms with toilets in them, especially in small apartments. It's a way to save space.

マメ知識
ユニットバスは和製英語なので、そのままでは通じません。

典型的な日本の家では、トイレと風呂は別になっています。しかし最近、特に小さいアパートなどで、風呂場にトイレがついているところもあります。スペースの節約のためです。

🏠 ハイテクトイレ ⊜USE

The most basic version of a high-tech toilet has a heated seat, a bidet shower, and a drying function. You can even adjust the power of the bidet. Automatic flushing and automatic seat covers are common, too. Some toilets have a control screen so you can adjust the water temperature.

マメ知識
本来ビデとは「おしり洗浄機」のことを指す。小さなシャワーのようなものでヨーロッパの一部で使用されている。

ハイテクトイレの基本バージョンには、暖房シートとビデ機能、乾燥機能がついています。ビデの強弱も調整することが可能です。自動的に水を流したり自動的に便座のカバーを開閉する機能もふつうに備わっています。中には水の温度を調整するためのスクリーン式コントローラーが備わっているトイレもあります。

流水音

It's a sound that will cover up the noises a human body makes when using the toilet. You will find a button that says "flushing sound" in some public women's restrooms. Women actually used to flush the toilet to cover up sounds. So this function is not only convenient, but it also saves a lot of water.

自分のトイレの音を消すために使われる音のことです。女性の公衆トイレでよく「流水」と書かれているボタンを見かけると思います。日本の女性は、実際に自分のトイレの音を消すために本当に水を流していました。ですから、この機能は便利なだけでなく、節水にも役立っています。

Have you ever seen anything you found strange in a Japanese toilet cubicle? Some toilets have a little shelf so you can change your clothes there.

ほかに公衆トイレで何か珍しいものを見ましたか？　服を着替えるスペースを作るための板が備わっている公衆トイレもあります。

マメ知識
この習慣は日本人の羞恥心（sense of shame）をよく表していると言われている。

flush
水を流す

cubicle
小部屋

第二章 ● 住まい・生活

ウォシュレットはいつごろ登場したのですか？

In 1980, the toilet company Toto introduced the "Washlet." This is not a generic name—it's the brand name of the Toto product. At first Toto imported bidet-toilets from an American company, and then it developed its own version. The Washlet became popular all over Japan around 1982.

1980年にトイレの企業であるTOTOがウォシュレットを発表しました。ウォシュレットは一般名称ではありません。「ウォシュレット」はTOTOの登録商標です。TOTOがアメリカの企業からビデ付便座を輸入したのが始まりで、その後日本人向けに新たに改良されてきました。1982年頃には日本全国で名が知られるようになりました。

generic name
一般名称、～の総称

マメ知識
「温水でおしりを洗う便座が温かいもの」とされる器具の一般名称は「温水洗浄便座」と言う。

【ひと言目に使える表現】

● 文頭に使える表現のバリエーションを増やしましょう。 ●

・In short...　要するに、手短に言えば

・Briefly...　簡潔（簡単）に言うと

・Broadly speaking...　大まかに言うと

・Simply put...　簡単に言えば

・Needless to say...　言うまでもないけれど、もちろんのことだけれど

・Obviously...　言うまでもなく、明らかに

・As far as I know...　私の知っている限りでは

・In my opinion...　私の意見としては

・Honestly... / To be honest...　正直に言うと

・In my understanding...　私の理解しているところでは

・In my experience...　私の経験では

・Commonly...　一般的に、ふつうは

・Generally... / In general...　たいてい、通常、ほとんどの場合、一般に

・Most of the time...　たいていの場合、多くの場合

・Mainly...　主に、たいていの場合

・Usually...　ふつうは、通常は、いつもは

・In my generation...　私の世代では

・Officially...　おおやけには

第三章 ● 教育・社会生活

絵辞典
日本の制服

Tell me about the uniforms.
 I want to know all about them.

　日本と言えば「制服の学生」というイメージを持つ外国人も多いはず。海外で紹介されている日本のアニメやゲームにも学生服を着た人物がたくさん登場します。日本にはどんな制服があるのか、どんな着方があるのか外国人に教えてあげましょう。

幼稚園

Do kindergarteners wear uniforms, too?

p.105

What are those backpacks made of?

小学生

p.107

リクルート

Does everybody have to have the same bag, too?

p.113

学校

▶ Track 16

🔊 1年のサイクル 🟰

The school year starts in April and ends in March. Usually school entrance ceremonies are held in early April and graduation ceremonies are at the end of March.

学校の学年は4月に始まり3月に終わります。ふつう4月初めに入学式、3月の終わりに卒業式があります。

*school year = academic year

🔊 小中高の学期制度 ❓ 🔢

In most cases, elementary, junior high and high schools have three class terms. The first term is from April to July, the second is from September to December, and the third is from January to March. In between the terms are vacations. Recently, there are more schools that use a two-semester system.

ほとんどの小学校、中学校、高校が3学期制をとっています。1学期は4月から7月、2学期は9月から12月、3学期は1月から3月です。各学期の間には休みがあります。最近は2学期制を採用する学校も増えてきています。

term
期間

two-semester
2学期制

マメ知識

小学校、中学校、高校をまとめて、schools at all three levels と言うこともある。

➕ How long is the summer vacation in your home country? We usually get about six weeks.

あなたの国では夏休みの長さはどれくらいありますか？　日本ではふつう、だいたい6週間です。

🔊 小・中・高の年数 🟰 ❓

Basically, it's the 6-3-3 system. Six years of elementary school, three years of junior high school, and three years of high school. Elementary and junior high school are compulsory. Since high school is not compulsory, students have to pass an entrance exam to enter high school.

基本的には、6-3-3制です。小学校が6年間、中学校が3年間、高校が3年間です。小学校から中学校までは義務教育です。高校は義務教育ではないので、学校に行くためには生徒は入学試験に通る必要があります。

compulsory
義務の、必須の

entrance exam
入学試験

中高一貫制度

There are many top private schools with unified lower and upper secondary school systems. Not many public schools have that system, but they are gradually increasing in number. To enter these schools, children in elementary schools need to take an entrance exam. Recently, the students preparing for an entrance exam are increasing, especially in big cities like Tokyo and Osaka.

unified lower and upper secondary school
中高一貫校

私立の上位校には、中高一貫制のところが多数あります。公立では中高一貫校はあまり多くありませんが、少しずつ増えてきています。中高一貫校に入学するためには、小学校の生徒は入学試験を受けます。最近では、中学入試の準備をする生徒たちが、とくに東京や大阪などの大都市周辺で増えてきています。

第三章 ● 教育・社会生活

Q&A

高校はどのように選ぶのですか？　行きたい高校に行けるのですか？

It depends on what you plan to focus on for the future. Also, your academic performance in junior high school matters. There are several types of high schools, for example general academic high schools, specialized schools targeted for specific jobs in industry, and so on. Of course, schools are usually ranked by academic level.

academic
学校の、学業の

specific
具体的な、専門的な

将来何に重点的に取り組みたいと考えているかによります。それから中学校での成績も関係してきます。高校にはいくつかのタイプがあります。例えば、普通高校や特定の職種につくための勉強をする専門学校などです。もちろん、それぞれの学校はたいてい学力によってランク付けされています。

I've heard that high school is compulsory in some countries. How about your country?
高校も義務教育に含まれる国があると聞いたのですが、あなたのところはどうですか？

🏫 大学入学試験 📖

Each university has its own admission system. Some have their own entrance exam, some use the standardized national entrance exam, some conduct interviews, and some accept recommendations. Most universities have an admission system that combines several of these factors, so it's pretty complicated.

入学許可のシステムは大学によって異なります。独自の入学試験を実施する大学もあれば、共通の一斉テスト（大学入学共通テスト）を使用する大学、面接を行う大学、推薦入学というのもあります。ほとんどの大学の入学システムは、こうした方法を複数組み合わせているので、とても複雑です。

standardized
共通化された、標準の

interview
面接

recommendation
推薦

admission
入学、入ること

🏫 大学入学共通テスト 📖

The National University Entrance Test, held nationwide in Japan every January, is the most widely used of Japan's entrance examinations. Many universities require this exam as part of the application process. But for those students who would rather not take an entrance exam, there are universities without this requirement.

毎年一月に全国一斉に行われる大学入学共通テストは、日本で最も一般的な、大学入試のためのテストです。これを受けるよう指示している大学を希望する際は、受験が必要です。指示していない大学を希望するのであれば、受ける必要はありません。

🏫 学校の行事 📖

School events are held regularly, especially in elementary and junior high school. To name some, there are school trips, sports festivals, and cultural festivals. Of course, parents' day is also held a few times a year.

小学校、中学校では定期的に行われる学校行事があります。いくつか挙げると、修学旅行（遠足）、運動会、文化祭などです。もちろん授業参観日も年に数回あります。

マメ知識

school trip は修学旅行、遠足のどちらにも使える。遠足は feild trip と言うこともある。

to name some
～の名前を挙げる

学生服

▶ Track 17

😊 学生服の歴史

The first school uniform appeared in the Meiji Period, over 100 years ago. At first they were kimono-style, but later they changed to Western-style. The design of the boy's uniform was based on European military uniforms.

最初の制服が登場したのは明治時代、今から100年以上も前のことです。はじめは着物風でしたが、その後洋服になりました。男子の制服デザインはヨーロッパの軍服をモデルにしました。

😊 学生服と学校 [USE]

Basically, each school has its own uniforms. The majority of students at public junior high schools and high schools wear uniforms. Private elementary schools and kindergartens have uniforms, too.

基本的に制服は学校によって違います。公立の中学、高校では大多数の生徒が制服を着用します。私立の小学校、幼稚園でも制服を着ます。

> ➕ **What do you think of school uniforms? In Japan, there are both opponents and supporters.**
> 学校の制服についてどう思います？　日本にも反対派もいれば、賛成派もいるんです。

😊 セーラー服 [=] 🔤

Some girls' uniforms look like sailor suits. There's a big collar that's square in the back. There's often a ribbon or kerchief tied in front. A pleated skirt is worn with the top.

女子制服の中には、水兵服のようなものがあります。背中に大きな四角い襟がついていて、前にはリボンかスカーフが結ばれています。履くのはプリーツスカートです。

マメ知識

チェック柄は tartan。tartan skirt でタータンチェック柄のスカート。

kindergarten
幼稚園

collar
襟、カラー

kerchief
スカーフ、ハンカチ

pleated
プリーツのある

マメ知識

handkerchief「ハンカチ」から hand を取って kerchief だけにすると「スカーフ」の意味。

第三章 ● 教育・社会生活

女子学生の着こなし ▽ USE

Customizing their school uniform is a way for girls to express their individuality. Japanese school uniforms have became popular because of the way girls wear them. Some girls wear extremely short skirts, some wear soft, loose-fitting pants under their skirts; they have their own fashion culture.

individuality
個性

extremely
とても、極度に

制服をカスタマイズすることは、自己表現のひとつの手段です。おそらく、女子生徒の制服の着こなしが、日本の制服を有名にしたのでしょう。極端に短いスカートをはいて、中にはそのスカートの下にジャージをはいている子もいたり……。女子生徒には独特の文化があります。

➕ Don't their legs get cold? — Well, I suppose they think they have to suffer to be fashionable.
足が寒そうですよね。でも「オシャレは我慢」なんです。

男子の制服

There are two types of school uniform for boys — the *tsume-eri* and the blazer type. The *tsume-eri* uniform is modeled after Western military officers' uniforms. It is also called *gakuran*. It has a black or navy blue standing collar jacket with a collar that joins in the middle. Blazer-type uniforms are more like business suits.

blazer
ブレザーの

男子学生の制服は2タイプあります。詰め襟とブレザーです。詰め襟の制服は西洋の将校の制服をモデルにしています。学ランとも呼びます。黒か紺のスタンドカラーのジャケットで、襟の中央で留められるカラーがついています。ブレザーの制服はもっとビジネススーツに近いものです。

第二ボタン USE ?

The second button of the boy's uniform has a special meaning. It's the button closest to the heart, so sometimes a girl asks a boy for his second button as a way to declare their love*.

*declare their love
= show their love
（告白する、愛を示す）

男子学生の2番目のボタンには特別な意味があります。ハートに一番近いボタンなので、女の子が愛の告白の手段として、好きな男の子にそのボタンをもらいに行くのです。

➕ Do you have similar customs or traditions in your country?
あなたの国にもこのような習慣や伝統はありますか？

制服の変化

Gender-neutral uniforms, reflecting society's loosening rigidity toward gender, have become more common. Schools may now offer unisex uniforms for students to choose from.

社会の意識の変化にともない、制服のデザインのジェンダーレス化が動き始めました。主な改革は「男女兼用」と「組み合わせの自由化」です。前合わせを左右変えられるブレザー、女子生徒にスカートとパンツの選択肢を持たせる、といったものが代表例です。中には、デザインを男女統一にした学校もあります。

ランドセル

A *randoseru* is a special hard backpack for elementary school students. The word comes from the Dutch word "ransel," which means "backpack." In the past, all *randoseru* for girls were red, and all the ones for boys were black, but recently there's more variety in the colors. They're usually made of artificial leather. They may seem heavy, but actually they aren't. They're designed to be just the right size for textbooks and notebooks.

artificial
人工の

ランドセルは小学生用の特別なリュックです。ランドセルという名前はオランダ語でリュックを意味する「ransel」に由来しています。女の子は赤、男の子は黒と昔は決まっていましたが、最近は色のバリエーションも増えました。人工皮革で作られていて、重そうに見えるかもしれませんが、実際にはそんなに重くありません。教科書やノートを入れるのにちょうどよいサイズに設計されています。

マメ知識

ランドセルの素材は株式会社クラレが製造するクラリーノという人工皮革が主流。約7割を占めている。

Did you have a locker to keep your stuff in at school?
学校に荷物を置いておけるロッカーはありましたか？

学校教育で英語は使えるようになるのか

文・平田久子

　ひたすら酷評され続けてきた我が国の英語教育でしたが、平成の時代になって改革が進み、「インプットまあまあOK、アウトプット未だ立ち遅れ」というレベルに到達しつつあります。2020年には小学校での英語教育が必修化されました。それでも世間は学校教育を通した英語力の向上に対しては期待薄な姿勢のままです。

　実際、日本人には英語を学ぶにあたって不利な点がいくつもあります。

英語を学ぶにあたり、日本人に不利に働く要素の主だったもの

- **発音の複雑さ**：幾つもの新しい音を習得しなければいけない
- **冠詞の存在**：理屈で納得できるものばかりではない
- **明解さの差異**：「主語＋動詞＋目的語」で明解に表現する習性に適応しづらい
- **使用頻度の少なさ**：英語力が向上しなくても困らない

　ここで数学の話をします。中学生は皆、方程式を学びます。方程式には公式というパターンがあり、与えられた条件を公式に当てはめると、正解を得られます。しかし、公式を暗記しただけでは計算力は向上しません。正解を示した数式を眺め続けても、成果は期待できません。自分で幾度も繰り返し数式に挑み、間違いを犯し、正解を見出すことで、すらすらこなせるようになるのです。

　この図式は語学にも当てはまります。文法という公式があり、それらに沿って読み、聞き、書き、話す。幾度も繰り返し挑み、間違いを犯し、修正することで、すらすらこなせるようになるのです。

　海外からの観光客が急増した昨今、全国の駅員さんや店員さんは、急速に英語力を向上させています。日々経験する「挑む間違える修正する」という反復練習の成果が、顕著に現れているのです。

　このような英語漬けといった環境が理想なのは明らかですが、それを通常の学校教育の場に求めるのは無理な相談というものでしょう。

また、数学のように英語を学べれば理想的なのですが、そうはいかない現実が道を阻みます。

　数字が持つ値はどのように扱っても恒久的に不動です。同時に、「＋」「－」を始め、集合や三角関数他どの記号も役割に例外を許さない、という掟が備わっています。

　翻って英語の学習は、例外と変則を受け入れないことには前進が望めません。何匹いても fish は fish、hardly は hard の副詞形ではない、chicken と a chicken は異なる意味を持つといった例外の数々が頭痛の種となり、学習におけるモチベーションの低下を促すのです。

　幸か不幸か、日本には他の言語の使用を押し付けられたという歴史がありません。一部の国々のように、大学教育は○○語でしか受けられない、といった限定的な強要も経験しませんでした。

　自国の言葉を守り通すことができたのは、誇らしい歴史の一片です。しかしその間、日本は言語の鎖国とも呼べる環境を作り上げてしまいました。海外留学以外に言語の会得の術なしとの説に納得しても、誰もが留学できるわけではありません。

　幸いなことに、今はどこに居てもインターネットを通して勉強できる時代です。翻訳アプリに依存することなく、自分にあった学習法を模索しながら、失敗なくして成長なしと開き直りながら、コツコツと英語を学び続けて行くのが良いのではないでしょうか。

学校外での勉強

▶ Track 18

🐛 塾 ▽ USE ?

A *juku* is a school where students go after regular school for extra study. Children attend *juku* to keep up with school classes and prepare for entrance exams. Usually children go there around dinner time, so some mothers make *obento* dinners for them to take.

> 塾は普通の学校が終わった後にさらに勉強するために通う学校です。子どもたちは、学校の勉強についていくため、また受験に備えて塾に通います。夕食の時分に行くことになるので、お弁当を作る母親もいます。

マメ知識

英語で塾や予備校に値する言葉として、cram school、preparatory school がある。

🐛 予備校 ▽ USE ?

A *yobiko* is a cram school where students prepare for university entrance exams. In order to get into their "dream school," many high school students attend *yobiko*. The tuition is quite expensive, but the quality of the preparation courses is high.

> 予備校は大学入試に備えるための塾です。「夢の大学」に合格するため、多くの高校生が予備校に通います。授業料はかなり高いですが、試験対策に的を絞った質の高い授業を提供しています。

tuition
授業料、月謝

🐛 浪人 ＝ ✎

You may have heard the word *ronin*. I think it means "masterless samurai" in English. But in Japan today, it refers to high school graduates who didn't pass their entrance exam and plan to try again next year.

> 浪人という言葉を聞いたことがあるかもしれません。英語に訳すと「主人のいない侍」となるでしょう。ですが現在の日本では、大学入試に合格できず来年もう一度試験を受けてみようという高校卒業生のことを指します。

➕ **What do you call people like *ronin* in English?**
英語では「浪人」のことを何と呼びますか？

インターネットを使った勉強 [USE]

App-based and web-based (YouTube, etc.) study options have become increasingly popular. They are inexpensive compared to cram school or prep school tuition and permit students to study in their spare time and at their own pace. Animated videos also allow students to more easily absorb information and to stay motivated.

アプリや YouTube を活用する勉強法が、近年増加しています。塾や予備校の授業料と比べて安価で、バスや電車を待つ間といった隙間の時間を使っての勉強が可能です。アニメ仕立てのものには、情報が頭に入りやすい、モチベーションをキープしやすい、という利点も見られます。

就職活動

▶ Track 19

新卒採用制度 ▽ ?

The *shinsotsu saiyo seido* is a system for collectively recruiting fresh college graduates. The government uniformly sets rules for the system, with PR activities held in March, recruitment and selection occurring in June, and official job offers made in October or later. It is often pointed out that the system has not made full use of human resources, as new hires are unable to utilize skills learned at university, or they leave companies soon after joining. Thus, a review of the system is required.

大学を卒業したばかりの社会人未経験者を一括して採用するシステムが「新卒採用制度」です。政府が一律にルールを定めていて、３月に広報活動、採用選考活動が６月、正式内定が 10 月以降に行われます。現代では大学で学んだ専門性を活かせなかったり、入社後の離職につながったりと、人材を十分に活用できていないとよく指摘され、制度の見直しが求められています。

Q&A

経験者ではなく新卒を採用する会社が多いのはなぜですか？

Actually, I had never thought about that. In my opinion, it could be related to Japanese culture, which values a fresh point of view and looks for young potential. But recently I have the feeling many companies are looking for mid-career people instead of recent graduates.

fresh point of view
新鮮なものの見方

potential
将来性、潜在力

実のところ、そんなこと考えたこともありませんでした。若い人の新鮮なものの見方と若い人のもつ可能性に価値があるとする日本文化に関係あるのかもしれません。ですけれど、最近は新卒者よりも経験者を求めている企業が増えてきているように感じます。

就職活動 ?

Usually, university students start job hunting in their third year. They continue until they get a job. For many years, getting a job in big companies* was regarded as a status symbol, but today people have revised their opinion of small-to-mid-sized companies due to the slow economy*.

ふつう大学3年生になると就職活動を開始し、職が決まるまで続けます。長い間、大企業に就職することがステータスと見なされてきましたが、最近は不景気の影響で、中小企業も見直されてきています。

status
地位

***big company = prestigious company**
（大企業、一流企業）

small-to-mid-sized company
中小企業

***slow economy = recession**
（不景気）

就職活動の流れ 1,2

1. Do research on companies or attend a job fair
2. Register and send in application forms (usually done online)
3. Attend a special explanatory seminar
4. Visit alumni of your school if you wish
5. Take exams and have interviews (usually two or three times)
6. Start working after graduation

1: 企業について調査をする、もしくは企業説明会に参加する
2: エントリーシートを送る（通常インターネットで行う）

register
登録する

explanatory
説明のための

alumni
卒業生 ※（OB/OG のこと）

マメ知識

OB/OG は日本語として一般化しているが、英語圏では日本語のような「先輩」と言う意味で使うことはほとんどない。

3: 企業の説明会に参加する
4: 希望する会社にいる自分の大学の先輩を訪問する(希望する場合のみ)
5: 入社試験を受け面接を行う(通常面接は2次か3次まで)
6: 大学を卒業して、会社に就職する

マメ知識

「エントリーシート」は
和製英語。

➕ **What is a typical job hunting pattern in your home country?**
あなたの国では、典型的な就職活動はどのようなものですか?

リクルートスーツ

It's very easy to tell who is job hunting in Japan, because they all wear the same outfit — a dark suit and a white shirt, which is known as a "recruit suit."

日本では、就職活動中の人を見分けるのはとても簡単です。リクルートスーツと言われている、黒いスーツに白いシャツを身につけているからです。

フリーター

A "freeter" is a person who works part-time or temporary jobs. The word "freeter" seems to have come from the English word "free," the German word "Arbeit," which means "work," and "-er," which refers to a person who does something.

アルバイトで仕事を続けている人たちのことを「フリーター」と言います。「フリーター」という言葉は3つの言葉に由来しています。英語の free、ドイツ語で労働を意味する Arbeit、「〜する人」を意味する -er です。

➕ **If you worked at a part-time job in Japan, what would you want to do?**
もし日本でアルバイトするとしたら、何がしたいですか?

第三章 ● 教育・社会生活

会社と人間関係 ▶ Track 20

🎬 終身雇用制

In Japan, the traditional employment system is the so-called "lifetime employment system." This means people work at the same company until they retire. This has been considered the best way to avoid losing a job. It also means people's salaries depend mainly on how long they've been working.

so-called
いわゆる

lifetime employment sytem
終身雇用制

　日本には伝統的な雇用形態があります。いわゆる終身雇用制です。つまり、同じ会社で定年まで働くというものです。それが失業しないですむいちばん良い方法だからです。また、昔から給料は雇用期間の長さで決まるものとされていました。

🎬 転職

Lifetime employment used to be the norm in Japan. But societal resistance to workers changing jobs continues to decline. Companies (web-based and in-person) that help people find new jobs are increasing in number. In the future, more workers will change jobs two to three times in their careers.

　長年、終身雇用は当たり前と捉えられてきましたが、今はそうではありません。社会の転職に対する抵抗感は急速に薄まって行っています。転職を手伝うサイトや会社は増えていて、今後は二度三度と転職する人も増えていくでしょう。

Q&A

 現在も終身雇用制は続いているのですか。

I think it's gradually changing. Companies are offering fewer lifetime job opportunities. In addition, more companies are hiring part-timers and contract workers to cut costs.

in addition
さらに

contract worker
契約社員

　少しずつ変わってきていると思います。終身雇用を保証する企業は少なくなっています。さらに、多くの企業はコスト削減のためにアルバイトや契約社員を雇用するようになってきています。

🐧 自由な働き方 ⊟ ❓

The most common working style for Japanese company employees has been "working at the same company all the way to retirement." But recently, various working styles have emerged. There are both non-regular and regular employment systems, and it is possible to have a second job if time permits. Many companies also stipulate that employees are not required to wear a suit and tie, depending on the department and the day's schedule. At the same time, there is a movement to abolish uniforms for female employees.

In addition, offices and employees tended to be concentrated in large cities. However, the COVID-19 pandemic has made it easier for people to telecommute, and the number of people living away from cities is gradually increasing. Companies are also moving to small and medium-sized cities to start new businesses or relocate their headquarters.

In Japan, as in many other countries, making money through online activities, such as on YouTube or as an influencer, has become a coveted occupation for young people.

「定年までずっと同じ会社で働く」というのが常識とされてきた日本人オフィスワーカーの働き方ですが、最近では様々なスタイルが見られるようになりました。雇用体系には非正規雇用・正規雇用とあり、時間さえ許せば副業を持つことも可能です。服装も、部署やその日のスケジュールによっては、スーツにネクタイ姿でなくても良いと定める会社も多く見られます。同時に、女子社員の制服廃止の動きも見られます。

また、オフィスも人も大都市に集中する傾向がありました。しかしコロナのパンデミックをきっかけに在宅勤務がしやすくなったことで、都会から離れて暮らす人も徐々に増えています。また企業の側でも、小規模中規模の都市に起業する、本社の場所を移す、といった動きも見られます。

さらに諸外国同様、日本でもユーチューバー、インフルエンサーといったネット発信で稼ぐことが、若者の憧れの職業になっています。

👆 覚えておきましょう

在宅勤務することは work from home と言います。work at home は間違いではありませんが、一般的には "from" を使います。

🏮ほうれんそう [USE] [?]

Horenso, the Japanese word for spinach, also has another meaning: it denotes an essential communication practice for workers to follow: report (*HO-koku*), contact(*REN-raku*), and consult(*SO-dan*).

spinach
ほうれん草

denote
示す、意味する

「ほうれんそう」とは、野菜のほうれん草を意味しましたが、いつしか報告＋連絡＋相談という、社会人のコミュニケーション必須ツールを示す言葉にもなりました。

🏮接待 [USE] [?]

Settai is a word that means taking clients out for lunch, dinner or drinks. Bosses ask tell employees to do *settai* to form a good connection with clients.

接待はランチや夕食、またはお酒の席に連れていって得意先をもてなすことです。上司は部下に、接待をして得意先と良い関係を築くようにとよく指示を出します。

🏮忖度 [USE] [?]

Sontaku means doing something based on someone's perceived wishes, even if that person did not ask you to. One example is doing something that you think would make your boss happy, even if your boss didn't ask you to.

「忖度」とは、人が望んでいそうなことを思いはかって、本人にそうしてくれと頼まれずとも、してあげることを意味します。一例を挙げると、上司が喜ぶだろうと思うことを、本人に頼まれなくてもしてあげることです。

🏮ブラック企業 [▽] [=]

Black kigyo is a type of company in which the employees are forced to work in poor and exploitative working conditions. In many cases, a *black kigyo* makes the employees work overtime to an almost illegal extent, eventually causing them to quit the company — or in the worst cases, leaving employees mentally or physically ill.

exploitative
搾取的な

mentally
精神的に

physically
体力的に

「ブラック企業」とは、従業員が劣悪で搾取的な労働環境での勤労を余儀なくされるような種類の企業です。多くの場合、「ブラック企業」は従業員に違法スレスレで低賃金での過重労働を強い、最終的に離職に追い込んだり、最悪の場合、彼らの心身の健康を害する結果をもたらします。

🗨 上下関係

In the era of lifetime employment, all the companies took for granted that supervisors were older than subordinates. Now that it's easier to change jobs or start a new business, it's not uncommon to find older subordinates and younger supervisors. In Japanese society, where sensitivity to age differences is strict, one should always be careful how to talk to coworkers. Today's society may be challenging for the people who have difficulties adjusting to such role reversals.

supervisor
管理者、監督者

subordinate
部下

challenging
難しい、困難のある

終身雇用が当然の時代においては、上司は年上、部下は年下、という序列が当たり前でした。しかし転職や起業がしやすくなった今では、年上の部下や年下の上司がそう珍しくもなくなりました。日本は年齢差に敏感な社会で、言葉遣いにもしっかり気を配らなければいけません。このような逆転現象に適応しづらい人にとっては、難しい時代になりました。

ゴミの捨て方

▶ Track 21

🗨 ゴミの分別

The first thing you need to do is understand what is burnable and non-burnable garbage. It differs depending on where you are. For example, plastic is considered burnable in some parts of Tokyo, and non-burnable or recyclable waste in others.

burnable
燃える

non-burnable
燃えない

recyclable waste
資源ゴミ

まず何が燃えるゴミで何が燃えないゴミかを理解することが必要です。住んでいる場所によって分類が異なります。例えば、東京の中でもプラスチックを燃えないゴミとするところもあれば、燃えるゴミ、もしくは資源ごみとするところもあります。

➕ How do you classify garbage in your home country?
あなたの国ではどうやってゴミを分別しますか？

classify
分類する

缶・瓶・ペットボトル

In general, you need to separate cans, glass bottles, and plastic bottles. They'll be recycled after they're collected. Pickup for those items is usually scheduled on different days of the week. You're supposed to remove the labels and caps from plastic bottles before you throw them away.

一般的に、缶と瓶とペットボトルを分ける必要があります。回収された後にリサイクルされます。ふつうそれぞれのゴミの回収日は異なる曜日に設定されています。ペットボトルはラベルをはがし、フタを外してから捨てます。

> ➕ The labels on plastic bottles have instructions on how to take them off. Check it out next time.
> ペットボトルのラベルにはどのようにそれをはがしたらよいかの指示が書いてあります。次に飲むときに見てみてください。

家庭ゴミの出し方を知る

If you live in an apartment, you'll probably see a poster explaining how to dispose of trash. Or you can go to the ward office and ask, or check the ward office website. Many ward offices have an English site. You'll find out what types of trash to take out on what days, what kind of bags to use, and where to put the trash.

もしマンションに住んでいるのであれば、おそらく掲示板にゴミの捨て方についてのポスターがあるはずです。区役所に行って尋ねたり、ウェブサイトで確認することもできます。たいてい、英語のサイトもあります。何のゴミがどの曜日に回収されるのか、そして使用するゴミ袋と回収場所を確認します。

> ➕ If you're having trouble, let me know. I can help.
> もし難しいようだったら教えてね。私が教えてあげられるので。

マメ知識
ペットボトルは和製英語。英語圏ではふつう plastic bottle と言う。

pickup
回収の

マメ知識
pickup という一語の形で名詞、形容詞として使うことができる。pick up「拾う、回収する」は動詞＋副詞。

dispose
処分する

ward office
区役所

🗑 家庭ゴミを出す [1.2]

Usually, in a big apartment building, you can put garbage in the trash room any time you want. However, for smaller buildings or private homes, you have to take out your garbage at the right time on the right day — or your neighbor may yell at you.

たいてい大きいマンションにはいつでもゴミが捨てられるゴミ置き場があります。小さいマンションや戸建ての家の場合は、決められた日に決められた場所にゴミを出さないといけません。ちゃんと守らないと、近隣の人たちから叱られてしまいます。

> ➕ Have you seen a garbage pickup area in Japan? They put nets on the garbage to keep cats and crows away.
> ゴミ収集場所を見たことはありますか？　ネコやカラスにゴミを荒らされないようにネットがかけてあります。

🗑 粗大ゴミ [=] [1.2]

Garbage with a side or diameter of 30 cm or more is called *sodai* (oversized) *gomi*. To throw away the items such as futons, chairs, chests, etc, you first contact your local government's website, and arrange for pick-up. Next, you purchase sodaigomi fee tickets from a convenience store or supermarket. In the morning of the pick-up date, you leave the items outside your door. Make sure each item has the ticket attached. You may also deliver the items to the local collection point.

粗大ゴミとは「辺または径が30cm以上のゴミ」を示します。それに当てはまるもの、例えば布団、椅子、チェストといったものを捨てたい時は、自分が住んでいる自治体のウェブサイト上で申し込み、日時と費用を確認します。その後コンビニやスーパーで自治体指定の手数料券を購入してゴミに貼り付けて、指定された日の朝にドアの外に出しておく、または自分で収集所に持ち込む、という捨て方をします。

マメ知識

trash は一般的な「ゴミ」を指すことが多いが、garbage は「生ゴミ」を指す場合が多い。また、主にイギリスでは rubbish もよく使われる。

keep away
近づけない

municipal
地方の、地方自治体の

第三章 ● 教育・社会生活

街の中　▶ Track 22

● エスカレーターの左右　□□

In the Kanto area, the left side is for standing and the right side is for walking. But in the Kansai area, it's the opposite. I think each country is different. But it might seem a little strange to have both ways in the same country.

マメ知識

ロンドン、香港は右待ちの左越し、シンガポールは逆。

関東地方では、左側が立ったままの列で、右側が歩く人のための列です。しかし関西では逆になっています。これは国によって違うものだと思いますが、ひとつの国の中でふた通りのルールがあるのは不思議に思えるでしょう。

➕ **Which side do you stand on in your country?**
　あなたの国ではどちらに立ちますか？

● ティッシュ配り　▽□

It's a kind of advertising tool. Companies give out free pocket tissues with advertisements of their products or services inside.

method
方法、手段

give out
配布する

広告手段のひとつです。自社の製品やサービスの広告を入れたティッシュを会社がタダで配っているのです。

● 歩きスマホ　□

"*Arukisumaho*" is walking while looking at your smartphone's screen. The act alone is not a punishable offense (as of 2023), but it is causing more and more accidents. In serious cases, such as a fall from a station platform, the person responsible may be criminally charged and/or sought compensation

「歩きスマホ」とはスマートフォンのスクリーンを見ながら歩くことです。2023 年現在、その行為だけでは処罰の対象にはなりませんが、それが原因での事故は増えています。駅のホームからの転落といった深刻なケースでは、過失傷害罪が適用されたり、賠償金を請求されたりします。

🗣️ 年齢確認 [USE] [1・2]

In Japan, the legal age for smoking and drinking is 20. You need to show your ID to prove your age when buying alcohol or cigarettes. But in reality it's a gray area. For example, at a convenience store, you just push Yes or No on a panel asking if you are over 20. Showing an ID isn't required.

ID
身分証明書

gray area
グレーゾーン、曖昧な部分

日本では、飲酒、喫煙のできる法定年齢は20歳です。たばこやお酒を買うためには、年齢を証明する身分証明書を提示する必要があります。ところが、実際のところはグレーゾーンです。例えばコンビニでは、「あなたは20歳以上ですか？　はい、いいえ」と表示されたパネルのボタンを押すだけです。身分証明書は要求されません。

🗣️ 成人年齢引き下げ [?]

In 2022, the legal age of adulthood was lowered from 20 to 18. As a result, any 18-year-old can sign contracts for cellphones and loans, obtain credit cards, and rent a room without parental consent. However, the legal age for alcohol drinking, smoking, and. public gambling, such as horse racing, is still 20.

2022年に法改正が施行され、成人年齢が20才から18才に引き下げられました。これにより18才に達した個人は、携帯電話やローンの契約、クレジットカードの作成、一人暮らしの部屋を借りる手続きなどが、親の同意なしに可能になりました。しかしながら、飲酒、喫煙、競馬などの公営ギャンブルは、20才の誕生日まで待たなくてはなりません。

バス・電車

▶ Track 23

🗣️ 切符の買い方 [1・2]

First find your destination on the chart, then find the price and what line to take. Next, at the ticket vending machine, select the ticket price. Last, put money in the machine and the ticket will come out of the slot.

destination
行き先、目的地

まず、路線図で目的地を見つけ、料金とどの電車に乗ればよいかを確かめます。次に、券売機で、乗車券の料金を選択します。最後に機械にお金を入れると、スロットから乗車券が出てきます。

🚇 交通系カード 📋 USE

Smart cards are distributed in different parts of Japan, depending on the issuing company: Suica and PASMO (Tokyo metropolitan area), ICOCA (Kansai), SUGOCA (Kyushu), and so forth. Originally, these cards were designed to pay bus and train fares locally. Now the card can be used to purchase items at convenience stores and various other outlets. The use of these cards is not restricted to the area where they were purchased. A deposit of 500 yen is necessary to obtain the card, but this will be refunded when the card is returned.

deposit
デポジット、保証金

首都圏は Suica や PASMO、関西は ICOCA、九州は SUGOCA など、発行する会社によって名前の異なるスマートカードが全国に流通しています。もとはバスや電車の運賃を払う目的のカードでしたが、現在ではコンビニ他様々な店で買い物の代金を払うことができるようになりました。自分の地元ではない地域でも使えます。カードを入手するときに 500 円の保証金が必要ですが、カードを返却するとその 500 円は返金されます。

🚇 路線地図と電車の種類 🚃

The Tokyo train network is often called the spaghetti tangle. But once you become familiar with the system, it's very easy. You just need to remember that there are three types of trains—overground trains, subways, and monorails.

tangle
からみ、もつれ

overground
地上の

東京の鉄道システムは、からまったスパゲティのようだと言われることがあります。しかし、一度その体系を覚えてしまえば、とても便利なものです。まず 3 つのタイプの電車があることを覚える必要があります。地上を走る電車、地下鉄、それからモノレールです。

🚇 満員電車 🚃

Imagine the rice of pressed sushi. That is how you feel in the most crowded train. In extreme cases, the train staff pushes people in to make sure they don't get caught in the doors. It is so cramped on crowded trains that you can hardly move, but there are at least a lot of nice advertisements to look at. The overhead posters are called nakazuri koukoku, or hanging advertisements. Recently, some trains have digital displays showing TV advertisements too.

押し寿司のご飯を想像してみてください。あなたが満員電車の中で感じるのは、それです。ひどいときには、鉄道のスタッフが、乗客がドアに挟まれないように乗客を電車の中に押し込みます。満員電車の中は身動きが取れないほど窮屈ですが、そんなときは車内広告を見るのもいいでしょう。頭上にあるポスターは「中吊り広告」と言います。最近では動画広告が流れるディスプレイ搭載車両もあります。

➕ Just remember not to take the last train on Friday night. It's the most extreme case.
金曜日の終電は避けたほうがいいですよ。最悪のケースです。

警察・消防・病院
▶ Track 24

🚓 警察への通報・相談 USE 1.2

Everyone should memorize emergency phone numbers. If you have an emergency such as a theft, assault, or traffic accident, the number to call is 110. If you have concerns about a particular crime such as stalking, fraud, e.g. you call 9110 and speak to the local police. This service is available from 8:30 am to 5:15 pm on weekdays. Because this is not a case of emergency, you will be charged for the call. Some police departments may provide service during the night or on holidays.

municipality
自治体

いざという時のために、緊急通報用電話番号を覚えておきましょう。盗難、傷害事件、交通事故といった緊急事態に巻き込まれた際には、「110」で警察に通報します。また、ストーカーや詐欺被害といった心配事があるときには、「9110」に電話して地域の警察に相談します。対応は原則平日の8:30から17:15までです（自治体によって違うことも）。緊急対応ではなく相談窓口なので、通話料がかかります。夜間や休日にも対応してくれる自治体もあります。

第三章 ● 教育・社会生活

消防署への通報

The number for fire department is 119. Once the call is connected, you will first be asked if the emergency is a fire or medical. You should state clearly "it's fire," or "need an ambulance". You will then be asked for your location. If you do not know the exact street address, you give the name of an office building or intersection nearby. Ambulance transport in Japan is free of charge, but should only be used in real emergencies.

fire truck
消防車

ambulance
救急車

消防署の番号は 119 です。電話がつながるとまず、「火事ですか救急ですか」と尋ねられます。返事が曖昧だと要請が消防車なのか救急車なのかわからないので、「火事です」「車の事故です」などと、はっきり伝えます。その後、所在地や状況を尋ねられます。正確な番地がわからない場合は、周りに見えるオフィスビルや交差点の名前を告げます。日本の救急車は無料で呼べます。だからと言って、気軽に呼んではいけません。

医者にかかる

The larger, highly specialized hospitals may require referrals or special fees for making an appointment. It may be wise to visit a small or medium-sized hospital if your condition does not seem so serious. Check each hospital's website to find out if an appointment is needed. A consultation fee will be charged for the first visit.

大規模で高度な医療を提供する病院は、特別料金や紹介状を要する所もあるので、深刻ではなさそうな症状の際は、小規模中規模の病院にかかるのが賢明です。予約の要不要は施設によって異なるので、ウェブサイトでチェックします。初診の際は初診料が請求されます。

処方箋で薬を入手する

Today, hospitals with on-site pharmacies are rare. The common procedure is the patients receive a prescription from their doctors and obtain medication somewhere outside. Unless your medication is a highly specialized type, you will not be told where to go any pharmacy.

pharmacy
薬局

prescription
処方箋

薬局を併設している病院は少なくなり、処方箋をもらって街の薬局で薬を購入するという形式が多くなりました。よほど特殊な薬を入手するのでない限り、特定の薬局に行くよう指定されることはありません。

🗨️ お薬手帳 USE [1₂]

A Medication Notebook is a personal history of current and pre-existing medical conditions, allergies, and medications (including dosage). When visiting a hospital or pharmacy, it is important to bring the notebook with you. If you do not have one, it may be obtained from any pharmacy free of charge. An app version is also available.

お薬手帳は、所有者の既往症、アレルギー、過去に処方された薬品の名称や量などを記載しておくノートです。医療機関にかかる際には、お薬手帳を持参します。処方薬を薬局で購入する際には、「お薬手帳をお持ちですか」と尋ねられます。持っていないのであれば、一冊手に入れましょう。どこの薬局でも、無料で渡してくれます。アプリ版も出回っています。

文字

▶ Track 25

🗨️ 漢字・ひらがな・カタカナ・ローマ字 = USE

Kanji, hiragana, katakana, and romaji are the main notation forms used in Japanese writing. Kanji are the traditional Chinese characters used for most words. Hiragana and katakana are phonetic alphabets. Hiragana are used for grammar particles and basic words, and katakana are usually used for loan words from other languages. Romaji is the use of Latin when writing Japanese. Using Romaji is the most common way of writing Japanese on a computer.

「漢字、ひらがな、カタカナ、ローマ字」は、日本語を書く際に用いられる主な表記法です。「漢字」は伝統的な中国の文字で、ほとんどの単語に用いられています。「ひらがな」と「カタカナ」は表音文字です。「ひらがな」は不変化詞や基本語に用いられ、カタカナはふつう、外来語に用いられます。「ローマ字」はラテン文字で日本語を書くときの表記法です。ローマ字は日本語をコンピューターに入力する際に最もよく用いられる方法です。

character
文字

phonetic
表音の、音声を表す

grammar particle
不変化詞。副詞、接続詞、連体詞、助詞の総称。

マメ知識
英語で絵文字は emoji と言います。

【あいづち】

●会話の合間やちょっとした投げかけに使える表現です。●

- That's right.　そうそう、その通り
- That's true.　そうですね、本当だね
- Exactly.　その通り
- Right.　そう、その通り
- Really?　本当に？
- Are you sure?　本気？
- Are you positive?　絶対に本当？
- Of course.　もちろん
- Of course not.　もちろん違います
- Absolutely.　もちろんです
- Let me see.　えーと、ちょっと待ってね
- You know...　えー（ことばに詰まったとき）、あのね、ところで
- I see.　なるほど、ふーん
- See!　ほらね
- You must be kidding/joking!　冗談でしょ！
- Maybe.　そうかも
- Guess what?　聞いて
- Bingo!　あったりー、ピンポーン
- Go ahead.　どうぞ
- Follow me.　ついてきて
- This way.　（道を案内しながら）こっち
- That sounds great!　いいね！
- That's a good idea.　それはいい！
- That's not a good idea.　それはやめておこう
- Why not?　そうしましょう
- No way.　だめ

第四章 現代ニッポン

現代ニッポン

新幹線　*p.*144

A bullet train!

How fast can they go?

What is a Green Car?

　　現代の日本を象徴するモノや街について見てみましょう。日本ではおなじみのホワイトデーですが、実は欧米の文化にはありません。パワースポットとはどんなところでしょう？　さらに、観光地としても人気の街の魅力も簡単に説明してみましょう。

パワースポット　*p.*143

What kind of spot is that?

How do you get power?

ホワイトデー　*p.*151

White day

What's White Day?

明治神宮

秋葉原

秋葉原の街
p.131

So many electronic stores and anime shops!

電気街

電気街口
Akihabara Electric Town Exit
电器街出口 전기 상점가 출구

Electric city!

歩行者天国

A vehicle-free day!

電気街の中

Wow, what a selection of goods!

原宿
p.130

自転車

I see. People who like anime gather here.

竹下通り

What kind of people come here?

原宿スナップ

Why do they make the "peace sign"?

They look cute... saying "*kawaii-ne*" is OK?

現代を代表する街

渋谷 ▽ ≡

Shibuya, along with Harajuku, is a center of Japanese youth culture and art. The famous Shibuya Scramble Crossing is a landmark representing the densely populated Tokyo area. In recent years, on Halloween, many young people gather in costumes.

渋谷は原宿と並ぶ日本の若者文化の発信地であり、芸術の街でもあります。東京の人口密集を表すランドマークとして有名な「スクランブル交差点」も渋谷にあります。近年はハロウィンになると、多くの若者が仮装やコスプレをして集まります。

マメ知識

「コスプレ」はもともと日本発祥の言葉だが、欧米でも人気が高く、最近は cosplay という英語で通じる。

原宿 ▽ ≡

Harajuku is a popular area among young people. It's known throughout the world as a trendy fashion district. The famous Takeshita-dori is a pedestrian street lined with fashion boutiques, cafés and restaurants on both sides. You can see many people wearing unique costumes. Originally these people gathered only in Harajuku. But recently they've been gathering in Akihabara, too.

pedestrian
歩行者の

原宿は若者に人気のエリアです。ファッションの最先端地区として世界的にも知られています。有名な竹下通りは、ファッション・ブティック、カフェやレストランなどのお店が両脇に並ぶ歩道です。個性的なファッションに身をつつんだ人々をおおぜい見かけることができます。もともとこういった格好を楽しむ人たちは原宿に集まっていたのですが、最近は秋葉原にも集まるようになりました。

➕ Have you ever heard of the area called Jimbocho? It's close to Akihabara. It's known for having a lot of used bookstores.
神保町という町の名前を聞いたことがありますか？ 秋葉原の近くにある地区で、古本屋の町として知られています。

🦋秋葉原

Akihabara is a district in central Tokyo. It used to be known as an electronic product paradise, and its nickname was "Electric Town." But now it attracts so-called *otaku* as well as technology geeks. There are a lot of shops with anime, *manga*, video games and "idol" goods.

秋葉原は東京の中心部にある地区です。以前は電化製品の繁華街として知られ、「電気街」と呼ばれていました。現在では、テクノロジーマニアだけでなく、オタクと呼ばれる人たちも引き寄せています。アニメやマンガ、テレビゲーム、それにアイドルショップなどの店がたくさんあります。

➕ **Would you like a little tour?**
ちょっとぶらぶらしてみる？（ちょっとひと周りしてみる？）

🦋六本木

Roppongi is one of Tokyo's most upscale neighborhoods. Roppongi Hills and Midtown Tower are home to many foreign-affiliated companies and IT firms, and having a location there is a status symbol in itself. It is a town where successful and wealthy people gather. Originally an area where GHQ was stationed after World War II, it has developed into a multinational city center.

六本木は東京の街の中でも「洗練された大人の街」としてイメージされます。六本木ヒルズやミッドタウンタワーには外資系企業や IT 企業が多く、そこに住所を持つこと自体がステータスです。成功者や富裕層が集まる街と言えるでしょう。もともとは第二次世界大戦後に GHQ が駐留した地域で、外国人向けの繁華街として発展してきました。

district
（ある特定の）地区、エリア

geek
（ある分野の）マニア
※特に PC やネットワークのマニアを指す

video game
ディスプレイに映して遊ぶゲーム。
※テレビゲーム、パソコンゲーム、ゲームセンターのゲームなど

マメ知識

行政上の「区」は ward、「市」は city。district は区や市ではなく特定の地域を表す。秋葉原は Chiyoda Ward（千代田区）の一区画。

第四章 ● 現代ニッポン

131

現代文化　▶ Track 27

✈嗜好の多様性　[USE][📢][?]

When planning a party, it is important to ask if your guests have any food restrictions. A host should consider food allergies, religious dietary rules, vegetarian diets that exclude meat and fish but may include dairy, and vegan diets that exclude all food products derived from animals. Dashi, an integral part of Japanese cuisine, is based on dried bonito flakes, dried sardines, or kelp. For vegetarian and vegan guests, dashi should be made exclusively from kelp. As gelatin is made from collagen extracted from the bones and skin of animals, consider avoiding jellies and bavarois.

dairy
乳製品

integral
不可欠な、本質的な

　会食を企画する際は、アレルギーだけでなく、個人的宗教的制約の有無も聞き出しておくのが賢明です。ベジタリアンには、魚・卵・乳製品の摂取に個人的な違いがあります。ビーガン（完全菜食主義者）は一致していて、肉や魚の他、卵・乳製品・蜂蜜も口にしません。日本料理に不可欠な出汁は、鰹節、煮干し、昆布のいずれかをもとにしています。ベジタリアンやビーガンに対応できるのは、昆布のみでとられたものです。ゼラチンは動物の骨や皮から抽出したコラーゲンで作られているので、煮こごり、ゼリー、ババロアも要注意です。

Q&A

 お寺で出される精進料理は、ビーガンにぴったりなのでは？

Yes, it is. You can eat the food served at a shukubo without worry. There are exceptions to this rule, and some lodgings have relaxed food restrictions, so please check with them before you consider using their services.

　そうです。宿坊で出される食事は心配なく食べられます。例外的に、食物の規制を緩めている宿坊もあるので、利用を検討する際は確認しましょう。

おたく

Otaku are people who have a strong interest in something. The term used to refer only to anime and manga enthusiasts, but nowadays it is used to refer to other things, like music. In the past, there was a strong prejudice against *otaku*, and the term "*otaku kakushi*" (hiding one's *otaku* identity from one's friends and family) and "*otabare*" (unintentionally revealing one's *otaku* identity) were used. However, these days, many young people are proud to be an *otaku*. Some even describe themselves as "light *otaku* (shallow *otaku*)" as a sign of modesty.

prejudice
偏見、先入観

unintentionally
意図せずに

オタクは、ある特定の分野に対して強い興味を持ち引きこまれている人たちのことです。前にはアニメ・マンガ好きを指す言葉でしたが、最近ではジャンルを問わなくなってきました。かつてはオタクに対する偏見が強く、オタ隠し（自分がオタクであることを現実の友人や家族に対して隠すこと）・オタバレ（自分がオタクであることが意図せず知られてしまうこと）という言葉がありました。しかし最近では多くの若者がむしろ何らかのオタクでありたいという意識をもっているそうです。人によっては、謙遜の意味をこめて自らを「ライトオタク（浅いオタク）」と表現することもあります。

覚えておきましょう

「オタク」に近い英語表現です。それぞれ微妙にニュアンスが違います。

geek: a computer expert or enthusiast
⇒（コンピューター系などの）技術オタク

nerd: an intelligent but single-minded person obsessed with a non-social hobby or pursuit
⇒インテリではあるが、非社会的な趣味を追いかけたり心がとらわれていたり、ひとつのことに専念しているオタク

maniac: any intemperate, overly zealous or enthusiastic person
⇒自分の趣味に熱狂的な情熱を注ぐ人。日本語のマニアに近い

freak: similar to "maniac" but even stronger in nuance
⇒奇抜な人、〜狂、中毒者。maniac より強烈な意味合いを含む

※ Random House Dictionary より

ニート 🟰

NEET is a term used to describe young people between the ages of 15 and 34 who are not in school, unemployed, and not in job training. It is incorrect to define NEETs as those who are unable to adapt to society, as some are in the process of working toward schooling or employment.

ニートは、就学・就労していない、または職業訓練を受けていない 15 才から 34 才までの若者を指す用語です。就学・就労に向けて努力している人もいるので、ニートを社会に適応できない人と定義づけるのは正しくありません。

両親と同居して面倒を見てもらっている独身者のことを parasite single という。

ネット弁慶 🟰

This term was associated by the old expression "*uchibenkei*" with the Internet. "*Uchibenkei*" is a person who appears strong at home but is quiet outside. So, a person who is bossy on the Internet but not so in the real world is called "*net-benkei.*"

昔からあった「内弁慶」という表現を、インターネットと結びつけた造語です。内弁慶とは、家の中では強そうにしているのに、外ではおとなしくする人のことです。これをもじって、ネット上では強気なのに現実の世界ではそうではない人を、ネット弁慶と呼びます。

ひきこもり 🔽🟰

"*Hikikomori*" is a person who stays at home for six months or longer without going to school or work and avoids interacting with mostly everyone outside their family. In the majority of cases, this happens due to a relationship breakdown or restructuring in the workplace. The government estimates that there are more than 1 million *hikikomori* in Japan.

breakdown
壊れる、破綻する

「ひきこもり」とは、学校や仕事に行かず、また家族以外の人とほとんど交流せずに、六ヶ月以上続けて自宅にこもっている人を指します。人間関係のこじれや職場のリストラからそうなってしまうケースが大多数です。日本にひきこもりは 100 万人以上いると、政府は発表しています。

➕ Is there any word that describes *hikikomori* in your country?
あなたの国でひきこもりを表す言葉はありますか？

 Z 世代

Generation Z is a term created in the U.S. that refers to young people (born 1997-2012). They are raised in a digital landscape of smartphones, laptop computers, and tablets. They constantly use these devices to consume news and entertainment on the web; send and receive information via email, text, and social media; and shop online. They don't tend to turn to traditional mass media formats such as television, radio, newspapers, and magazines. Gen Zers are concerned about their way of living and social issues, and are open to diversity. In Japan, the number of Gen Zers who share these elements is raising.

Z世代はアメリカで誕生した用語で、家に PC や携帯電話があるのが当たり前という環境に生まれ育った、1997 年から 2012 年生まれの若者たちを指します。ウェブで娯楽を楽しむ、情報を受信発信する、買い物をする、と I.T. 機器をフルに活用する一方、TV や新聞といった従来のマスメディアにはあまり目を向けません。自分の暮らし方にこだわり、社会全体が抱える問題に対する関心を持ち、多様性に寛容といった特性が顕著です。日本でも、Z世代特有の気質を持った若者は増えてきています。

マメ知識
Z世代は英語で「Gen Z」「Gen Zers」と書かれることもあります。

LGBTIQA+

Society's understanding and acceptance of evolving gender identification and same-sex or non-binary relationships has grown rapidly. Institutional reforms such as those legalizing same-sex marriage now exist around the globe. However, gender discrimination, bias and bullying persist on an individual level. Those in the LGBTIQA+ community must remain vigilant to protect themselves and their rights.

近年、社会の性的嗜好の多様化に対する関心や理解は急速に高まっていて、同性間での事実婚カップルに対する制度改革が進んでいます。しかし個人レベルでの差別やいじめは存在していて、性的マイノリティがカミングアウトするにあたっては、多大なる勇気が必要です。 LGBTIQA+ の人々が自分たち自身とその権利を守るためには、未だ注意が必要です。

discrimination
差別

persist
持続する、根強く残る

覚えておきましょう

アメリカでは Z を「ズィー」と、イギリス・カナダ・オーストラリア・ニュージーランドといった英連邦の国々では「ゼッド」と発音します。

リア充

Riaju is a person who is leading a fulfilling life, for example at work or in a romantic relationship. This word originally comes from "real *jujitsu gumi*," which means people whose "real lives," not their lives on the Internet, are fulfilling and productive.

fulfill
満たす

「リア充」は、例えば仕事や恋愛などで充実した日常生活を送っている人のことです。この言葉はそもそも「リアル充実組」から来ています。その意味は、インターネット上の生活ではなく「リアルな生活」が充実度の高い生産的なものである人たち、ということです。

カラオケ

Karaoke is singing songs with music accompaniment only. There are karaoke boxes, which are specialized premises where small private rooms with soundproofing can be rented by the hour. In addition to singing, some karaoke boxes offer places to play musical instruments, watch live idol performances, or watch DVDs.

accompaniment
伴奏

instruments
器具、楽器

カラオケは伴奏のみの音楽に合わせて歌う遊びです。カラオケボックスというカラオケをするための専門店があり、防音対策をした小さな個室を時間制で借りることができます。カラオケボックスでは歌う以外にも、楽器の演奏やアイドルのライブ配信、DVD鑑賞ができる場所もあります。

ゲームセンター

Japanese game arcades offer several types of machines, including prize games where players can win items such as stuffed toys, *purikura* where instant photos can be taken and processed, chassis games where players use their bodies to play shooting games and such, and medal games where players gamble for tokens rather than money. In recent years, some places specialize in games using virtual reality (VR).

win
勝利する、獲得する

日本のゲームセンターでは、ぬいぐるみなどの景品を獲得できるプライズゲーム、インスタント写真の撮影加工ができるプリクラ、ガンシューティングなどの体をつかって遊ぶ筐体ゲーム、金銭を目的としないギャンブルをするメダルゲームなど、複数のゲーム機が設置されています。近年は仮想現実（VR）を用いたゲームを専門として遊べる場所もあります。

マメ知識
プリクラは1995年に生まれた「プリント倶楽部」の略称で、「プリントシール機」が一般的な名称です。

✈マンガ

Manga is the same as comics or cartoons. However, when we speak of manga in English, we're usually only referring to Japanese comics. The drawings in manga go from right to left, just like the flow of Japanese text. As in anime, the characters have very large eyes. In recent years, webtoons, or full-color manga in a vertically scrolling format optimized for smartphone viewing, have been gaining momentum. Traditionally, manga were released as books by publishers, but webtoons are characterized by a revenue structure that encourages users to pay to read a single story on a platform.

comic
一般的には描かれたマンガ（本）を指す

cartoon
一般的には日本語のアニメと同じような＜動画＞を指す

マンガはコミックやカートゥーンと同じです。しかし、英語で manga といえば、ふつうは日本のコミックのみをさします。マンガの絵は、日本語の文章の流れと同じように、右から左へと進みます。アニメと同じように、登場人物はとても大きな目をしています。近年ではスマホでの閲覧に最適化した、webtoon と呼ばれるコマ割りを廃した縦スクロール形式のフルカラーマンガが盛り上がっています。従来は出版社を通して書籍単行本化するのが基本でしたが、webtoon はプラットフォーム上で単話を読むために課金を促す収益形態が特徴です。

第四章 ● 現代ニッポン

Q&A

 マンガにはどんなものがありますか？

There are too many to explain in simple terms, but broadly speaking, *manga* can be divided into four categories: *manga* for girls, for boys, for teenagers, and for adults. *Manga* are not just for entertainment—some are educational. For instance, there are *manga* about history, cooking, and social situations.

broadly speaking...
大まかに言って

divide into
～に分類する

たくさんありすぎて一概には言えませんが、大まかにいうと、マンガは4種類に分けられます。少女マンガ、少年マンガ、児童マンガ、成年マンガです。娯楽のためだけでなく、学習のためのものもあります。歴史や料理、今直面している社会問題などを描いているものもあります。

マンガ喫茶 (=) 🈁🈁 (USE)

A *manga kissa* is like a *manga* library that has areas with computers and headphones. While you're there you can read or watch anything that can be rented from the shop, including *manga*, magazines and movies. Free drinks are provided, too! Normally, the price is around 500 yen per hour.

マンガ喫茶はマンガ図書館のようなもので、パソコンとヘッドフォンを備えた個室があります。喫茶内では、マンガはもちろん、雑誌、映画などお店から借りられるあらゆるものを楽しむことができます。フリードリンク付きです。利用料はふつう1時間500円くらいです。

➕ Some people use them as a nap space or a place to spend the night when they miss the last train. Don't be surprised if you hear snoring.

昼寝をする場所や終電を逃したときに一晩過ごす場所として使う人もいます。いびきが聞こえてもびっくりしないように。

メイド喫茶 (=) (1.2)

Meido kissa are cafés with waitresses who wear maid uniforms. When you enter the shop, a "maid" greets you with a polite bow and says, "Welcome back, my lord." The menu may include something called "favorite drink." If you order this, the maids will choose a drink they think suits you best.

maid
メイド、お手伝いさん

lord
主人
※[英] (称号の) 伯爵などの意味もある

メイド喫茶はメイドの格好をしたウェイトレスが給仕をしてくれる喫茶店です。店内に入ると、メイドが丁寧にお辞儀をして「お帰りなさいませ、ご主人さま」といってあなたを出迎えます。メニューには「お気に入りの飲み物」というようなものがあるかもしれません。これを注文すると、メイドがあなたに合った飲み物を選んでくれます。

➕ Don't be surprised if the maids stir your drink or wink in a cute way.

メイドが飲み物をかき混ぜてくれたり、かわいくウインクしたりしても驚いちゃダメですよ。

ネコカフェ・ふくろうカフェ

Cat cafés and owl cafés let you spend time with animals while you have a drink or a snack. Some even let you hold and pet the animals. These cafés have become more and more popular. In 2005, there was just one cat café in Tokyo. In 2015, there were 58.

「ネコカフェ」や「ふくろうカフェ」では、飲み物や軽食を飲食するする間、動物といっしょに時間を過ごさせてくれます。動物を抱いたりかわいがったりさせてくれるところもあります。このようなカフェはますます人気が出てきました。2005年にはネコカフェは東京に1軒だけでした。2015年には58店舗ありました。

カワイイ

Kawaii is a word that includes the nuances of cute, lovely and pretty. It can be used to describe any item and people of all generations, just like "cute" in English. The phrase you hear the most frequently might be "*kawaii ne,*" which means "Isn't it cute?" People really say it a lot.

nuance
ニュアンス

frequently
高い頻度で、しばしば

カワイイは、cute（愛嬌がある）、lovely（美しくて愛らしい）、pretty（かわいらしい）といったニュアンスを含む言葉です。何に対しても、また年齢に関係なく誰に対しても使える、英語の cute のような言葉です。もっとも耳にするフレーズは *kawaii ne* でしょう。これは「かわいいですよね？」の意味で、本当によく聞く言葉です。

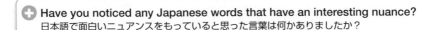

Have you noticed any Japanese words that have an interesting nuance?
日本語で面白いニュアンスをもっていると思った言葉は何かありましたか？

ゆるキャラ 〓 USE

A *yuru-kyara* is a mascot character that is created in order to promote a region, a company or an organization. *Yuru-kyara* are usually cute and innocent-looking. They often incorporate motifs that represent local culture or the company's products.

「ゆるキャラ」とは、マスコットキャラクターで、ふつう場所や地域や企業、団体のプロモーションを目的 に作られるものです。愛らしく素朴な性格付けがなされます。多くの場合、地域の文化や歴史・物産、企業の製品を表すモチーフを体現しています。

➕ Can you think of any character which fits the idea of *"kimo-kawaii"*?
　キモカワイイと言えるようなキャラクターが何か思い浮かびますか？

Q&A

 なぜ日本では子どもっぽいキャラクターやアイドルが好まれるのですか？

One possible reason is that people in Japanese society, especially men, traditionally tend to favor innocent people who have not yet built up much knowledge. This could also be why many Japanese companies prefer to hire freshmen straight out of college rather than experienced people.

ひとつ言えるのは、昔から日本の社会では人びと、特に男性が、完全に知識を吸収しきっていない無垢な人を好む傾向があるからかもしれません。もしかすると、これは日本の企業が経験者より大学新卒者の採用を好む理由でもあるかもしれません。

アイドル業界 [=]

The "idol industry" that produces young male and female pop stars is a huge market in Japan. These "idols" don't always become famous because of their singing or dancing skills. Often it's because of their appearance and personality.

少女や少年のポップスターを生み出す「アイドル産業」は、日本ではとても大きな市場となっています。こういったアイドルたちは、必ずしも歌やダンスの技量によってではなく、ルックスやパーソナリティで有名になります。

idol
（むやみにあがめられる）
崇拝の対象、アイドル

海外では idol ではなく、pop star と呼ばれることが多い。世界的スターになると icon と呼ばれることもある。

女性アイドルグループ [=]

Girl idol groups usually consist of members who are teenagers or in their early twenties. Their devoted fans could be described as "idol *otaku*." Girl idols are commonly portrayed as cute, sweet and lovable. Since there are so many young people who hope to become the next idol, it is a very competitive industry.

少女アイドルグループはたいてい 10 代から 20 代前半の女の子のグループです。熱狂的なファンは「アイドルオタク」と呼ばれることもあります。少女アイドルはふつう、キュートでかわいく愛らしいイメージで売り出されます。次世代のアイドルになろうと控えている予備軍が多いため、とても競争の激しい業界です。

devote
打ちこませる、（時間を）充てる

portray
表現する、演じる

competitive
競争の激しい

男性アイドルグループ [画] [=]

Boy groups are just like girl groups. They have diverse female fans, from elementary school children to housewives. Each member also works individually outside of the group in jobs like acting, narrating and so on.

少年アイドルグループも少女アイドルグループの場合とよく似ています。小学生から主婦まで幅広い年齢層の女性ファンをもっています。メンバーの一人ひとりが、俳優やナレーターなどとしてグループ外の個人の活動もおこなっています。

housewife
主婦
※アメリカでは
homemaker がよく使われる。

individually
個人としては

 *♥ ♥ ♥ のところに、自分の関心のあるグループの固有名詞を入れてみましょう。
Do you think a Japanese idol like ♥ ♥ ♥ could be popular in your country?
日本の ♥ ♥ ♥ のようなアイドルはあなたの国でも人気が出ると思いますか？

インフルエンサー・配信者 =

Influencers and distributors are also active as Internet celebrities in Japan. Influencers mainly use Twitter, Instagram, and TikTok, while distributors use social media services such as YouTube and Twitch. In recent years, influencers and YouTubers have become some of the most popular dream occupations for children in Japan.

日本でもインターネット上の有名人として、インフルエンサーや配信者が活躍しています。インフルエンサーは主に Twitter や Instagram、TikTok を使い、配信者は YouTube や Twitch といった SNS サービスを使用しています。近年インフルエンサーや YouTuber は、日本の子どものなりたい職業ランキングで上位にもなっています。

パチンコ = USE

Pachinko is a game like pinball. It's a form of entertainment that creates excitement, like gambling. If you win, you are given chips, not money. These chips can then be exchanged for cigarettes or sweets, etc., or you can take them to a different shop and exchange them for money. You have to be 18 or over to play *pachinko*.

パチンコはピンボールのようなゲームです。パチンコはギャンブルに似た興奮させる要素をもつ娯楽です。勝つとお金ではなくチップが渡されます。このチップでたばこやお菓子やそのほかのものと交換することができます。あるいは、別の場所に持っていくとお金と交換することもできます。パチンコをするには 18 歳以上でなくてはなりません。

パチンコと法律 ?

Gambling in public is mostly illegal, but not *pachinko*, because it is regarded more as a game than as gambling. Winning money directly from a game is illegal. But in *pachinko*, the winnings are exchanged for money later.

illegal
不法、違法

winning
賞金、賞品、もうけ

日本では人前での賭博は違法ですが、パチンコはそうではありません。なぜならパチンコは、賭博というよりゲームを楽しむ場所と見なされているからです。賞金をその場で受け取ってしまうと賭博とされますが、パチンコでは、得られた賞品を別の場所でお金に換えます。

Would you like to go to a *pachinko* parlor? Well, the balls usually sell out quickly, so don't be disappointed.

パチンコに行ってみますか？　でも、ふつう、あっという間に玉はなくなってしまいますから、がっかりしないでね。

デパ地下

The word *depachika* is a combination of the words "department" (like "department store") and "*chika*," which means underground*. In *depachika*, you'll find an amazing variety of foods, beautifully displayed. It's like a food paradise.

***underground = basement level** (地下)

英語の department はお店としてのデパートよりも、政府や企業の部署や課を表す用語としてよく使われる。

デパ地下は、department と「地下」を意味する chika が組み合わさってできた言葉です。デパ地下には、何種類ものおいしそうな食べ物がきれいに並んでいます。まるで食べ物天国です。

 My favorite is the sweets section. Which is yours?
私のお気に入りはお菓子のコーナーです。あなたのお気に入りのコーナーは何ですか？

パワースポット

"Power spots" are sacred places filled with an energy known as "qi." Power spots are a recent fad. "Qi" is one of the basic concepts of feng shui, and it is believed to be a kind of invisible energy. Popular power spots usually have historical or religious roots, like Meiji Jingu, the Imperial Palace, and so on.

qi
(東洋医学）気

fad
一時的な流行、ブーム

feng shui
風水

パワースポットは「気」と呼ばれるエネルギーで満たされている神聖な場所です。パワースポットは最近流行の場所です。「気」は（中国の）風水の基礎となる概念のひとつで、目に見えないエネルギーだと考えられています。よく知られているパワースポットは、ふつう歴史的、宗教的由緒をもっています。例えば明治神宮や皇居などがそうです。

feng shui（風水）は中国語のピンイン表記がもとになっている。

新幹線

▶ Track 29

✈ 新幹線 (=) [USE]

The *Shinkansen* is Japan's high-speed train. It has a maximum speed of 300 km per hour. In English it's often called the "bullet train" because of its speed and design — the front of the train looks like a bullet. *Shinkansen* have different names for different routes. For example, the Shinkansen from Tokyo to Aomori is called the Hayabusa.

新幹線は日本の高速列車です。最高スピードは時速 300 km です。弾丸のように速く、正面が弾丸に似た形をしていることから、英語ではよく「弾丸列車」と呼ばれます。新幹線は路線によってそれぞれ名前をもっています。例えば、東京発・青森行きの新幹線は「はやぶさ」と呼ばれています。

➕ Have you ever heard the word Hayabusa used for something other than the *Shinkansen*? It's the name of a Japanese unmanned spacecraft, too. Hayabusa means "falcon."

新幹線以外で、はやぶさということばを聞いたことはありますか？ 日本の無人宇宙探査機の名前でもあります。「はやぶさ」を英語でいうと falcon です。

✈ 席の種類 (1₋2) [USE]

There are two types of seats on the *Shinkansen*: reserved and non-reserved. The cars are divided according to the type of seat. Reserved seat cars include Green Car and Grand Class, which have upgraded seats and services. Non-reserved seats are first-come-first-served, so if all the seats are occupied, you can either stand or wait for the next train.

新幹線には、指定席と自由席の２種類の座席があります。座席の種類によって車両が分かれています。指定席にはグリーン車とグランクラスといって、座席やサービスがグレードアップされているものもあります。自由席は早い者勝ちなので、座席が全部埋まっている場合は、立ったまま乗る、または次の電車を待つ、のどちらかを選びます。

マメ知識

新幹線の定義は「主たる区間を列車が 200 km/ 時以上の高速度で走行できる幹線鉄道」とされている。2011 年現在の日本の新幹線（東北新幹線）の最高営業運転速度は 300km/ 時。

bullet
弾丸、銃丸

unmanned
(乗り物が) 無人の

***car = carriage**
(車両、客車) ※電車の文脈で使われているとき、car は車両の意味。

Green Car
グリーン車

first-come-first-served
早い者勝ち

青春 18 切符 USE 1.2

"*Seishun zyuhachi kippu*" is a one-day ticket that can be used for unreserved seats on regular local JR trains throughout Japan. It is not valid for Limited Express or Shinkansen trains. It is available for a limited time each year in spring, summer, and winter. The period of use is also limited. It is a five-piece coupon ticket and can also be used by people other than the purchaser. The name of the ticket might lead one to imagine that this ticket is only for young people, but there is no age limit.

青春 18 切符は全国の JR 普通列車（各駅停車）の自由席で使用できる一日券です。特急や新幹線には乗車できません。毎年春、夏、冬に期間限定で発売されます。利用期間も限定されています。五枚綴りの回数券で、購入者以外の人も利用できます。切符の名称からこの切符は若者限定と想像してしまいますが、年齢制限はありません。

夜行バス USE 1.2

Night buses connecting major cities and towns are popular because they allow passengers to travel while they sleep and are inexpensive. Compared to the Shinkansen, they can be more than 50% cheaper, although this varies depending on the season and day of the week. Tickets can be purchased at major convenience stores.

主要な都市と都市を結ぶ夜行バスは、寝ている間に移動ができる上、料金が格安なので人気です。季節や曜日によって異なりますが、新幹線と比較して値引き率は 50% を上回ります。切符は大手のコンビニエンスストアで購入できます。

夜行バスの乗車風景   © show999/stock.adobe.com

現代の生活習慣　▶ Track 31

🐝女子会 〔=〕〔USE〕

A *joshi-kai* is a party or get-together for women only. Similar to office workers' drinking parties, many *joshi-kai* are held among friends or women working in the same office. But it's said that the main purpose of a *joshi-kai* is to exchange information or gossip that they would not like to reveal to men.

gossip
うわさ話、陰口

「女子会」は、女性だけが参加するパーティーや集まりのことです。職場の飲み会と同様に、友だちや同じ職場で働く女性たちの間で開かれます。しかし、女子会を催す主な目的は、男性には明かしたくない情報やうわさ話を交換することだと言われています。

🐝婚活 〔=〕〔USE〕

Konkatsu is a series of activities designed mainly for single women and men who would like to marry but have had difficulty finding a partner. A lot of single people are encouraged to participate in various activities including matchmaking parties, and to use marriage-related information services.

design
（特定の目的で）作る、
意図する

「婚活」は主に、結婚したいのにできない女性が結婚するための、一連の活動のことです。多くの独身者が、お見合いパーティーへの参加や結婚情報サービスの利用など、さまざまな活動をするよう促されています。

🐝マッチングアプリ 〔=〕〔USE〕〔?〕

With the coronavirus pandemic reducing the number of direct encounters, the use of matching apps has surged. They allow people to communicate over the Internet based on their registered profile information, and can lead to real-life encounters. However, one must be very careful because some people are using them for scams or solicitations.

surge
急激に高まる

コロナ禍で直接的な出会いが減ったことで、マッチングアプリを利用した婚活が定着しました。登録されたプロフィール情報をもとにインターネット

上でやり取りをし、リアルでの出会いにつなげる場です。ただし、詐欺や勧誘が目的の人もいるため十分に注意しなければいけません。

既読スルー （＝）（USE）（?）

Kidoku-suru is something that people do sometimes when exchanging messages on social media services. It means "leaving a read message unanswered." Once a message that you send has been read by the receiver, your screen indicates that it's "already read." It's regarded as bad manners not to reply to a message immediately, so *kidoku-suru* is often criticized. Also, leaving a message without checking it in the first place is called "*midoku-suru*." In some cases, the messages may simply be left alone, but you can also avoid a "read" mark by checking messages while using airplane mode and such.

leave
そのままにする

「既読スルー」は、SNS でやり取りをする際の態度のひとつです。この言葉は「読んだメッセージを、返答しないまま放っておく」という意味です。あなたが送信したメッセージを受信者がいったん読むと、あなたの画面に「既読」と表示されます。メッセージにすぐに返答しないのはマナー違反とみなされるので、「既読スルー」は往々にして批判されます。また、そもそもメッセージを確認せずに放置することは「未読スルー」と言われます。本当に確認していない場合もありますが、「未読スルー」と言われないために、機内モードなどを駆使して既読がつかないように確認することもできます。

終活 （＝）（　）（　）

Shukatsu sounds like the word for job-hunting, but the *kanji* are different. This *shukatsu* literally means "final actions." *Shukatsu* is what some elderly people do to prepare for death in order not to cause trouble for their family and society. An example is getting one's funeral plan and other things ready ahead of time.

「終活」は「就活」と同じに聞こえますが、漢字が異なります。この「終活」は文字通り、「最期のための活動」という意味です。「終活」とは、年をとった人たちが家族や社会に迷惑をかけないように、自分の最期の準備をするために行う活動です。一例を挙げると、あらかじめ自分の葬式やそのほかの準備をしておくことです。

 イクメン

Ikumen is a man who is actively involved in childrearing. Iku comes from *ikuji* – "child-rearing" – and *men* probably means "man." Ikumen may also be a play on words related to an older term, *ikemen* (which refers to a good-looking man).

「イクメン」は、子育てに積極的に関わる男性です。「イク」は育児から来ており、「メン」はおそらく男性のことです。「イクメン」にはまた、（顔立ちのよい男性を指す）「イケメン」という以前からの造語に引っかけた言葉遊びかもしれません。

➕ Do you have a word like *ikumen* in your home country?
あなたの国にもイクメンに当たる言葉はありますか？

Q&A

 日本語にはどんな略語がありますか？

Japanese has many shortened words. Some of them are short versions of long *kanji* combinations — for example, *shukatsu* is short for *shushokukatsudo*, meaning "job hunting." *Shukatsu* is used in the media and daily conversation. There are also shortened versions of many words without *kanji*. In many cases we connect the first part of each segment of the original word.

segment
区切り、断片

日本語には多くの略語があります。漢字が組み合わさった長い言葉を短くすることがあります。例えば、就活は job hunting を意味する「就職活動」の略語です。メディアや日常会話では、就活が使われます。漢字を使わない言葉にも多くの略語が存在します。多くの場合、元の言葉の各断片の最初の部分をつなぎ合わせます。

マスク（花粉症）

For a long time, Japanese people have had the habit of wearing masks because they have caught a cold, do not want to catch a cold, or cause trouble to those around them. With the proliferation of hay fever, mask wearing has increased dramatically, and spring has become the season for masks. During the recent COVID-19 pandemic, masks were worn throughout the country, and while this was viewed favorably, it was also seen as an overreaction, making it a difficult issue.

🌱マメ知識

風邪予防などの医療用マスクは surgical masks という。mask だけだと仮面の意味。

昔から日本人は、風邪を引きたくない、引いた、周囲の人に迷惑をかけたくない、といった理由でマスクを着用する習性がありました。花粉症が拡大すると、マスクの着用率が一気に高まり、「春はマスクの季節」といった風潮になりました。近年のコロナのパンデミックでは、国中一斉マスク着用という状態になり、好意的に取られる一方、過剰反応とも評され、難しい問題となりました。

 When do you wear surgical masks? Do you wear them when you have a cold?
医療用マスクはどのようなときに使いますか？ 風邪を引いたときにマスクを使いますか？

Q&A

 なぜ写真を撮るときにピースサインをするのですか？

automatically
無意識に、自動的に、

To be honest, nobody knows the real reason, but it is true that we automatically make the "peace sign" sign when having our photo taken. Some people say that a certain Japanese actor was the first to make the sign in a TV commercial back in the 1970s.

🌱マメ知識

「写真を撮る」は take a photo、「写真を撮ってもらう」は have a photo taken。日本語は撮る側と撮られる側を意識することなく「写真を撮る」と言いますが、英語では意識しましょう。

正直に言って、誰も本当の理由を知りませんが、確かに私たちは写真を撮られるときに無意識にピースサインをしますね。1970年代のCMである俳優がVサインをしたのが最初だという人もいます。

When we have our photo taken, we say "Cheese!" What about in your country?
日本では、写真を撮るときに「チーズ」と言いますが、あなたの国では何と言いますか？

✳クリスマス 🖥️ USE

We celebrate Christmas in a similar way to the West. Usually we have a special dinner, and children receive gifts from Santa Claus. The difference is that it is more an event for couples than families — usually for the younger generation. Couples exchange gifts, and visit places illuminated with lights and other special events. To many of us, Christmas is one of many yearly events. There is almost no consciousness of its religious aspect.

クリスマスは西洋と同じようなやり方でお祝いをします。一般的には、ごちそうを食べて、子どもたちはサンタクロースからプレゼントをもらいます。異なるのは、家族で行うイベントというよりもカップルのための、特に若い世代のカップルのためのイベントという色彩が強いことです。カップルでプレゼント交換をします。イルミネーションを見に行ったりイベントに出かけたりします。多くの日本人にとって、クリスマスはたくさんある年間行事のひとつであり、宗教的な側面はほとんど意識されません。

Q&A

 なぜクリスマスをチキンでお祝いする人がいるのですか？

You'll see many commercials and posters showing fried chicken during the Christmas season. Naturally, that makes people want to have chicken for Christmas dinner. Obviously, it's a promotional scheme, and it became a big success. Another reason may be that turkey is not as popular in Japan as in other countries.

promotional
宣伝の、販売戦略の

turkey
七面鳥、ターキー

クリスマスに七面鳥を食べるのはイギリスの風習。そのほかの国では、それぞれ独自のごちそうや伝統料理を用意して家族でお祝いをするのが一般的。

クリスマスの時期になるとフライドチキンが登場するコマーシャルやポスターが至るところに現れます。ですから、人々がクリスマスにチキンを食べたいと思うのは自然なことでしょう。明らかにプロモーション戦略のひとつですが、うまくいっているようです。また、もうひとつの理由として、日本では海外と比べると七面鳥が一般的ではないからかもしれません。

➕ Do you celebrate Christmas? What is the biggest holiday in your home country?
クリスマスをお祝いしますか？　あなたの国でいちばん盛り上がるお祝い行事はなんですか？

ホワイトデー

The 14th of March is White Day in Japan. On Valentine's Day, women give chocolates to men. The men who received chocolates buy candy or other sweets to give back to the women on White Day. It is said that chocolate and candy companies created these traditions as a marketing ploy.

日本では3月14日はホワイトデーです。バレンタインデーには女の子が男の子にチョコレートをあげます。チョコレートをもらった男の子は、ホワイトデーにキャンディーか何かのお菓子を買って女の子にお返しをするのです。チョコレートや菓子の会社のマーケティング戦略によって作られた習慣だと言われています。

マメ知識

ホワイトデーがあるのは、日本、韓国、台湾、中国の一部。

ploy
策略

➕ Do you give something back if you receive something on Valentine's Day?
バレンタインデーに何かもらったら、お返しをしますか？

ハロウィン

Originally held in ancient Ireland, Halloween was a festival to welcome ancestors home. It has become a festival in the U.S. and other English-speaking countries. In recent years, Halloween has been celebrated in Asia as well. Following the custom, children in Japan dress up in costumes and visit houses to receive sweets, and adults also dress up and enjoy parties. Just like in other countries, some of the participants create problems after too much drinking and merrymaking. The general public feels that self-discipline is necessary among the festive participants.

もともとは、古代アイルランドで行われていた、先祖を迎え入れるという、お盆の祭事です。アメリカを始め英語圏の国々でお祭りとして定着した後、近年ではアジアでも祝われるようになりました。風習にならい、日本でも子どもたちが仮装をしてお菓子をもらいに家々を訪ねますが、大人たちも仮装を施してパーティーを楽しみます。しかし他の国と同様、お酒が過ぎる、はしゃぎ過ぎるといった問題が起こりがちで、参加者の自制が求められます。

第四章 ● 現代ニッポン

151

🐝大人買い (=) (USE)

Otona-gai is buying products in bulk. This word usually refers to buying a whole set or series of products, like a complete series of comic books.

「大人買い」とは、商品を大量に買うことです。この言葉はふつう、商品を全セット、あるいは全シリーズ買うことを指します。例えば、漫画本を全巻買うといったことです。

🐝日本の住所 (¹·₂) (USE)

In Japan, addresses are written in order of the largest place to the smallest. In general, the address goes: prefecture, city, ward, and then the district (cho or town), followed by a series of numbers. The numbers indicate smaller divisions like blocks and the number on a building.

日本では住所は大きな地域から小さな地域の順に表します。一般的には、県、市、区、町村の順に並び、その後にいくつかの数字が続きます。続きの数字はさらに詳細を表すもので、街区や住居の番号を表します。

indicate
示す、意味する

マメ知識

海外では street（通り）ごとに家が順番に並んでいるのが一般的。

現代的な表現

▶ Track 32

🐝若者言葉 (USE) (📎) (📖)

Have you ever heard words and abbreviations based on foreign languages and dialects such as "*emoi*," "*shirankedo*," and "*otsu*" in everyday life? It can be difficult to immediately understand these Japanese youth words. The best way to understand them is to observe people who use them and ask them what they mean. However, if you awkwardly try too hard to use them, you will be told that it is "*itai*"(cringy), so beware!

「エモい」「知らんけど」「おつ」といった外国語や方言を元にした言葉や省略語などを、普段聞いたことはありますか？　こういった日本の若者言葉をすぐに理解するのは難しいでしょう。理解するためには若者言葉を使っている人たちを観察したり、その意味を聞いてみるのが一番です。ただし無理して使おうとすると、「イタい」と言われてしまうのでご注意を！

痛い

Itai has recently been used to mean that something is poor, sickly or disgraceful. The original meaning of this word refers to physical pain. Later, the meaning of "costly" was added. *Itai* is usually used as an adjective in phrases like "*itai hanashi*" (a disgraceful affair) and "*itai saito*" (a poorly designed website).

sickly
弱々しい、情けない

disgraceful
恥ずべき、不名誉な

costly
犠牲の大きい

adjective
形容詞の

self-deprecating
自虐的な

「痛い」は近年、物事が情けないこと、哀れなこと、みっともないことを意味して用いられるようになっています。この言葉の本来の意味は体に痛みがあることで、後に「犠牲の大きい」という意味が加わりました。「痛い」はふつう形容詞として用いられ、「痛い話」や「痛いサイト」のような形で使われます。

Have you seen a car covered with illustrations of anime characters? Those cars are called "*itasha*," short for "*itai* car." Actually, the owners of those cars call them *itasha* with a self-deprecating meaning.

アニメのキャラクターが車の表面に描かれている車を見たことがありますか？ そのような車を「痛車」と呼びます。痛車の持ち主も、自虐的な意味を込めて自分の車を痛車と呼びます。

めんどくさい人

A *mendokusai-hito* is a person who is difficult to get along with. Some features of *mendokusai-hito* are: they don't like to be alone and are always seeking attention; they consult others on trivial things; they are stubborn and never accept others' advice; and they carry a grudge for a long time. *Mendokusai* originally means "bothersome" or "a pain in the neck."

「めんどくさい人」とは付き合いにくい人のことです。「めんどくさい人」の特徴は、ひとりが嫌いでいつも人にかまってほしがる、ささいなことで人に相談する、頑固で他人の忠告を受け入れない、いつまでも根に持つ、といったことです。「めんどくさい」はもともと「迷惑な」あるいは「イライラの元」といった意味です。

キョロ充 [=] [✎] [USE]

The onomatopoeic term "*kyoro kyoro*" is used to describe an impatient or restless person. *Kyoro-zyu* is Internet slang for a person who is always floating around different groups of people for fear of being left out, usually in order to belong to a more powerful group.

周囲をせわしなく見回し落ち着きのない様子を擬音で「キョロキョロ」と表します。キョロ充とは、力あるグループに属するために、孤立を恐れて人の顔色や状況に合わせようといつも「キョロキョロ」としている人を蔑むネットスラングです。

かまちょ [=] [✎] [USE]

"*Kamacho*" is an abbreviation of "*kamatte choudai*" (please be nice to me). The term is common with the younger generation. *Kamacho* has a negative connotation because it suggests the person is annoying.

「かまちょ」とは「かまってちょうだい」を略した言葉です。若者言葉の一つで日常的に使われる言葉です。しかし「かまちょな人」と表す場合は、うっとうしい人だというネガティブな響きの言葉なので注意してください。

残念な人 [=] [✎] [USE]

"*Zannen-na-hito*" is a person who always falls short of others' expectations, even though they do their best. *Zannen-na* is a Japanese adjective that refers to something disappointing or someone who makes others feel regretful or sorry.

fall short
(予想や基準を) 満たしていない

「残念な人」は、いつもほかの人の期待に応えられない人のことです。本人は最善を尽くしているにもかかわらず、駄目なのです。「残念な」は日本語の形容詞で、人をがっかりさせるような事柄や、他人を後悔させたり残念な気持ちにさせてしまうような人物を指して使われます。

ハンパない [✎] [USE]

"*Hanpa-nai*" means that the extent*, volume or level of something is very large, high or extravagant. The complete form of this expression is hanpa-dewanai, which is a negative expression meaning that something is half complete*. *Hanpa-nai* is a slangy word mainly used by younger people.

*extent = degree
(程度)

volume
量

extravagant
途方もなく、法外的な

slangy
俗語的な

*half complete = incomplete
(不完全、中途半端)

「ハンパない」は、物事の程度や量、水準が非常に大きい、高いあるいは法外であることを表すのに用いられます。この表現の完全な形は「半端ではない」で、これは物事が中途半端であることを表す言葉の否定形です。「ハンパない」は俗語的な言葉で、主に若い世代の人たちに使われます。

どや顔 ☰ 📖 USE

Doya-gao is a proud or triumphant look on someone's face. *Doya* originally comes from the expression "*Doya*!" which is mainly used in the Kansai area. When someone is proud of what they have done, they might say "*Doya*!" meaning "How about that?!" *Gao* is an alternative pronunciation of *kao*, which means "face."

triumphant
勝ち誇った、得意の

alternative
代わりとなる、別の

「どや顔」とは、したり顔または得意顔のことです。「どや」はもともと「どや！」という表現に由来しています。これは主に関西地方で、自分のやったことを得意に思ったときに使う言葉で、「どうだ、すごいだろう」という意味を表します。「がお」は「かお」の音便のひとつで、face を意味しています。

➕ **Can you make a *doya* face?**
どや顔やってみて！

なんちゃって 🖊 📖 USE

Nanchatte is originally an expression meaning "It's just a joke." This expression is still used, but people mostly use *nanchatte* in combination with a noun in humorous contexts. When *nanchatte* is used with a noun, it means "fake" or "not real." If you say "*Nanchatte eigo*," it means language that sounds like English but is not real English.

noun
名詞

「なんちゃって」は もともと「ほんの冗談だよ」という意味の表現です。この表現は現在でもまだ使われますが、たいていは皆「なんちゃって」を名詞と組み合わせて、面白おかしい文脈で用います。「なんちゃって」が名詞と組み合わされると、「偽の」または「本物ではない」の意味で用いられます。「なんちゃって英語」と言えば、英語のように聞こえるけれど本当の英語ではない言葉を意味します。

マメ知識

英語で「冗談だよ」と軽く伝えたいときは、Just kidding! も便利。

➕ **Once you get used to *nanchatte*, it can be very useful. You should try using it!**
「なんちゃって」の使い方を覚えると、すごく便利ですよ。ぜひ使ってみてね。

イケてる

Iketeru comes from the old expression, *ikasu*, which refers to something or someone attractive or cool. *Iketeru* is usually used to describe a person's appearance, but people sometimes use it to describe an interesting story or funny joke. The negative form of this expression, *iketenai*, was coined more recently.

coin
（新語などを）造り出す

「イケてる」は昔からある「いかす」という表現が元になっており、物事や人物が魅力的な、あるいはかっこいいことを表します。「イケてる」は通例、人の容姿を説明するのに使われますが、話が面白いこと、あるいは冗談がおかしいことを表現するときにも使われます。最近になって、否定形の「イケてない」も使われるようになりました。

SNS

The purpose of social media is to transmit information. Unlike in other countries, where Facebook is the mainstream, in Japan social networking is centered around Twitter and Instagram. Some people do not use their real names, but rather nicknames or other pseudonyms.

pseudonym
偽名、仮名、ペンネーム

ソーシャルメディアは情報を発信するのを目的としています。なかでもコミュニケーション要素が強いものがSNSです。Facebookが主流な海外とは異なり、日本ではSNSといえばTwitterやInstagramが中心です。人によっては本名を載せず、あだ名などを使用して匿名でSNSを利用することもあります。

炎上

The word *enjo* means to burst into flames. It also refers to receiving a great deal of critical feedback online. One example is when people write malicious comments on social media sites or video streaming sites. Basically, an *enjo* is a heated discussion. The term *bazu-ru* means buzzing — when something goes viral on the Internet.

「炎上」とは「炎となって燃え上がる」ことを意味します。しかし、これはまた、ネットで批判的な意見を大量に受け取ることも意味します。一例は、人々がSNSやビデオストリーミングサイトに悪意のあるコメントを書くことです。この言葉は、ネットワーク上での激しい議論を意味する英語の用語 flaming とある程度、似ています。反対に、良い意味でネット上で急激に拡散され注目を集めることを「バズる」と言います。英語の「buzz」が語源ですが、意味合いとしては「go viral」が近いと思います。

✈絵文字

Emojis are used in text to convey emotional expressions. Although now a global standard, they actually originated in Japan. There is also a technique called *kaomoji*, which is the use of symbols and letters to create facial expressions.

絵文字はテキストを彩り、感情表現をより伝えやすくするためのアイテムです。今では世界規格となっていますが、実は日本発祥なんですよ😲　絵文字の他にも、記号や文字で表情を表す顔文字 (*´ᵕ`ᵕ)('·ω·`) という手法もあります。

 覚えておきましょう

文法キーワード

　日本語ならではの表現を英語で伝えるためには、その表現が使われる文脈を説明するほかに、実際の文章でどのような使われ方がされるのか文法的な説明が必要なケースもあります。必須ではありませんが、いくつかのキーワードを覚えておくといざというときに説明しやすくなることもありますので、余裕があったらぜひ覚えておきましょう。

主語 : subject
動詞 : verb
名詞 : noun
形容詞: adjective

副詞 : adverb
複数形: plural / plural form
単数形: singular / singular form
敬語: honorific

便 利 用 語 集 4

【和製英語】
●英語の表現を覚えましょう。●

・アルバイト　part-time job

・アプリ　app

・エアコン、クーラー　air conditioner

・オーダーメイド　custom-made

・カッター　box cutter

・キーホルダー　keyring

・コインランドリー　coin-operated laundry、laundrette（英）

・サラリーマン　office worker

・シーズンオフ　off-season

・シュークリーム　cream puffs

・ショートケーキ　sponge cake with strawberries on top

・スキンシップ　physical contact

・ダンボール　cardboard

・タッチパネル　touch screen

・テレビゲーム　video game

・ノートパソコン　laptop computer

・バイキング　buffet

・ピーマン　green pepper

・ビニールシート　plastic sheet

・プリント　handout、printout

・フリーサイズ　one-size-fits-all

・フロント　reception

・ベビーカー　baby carriage

・ホッチキス　stapler

・ホームページ　website、web page

・ポイントカード　loyalty card

・メールマガジン　e-mail newsletter

・ロスタイム　added time

・ワンピース　dress

第五章 ● 昔から今につながる習慣

国民の祝日カレンダー

▶ Track 33

1月

1日・元日　New Year's Day

Family members gather to celebrate the start of the New Year.

家族で集まり、新しい年の始まりを祝います。

第2月曜日・成人の日　Coming-of-Age Day

Men and women who have turned 20 in the past 12 months celebrate their coming of age.

過去12カ月の間に20歳になった男女の成人を祝います。

2月

11日・建国記念の日　National Foundation Day

The day commemorating the coronation of the first Emperor, Jimmu. This is the day people show their appreciation for the foundation of the country.

初代天皇であった神武天皇の即位の日。この日は、国民が建国を感謝する日です。

commemorate
祝う、記念する

coronation
即位

マメ知識

日付は、『日本書紀』にある神武天皇が即位したとされる日に由来している。

3月

20日／21日・春分の日　Vernal Equinox Day

Families gather and often visit their ancestors' graves.

家族が集まって、先祖の墓参りをしたりします。

vernal equinox
春分、秋分　※昼と夜の長さがほぼ等しくなるとき

マメ知識

春分の日はまれに、19日／22日になる年があります。

4月

29日・昭和の日　Showa Day

Originally the birthday of Hirohito, the Showa Emperor.

もともとこの日は昭和天皇の誕生日でした。

5月

3日 • 憲法記念日 Constitution Memorial Day

The day commemorating Japan's constitution, which became effective in 1947.

1947年の現憲法の施行を記念する日です。

4日 • みどりの日 Greenery Day

This is a day when people appreciate the blessings of nature and think about the environment.

この日は国民が自然の恵みに感謝し環境について考える日です。

blessings of nature
自然のめぐみ、自然の恩恵

5日 • こどもの日 Children's Day

People pray for the health and happiness of children.

子供の健康と幸せを願う日です。

7月

第3月曜日 • 海の日 Maritime Day

This is a day when people appreciate the blessings from the ocean and hope for a good life*.

国民が海の恩恵に感謝するとともに、繁栄を祈る日です。

*good life =prosperity
繁栄

8月

11日 • 山の日 Mountain Day

Similar to Maritime Day, it's a day to appreciate the blessings from the mountains and learn about nature.

海の日と同じように、国民が山の恩恵に感謝し、自然に親しむ日です。

9月

第3月曜日 • 敬老の日 Respect-for-the-Aged Day

This is a day to honor senior citizens and wish for their longevity.

高齢者を敬い、長寿を祝う日です。

第五章 ● 昔から今につながる習慣

23 / 24日 ● 秋分の日 Autumnal Equinox Day

This is a day when people honor their ancestors. Families gather and often visit their ancestors' graves.

先祖を敬う日です。家族で集まって先祖の墓参りをします。

第2月曜日 ● 体育の日 Health-Sports Day

On this day, people take part in athletic events to promote good health*.

この日は、運動の催しに参加し、健康を培う日です。

***good health**
= well-being
（健康で安心なこと）

3日 ● 文化の日 Culture Day

The constitution was ratified on this day; now it is a day for promoting cultural awareness*, love, freedom and peace.

現憲法が公布された日です。現在では、自由と平和を愛し、文化をすすめる日とされています。

***awareness**
= understanding
知識

23日 ● 勤労感謝の日 Labor Thanksgiving Day

Originally, this was a day to express gratitude to the Shinto gods for an ample harvest. Nowadays, people express gratitude to each other for their daily work and production.

もとは神道の神々に豊穣を感謝する日でしたが、現在では、勤労を貴び、生産を祝い、国民がたがいに感謝し合う日になりました。

ample
（場所が）広々とした、ゆとりがたっぷりある

天皇誕生日 The Emperor's Birthday

The day when the nation celebrates the birth of the Emperor. The holiday is observed on the birthday of the reigning Emperor.

天皇の誕生を祝う日です。この祝日は今上天皇の誕生日に合わせて制定されます。

ⅲ ゴールデンウイーク 〓📖🔖

Golden Week is a period with four national holidays, between April 29th and May 5th. Like the New Year holiday, it's a popular vacation time. All business activities slow down during Golden Week.

ゴールデンウイークは４つの祝日が集まっている期間で、４月29日から５月５日までを指します。正月と同様、ゴールデンウイーク中は多くの人々が休みを取り、社会活動が減速します。

ⅲ ハッピーマンデー 〓📖🔖✏

Happy Monday is when a holiday is moved to Monday to make a three-day weekend. In the past, all national holidays had designated dates. Then, some national holidays were moved to the nearest Monday. The law changed again in 2000 and 2003, and now Coming-of-Age Day, Maritime Day, Respect-for-the-Aged Day, and Health-Sports Day fall on Mondays.

ハッピーマンデーとは、３連休を作るために休日を月曜日に移動した日のことです。過去には、祝日はすべて決まった日でしたが、いくつかの祝日が直近の月曜日に移されました。2000年と2003年に施行された法律により、成人の日、海の日、敬老の日、体育の日は指定された月曜日になりました。

 覚えておきましょう

commemoration

記念日を説明するときに便利な単語が commemoration です。意味は「祝賀する、記念する」。「〜の記念日」は　The commemoration day of ... と表現できるので覚えておくと便利です。もちろんこの単語がすぐに出てこないときは、The memorial day of ... と言い換えれば伝わります。

The day commemorating the coronation of the first Emperor, Jimmu.
→The day to remember the coronation of the first Emperor, Jimmu.

日本人がおみこしを担ぎながら町を練り歩く光景は、きっと外国人には珍しいものでしょう。「おみこし」をあなただったらどうやって英語で説明しますか？ A mini house for *kami* ...？ それもいいかもしれません。では、「わっしょい」は？ この章で見てみましょう。

祭り

わっしょい わっしょい

What is this?

What are they wearing?
Is that another uniform?

Is there anything inside?

Why do they shake
them so hard?

What is this festival for?
Who are they performing
for?

p.171

着物

日本に来た外国人ならきっと一度は着物を着てみたいはず。
手ごろなのは浴衣ですが、本物の着物も味わってほしいですね。
着物を着る際に使われる帯や足袋など、それぞれの特徴が説明
できるときっと役に立つでしょう。

かんざし

A hairpin used when wearing a kimono.

着物

Why is it always left over right?

帯

A kimono belt.

おはしょり

Drape.

たび

How are they different from regular socks?

草履

They're like flip-flops.

Can I put it on by myself?
When should I wear it?
How is it different from a *yukata*?

p.166

着物と浴衣

▶ Track 34

🏠 着物 ▽ 🖊

Kimono literally means "clothing." It's a traditional outfit made of silk, cotton, linen, or wool. Over a period of hundreds of years, the *kimono* evolved in style and design.

> 着物とは文字通りには「衣服」という意味です。絹、木綿、麻、ウールで作られている伝統的な衣服です。何百年もの間、着物のスタイルやデザインは進化をとげてきました。

outfit
服装ひとそろい

evolve
発展する、発達する

🏠 着物の今と昔 🎭 ? 🧴

Until the nation's period of modernization (the mid-19th century), everybody wore kimonos. As Western-style clothing entered the country, people began to switch. Apparently, Western-style clothing allows people to move faster and easier. Today, people wear decorative* silk kimonos during the New Year, at tea ceremonies, weddings, school graduations, and other formal gatherings.

> 日本の近代化の時代（19世紀半ば）までは、みな着物を着ていました。洋服が日本に入ると、人々は洋服を着るようになりました。洋服によって素早く楽に動けるようになったのでしょう。現代では、正月やお茶会、結婚式、卒業式、そのほかのフォーマルな集まりに装飾的な絹の着物を着ます。

modernization
近代化

apparently
どうも〜らしい、見たところ〜のようだ

*decorative = fancy
（飾りの、装飾的な）

🏠 足袋 ▽ = USE

Tabi are ankle-high socks. They're worn with *zori*. They have a division between the big toe and second toe. On formal occasions, white *tabi* are needed. On casual occasions (at a friend's house, for example), it's okay to wear colored *tabi*.

> 足袋は足首までのソックスです。草履と一緒に使います。足袋は親指と隣の指の間に切れ込みがあります。正式な場では、白足袋を履きます。カジュアルな場面（例えば友人の家）では、色のついたものでもかまいません。

division
（細長い）切れ込み

ⅲ 草履と下駄 ▽ USE

Zori and *geta* are footwear that go with kimono. *Zori* are worn on casual and formal occasions. With *zori*, you need to wear *tabi*. *Geta* is a casual form of footwear, worn with a *yukata*. With *geta*, you don't need to wear *tabi*.

草履も下駄も、着物を着るときに履く履き物です。草履はカジュアルな場からフォーマルな場まで履きます。草履を履くときは必ず足袋もはきます。下駄はカジュアルな履き物で、浴衣を着るときに履きます。下駄を履くときは、足袋ははきません。

> ➕ Have you ever seen *geta*? They look like wooden flip-flops with heels.
> 下駄を見たことはありますか？　木でできたビーチサンダルにヒールがついたようなものです。

flip-flops
ビーチサンダル

sandal は夏用の軽い履き物全般を指す。flip flop はサンダルの一種。

ⅲ 帯 ▽ = USE

An *obi* is a long belt or sash that holds a kimono in place. *Obi* are categorized according to their design, material, formality and use. Kimono and *obi* look beautiful and never go out of fashion.

帯は着物をまとめる長いベルトもしくはサッシュです。デザイン、形式、素材、用途によっていくつかのタイプがあります。着物と帯は美しく、決して流行に左右されません。

sash 帯
material 素材
formality 形式

蝶々結びは butterfly knot。

> ➕ The standard length of an *obi* is 3 to 4 meters, or 10 to 13 feet. Can you imagine how to tie them?
> 通常の帯の長さは 3 から 4 メートル、つまり 10 から 13 フィートです。どうやって結ぶか想像できますか？

👆 覚えておきましょう

　女性の着物姿を引き立てる重要ポイントの一つは、襟全体と首筋を見せることです。浴衣でも本格的な着物でも、髪が長めの方はえいっとアップにしませんか。首まわりをスッキリさせると、着物の魅力が一気に倍増します。ぜひご検討ください。

Q&A

 着物を着るのは難しいですか？

Yes, it takes a while to master the technique. The popular way to learn is to go to so-called "kimono fitting classes." The teachers will teach you every detail you need to know. If someone you know can teach you, then you should go ask them to teach you. Actually, I can't put it on by myself either.

この技術を習得するにはいくらかの時間がかかります。着付け教室に通うのが一般的な学び方です。知っておくべきことを先生が細部にわたって教えてくれるでしょう。もし身近に教えてくれる知り合いがいれば、その人たちに教えをこうといいですよ。実は、私もひとりでは着物を着ることができません。

Q&A

 YouTube でマスターしようと思うのですが……。

That's not a good idea. It's better to have someone teach you in person. Videos like those on YouTube are probably better for reviewing.

それはお勧めしません。どなたかに直接習いましょう。YouTube のような映像は、復習に使用するのがいいでしょう。

覚えておきましょう

指の名前

英語で足の指は toe と言います。指といえばまず finger が頭に浮かんでしまうかもしれませんが、これは手の指のみを意味します。足の話をしていて finger と言うと、聞き手は混乱してしまいますので、要注意です。

浴衣

A *yukata* is a cotton kimono. Both men and women wear *yukata* at outdoor summer festivals or fireworks events. The *yukata* is a lightweight, casual type of clothing*, so the *obi* worn with a *yukata* should also be lightweight and casual.

*type of clothing = garment
（衣類）

浴衣は木綿の着物です。男性も女性も屋外で行われる夏の祭りや花火大会に浴衣を着て行きます。浴衣は軽くてカジュアルな着物ですから、帯も軽くてカジュアルなものを締めます。

➕ *Yukata* are basically "one-size-fits-all," so if you want to wear one, you can try mine on.
浴衣は基本的にフリーサイズだから、もしちょっと着てみたいなら、私の浴衣を試してみる？

浴衣の今と昔

The original form of *yukata* was made of linen and called *yukatabira*. About 1,000 years ago, aristocrats customarily took steam baths. The *yukatabira* is a very thin *kimono* that prevents one's skin from burning. Later, cotton became less expensive and was used as the fabric for all *yukata*.

linen 麻
aristocrat 貴族
steam bath 蒸し風呂
prevent 防ぐ

浴衣はもともと麻で作られていて、湯帷子と呼ばれていました。1000年ほど前、貴族は蒸し風呂に入る習慣がありました。湯帷子は皮膚をやけどから守るための、とても薄い着物でした。後に木綿が安価になり麻に取って代わりました。

覚えておきましょう

着物は右の前身頃を体に沿って巻き込み、左前身頃を上からかぶせるように着ます。男女とも同じです。その逆は「左前」と呼ばれ、死者の装束に用います。着物文化に疎い現代人の中には、このルールを知らない人もいます。着付けがわかっている人でも、他人に着せるとなると（例えば外国人の友人に頼まれた場合）、自分に着せるのとは勝手が違いますので、襟を間違って合わせてしまいがちです。「左前」は単純なミスではありますが、「縁起が悪い」と悪印象を残してしまうものです。人に浴衣や着物を着せるときは、必ず襟の合わせ方を念を入れて確認しましょう。

お花見 〔=〕〔USE〕

Ohanami is cherry blossom viewing. When the flowers are in bloom, people go to parks to view them. A lot of companies have *hanami* parties. Many parks are crowded with people having picnics, drinking, singing and dancing under the cherry trees.

お花見とは桜の花を眺めることです。桜が咲くと、人々は花を見るために公園へ出かけます。多くの会社でお花見をします。公園は桜の木の下で飲食をしたり、歌ったり踊ったりしたりする人でにぎわいます。

➕ You should bring good food, good sake, and a plastic sheet to sit on!
お花見へは、おいしい食べ物とよいお酒と座るためにビニールシートを持って出かけましょう！

夜桜 〔🗓〕〔USE〕

Yozakura literally means "night cherry blossoms." People gather after dark to enjoy viewing the cherry blossoms at night. It is a popular style of *hanami*. At night, some places even light up the cherry blossoms.

夜桜とは文字通りには夜の桜という意味です。暗くなってから集まり、夜の桜を楽しみます。人気のある花見のやり方です。夜に桜をライトアップするところもあります。

➕ Weather is important for cherry blossom viewing. Let's hope tomorrow will be a nice day!
お花見は天気が重要なんです。明日は晴れるといいですね！

▶ Track 36

🏛 祭り 📖 USE ❓

Matsuri means "festival." Matsuri are held to wish for things like a stable harvest, business prosperity, safety, longevity, and world peace. A *matsuri* is also an occasion to thank our ancestors for the protection they provide to the family and the community.

stable
安定した

prosperity
繁栄

longevity
長寿

祭りとはフェスティバルのことです。祭りは豊穣、商売繁盛、無病息災、長寿、この世の平和などを祈願するために行われます。家族や共同体を守っていてくれる先祖たちに感謝を表す機会でもあります。

🏛 神輿 ＝ USE

A *mikoshi* is a portable wooden shrine. During a festival, some people wearing jackets called *happi* carry *mikoshi* around the neighborhood on their shoulders. The design of *mikoshi* and the way they're carried are different in each neighborhood.

御輿は木製の「持ち運びできる神社」のようなものです。祭りのあいだ、法被（はっぴ）と呼ばれる上着を着て、御輿を担いで近所を練り歩く人もいます。神輿のデザインや担ぎ方は地域によって異なります。

➕ Can you guess who we are praying to? We're praying to *kami*, or Shinto god. *Matsuri* are a part of the Shinto religion.

誰に祈願しているかわかりますか？　神道の神（*kami*）です。祭りは神道に関係しています。

🏛 春祭りと秋祭り ❓

Two major events in shrines are the spring festival and the fall festival. In spring, people pray for a stable harvest. In fall, people give thanks for an ample harvest. Festivals are also held in summer, when people pray for stable weather.

ample 十分な

神社の２大行事は春と秋の祭です。春には豊穣を祈る祭が、秋には豊穣を感謝する祭が行われます。夏にも祭が開催され、天候の無事が祈られます。

出店

Demise are booths appearing inside or near shrines during festivals. *Demise* sell toys and food. You can also enjoy catching goldfish, playing shooting games, and so on. You may also hear the sounds of Japanese instruments like whistles and drums in the background.

出店は、祭りの間に神社の境内や付近に設置される屋台です。出店ではおもちゃや食べ物を売っています。金魚すくいや射的などのゲームも楽しめます。笛や太鼓といった和楽器の BGM があることもあります。

わっしょい

People shout when carrying *mikoshi*. The most popular words used are "*wasshoi*," "*essa*," and "*seiya*." There are many explanations for these words, but nobody knows which one is true. The words may not mean anything at all. They may just be "spirit-lifting" chants.

"spirit-lifting" chants
気が高まる音

御輿を担ぐときは掛け声を上げます。「わっしょい」「えっさ」「せいや」といった掛け声が最も一般的です。いわれについてはいろいろな説がありますが、確かなものはありません。意味はなく、ただ気を高めるだけの掛け声なのかもしれません。

Q&A

 御輿は結構荒っぽく扱われますが、どうしてですか？

People think that shaking the *mikoshi* makes the spirits livelier. Sometimes the carriers let two or three *mikoshi* crash into each other.

the spirits
（この場合は）神霊

lively
活発な、元気にさせる

神輿を大きくゆすることで神霊を活気づかせると信じられているからです。ふたつあるいは 3 つの御輿をぶつけ合うこともあります。

チャレンジ

お祭りに関するものを説明してみましょう。回答例は次のページにあります。

風鈴

●どこにさげる？

chime: 鈴
clear, light sound: チリンと鳴る

盆踊り

●誰が参加する？

local: 地域
tower:（ここでは）やぐら
traditional folk song: 民謡

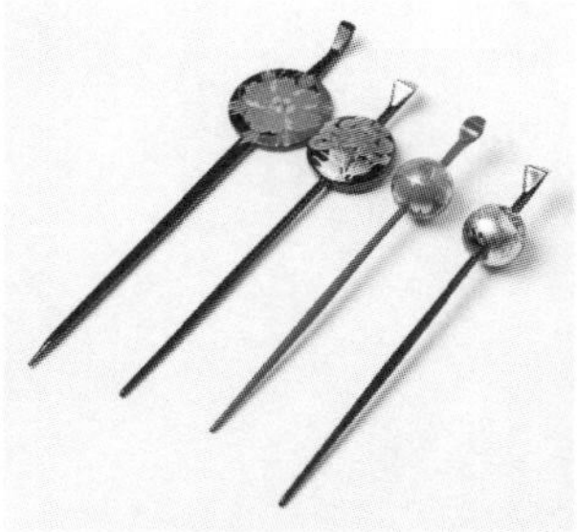

かき氷

●どこで食べられる？

shave: 薄く削る
flavored syrup: 味つきシロップ

かんざし

●昔はどのように使われていた？

decorative: かざりの
stick-shaped: 棒状の

提灯

●中には何を入れる？

portable: 持ち運びできる
ceiling: 天井／ bulb: 電球

ひょっとこ

●どこで登場する？

mask: お面
comical: ひょうきん

ラムネ

●名前の由来は？

glass ball: ガラス玉
push down: 押し込む

回答例は次のページ

風鈴 (=) (USE) 🔊

Furin are wind chimes. They're made of various materials, for example glass, iron or clay. They're hung outside by a window in the summer. When the weather is hot, the light, clear sound of the chimes makes people feel refreshed. When summer is over, people take down the chimes and store them until the next summer.

> 風鈴は wind chime です。ガラスや鉄、瀬戸物などいろいろな素材で作られています。夏の間、窓のそばにつるされます。夏の暑さの中で軽いチリンという音を聞いて人々はなごみます。夏が終わると風鈴は外され、次の夏までの間、しまわれます。

chime
チャイム、鐘

clay
粘土、土

盆踊り (▽) (=) 🎎

Bon odori is the local *bon* dance gathering, which community members participate in. *Bon* is the time when the spirits of our ancestors return from heaven. Some people describe it as the Japanese version of Halloween.

> 盆踊りは、地域の人々が踊りに参加する盆の集まりです。盆は天国から先祖の霊が帰ってくる期間です。日本版ハロウィーンと言えるかもしれませんね。

盆踊りの内容 (=) (USE)

In the local *bon* season, either mid-July or mid-August, each community hosts a *bon odori* to welcome ancestors when they come to visit. *Bon odori* is a form of entertainment; with cheerful *taiko* music and traditional folk songs, the dancers usually dance in a circle around a tower called a *yagura*.

> 7月の半ばもしくは8月の半ばの盆の季節になると、各地域で先祖を出迎えるために盆踊りを開催します。盆踊りは娯楽の一形態で、にぎやかな太鼓の音楽や昔からの民謡が流れ、踊り手たちはふつう、やぐらと呼ばれる塔の周りで輪になります。

What kinds of music are played at local festivals in your home country?

あなたの国では、地域のお祭りでどんな音楽が使われますか？

提灯 = USE 🔊

A *chochin* is a Japanese lantern. It's a traditional portable lighting device made of a bamboo frame and *washi* paper. Traditionally, there was a candle inside, but nowadays light bulbs are used for safety reasons. *Chochin* are essential for festivals and ceremonies. They can be hung from a hook or carried by hand.

bulb
電球

> 提灯は日本のランタンです。細長い竹の軸と和紙で作られている伝統的な携帯照明器具です。昔は中にろうそくを入れて使用していましたが、近ごろでは電球が使われています。お祭りや儀式には欠かすことができません。提灯はかぎから吊り下げることもできれば、手で持ち歩くこともできます。

ひょっとこのお面 ▽ USE

Hyottoko is a type of mask. It represents a comical male character. *Hyottoko* appear in traditional dances. In many cases, *hyottoko* appear with a female partner, *okame*.

> ひょっとこは、お面の一種です。ひょうきんな男性を表すもので、伝統的な踊りに登場します。女性のパートナーであるおかめと共によく登場します。

かき氷 ▽ USE

Kakigori is shaved ice. You find it at festivals or restauraunts in summer. If you buy an ice shaver, you can make it at home. You pour flavored syrup (lemon, strawberry, melon, etc.) on top, then eat it.

shave
～を薄く削る

> かき氷は削った氷です。夏には夏祭りや食べ物屋などで見かけるでしょう。かき氷機を買えば家庭でも作ることができます。いろいろな風味のシロップ（レモン、イチゴ、メロンなど）をかけて、食べます。

第五章 ● 昔から今につながる習慣

Cold food gives you an ice cream headache, doesn't it? Are you alright?

冷たいものを食べると頭がキーンと痛くなりますよね。大丈夫ですか？

ラムネ ▽ USE

Ramune is a type of soft drink popular among children. The name originally comes from "lemonade." *Ramune* comes in bottles and is sold mostly at festivals. At the top of the bottle there's a small glass ball that serves as a cap. The fun part is, you need to push the glass ball down into the bottle before you drink.

ラムネは子どもたちに人気のあるソフトドリンクです。ラムネという名前はレモネードに由来しています。瓶に入っていて、たいていはお祭りで売られます。瓶には飲み口のところにガラス玉がついていて、それが蓋の役目をしています。ガラス玉を強く瓶の中に押し込むところが楽しいです。

マメ知識

アルコールを含まない飲み物全般を soft drink と言う。炭酸飲料を明確にしたいときは soda。

cap
蓋

➕ Some shops collect the empty bottles and give them to a recycling company. So you should ask the shop owner if they are collecting them or not.

空き瓶を回収してリサイクル業者に渡してくれるお店もあります。だから、お店の人に瓶を集めているかどうか聞いてみましょう。

かんざし ▽ USE

Kanzashi are hair accessories used for women's traditional hairstyles. There are many different shapes of *kanzashi*. Some are decorative, but some have simple stick shapes. In the old days when men and women wore *kimonos* and traditional hairstyles, women commonly wore stick-shaped *kanzashi*.

かんざしは女性の伝統的な髪型に使われる髪飾りです。さまざまな形のものがあります。飾りのたくさんついたものもあれば、シンプルな棒状のものもあります。男性も女性も着物を着て伝統的な髪型をしていた昔は、女性は通例、棒状のかんざしをつけていました。

七五三

▶ Track 38

🎐 七五三 ▽ ☰

Shichi-Go-San is a celebration for children aged seven, five, and three. It's on November 15th. Generally, girls celebrate at the ages of seven and three, and boys celebrate at the ages of five and three. Children dress up nicely in either *kimono* or Western clothes and visit a shrine with their family.

七五三は、11月15日に7歳、5歳、3歳の子どもを祝う行事です。一般的には、女の子は7歳と3歳のとき、男の子は5歳と3歳のときに祝います。子どもたちはきちんと着物や洋服を着て、家族と一緒に神社へお参りに行きます。

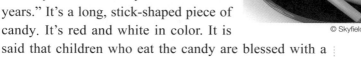

➕ We usually take commemorative photos on this day. Do you have any children's events like this in your country?

七五三の日には、記念写真を撮るのがふつうです。お国にもこのような子どもの行事はありますか？

🎐 千歳飴 📓 USE ❓

Parents buy *chitose ame* for their children on *Shichi-Go-San. Chitose ame* literally means "candy of a thousand years." It's a long, stick-shaped piece of candy. It's red and white in color. It is said that children who eat the candy are blessed with a thousand years of happiness.

© Skyfield/stock.adobe.com

七五三では、親は子どもに千歳飴を買い与えます。千歳飴は文字通りには「千年の飴」という意味です。長い棒状の飴で、紅白の色がついています。千歳飴を食べた子どもは千年の幸せに恵まれると言われています。

➕ What is the candy for Christmas called? It's shaped like a letter "J," and it's red and white in color.

クリスマスに食べるキャンディは何と呼ばれますか？　アルファベットのJの形で赤と白のキャンディです。

マメ知識

クリスマスのキャンディは candy cane と言います。

七五三のお祝いは 11 月 15 日にしなくてはいけないのですか？

 ?

No. It doesn't have to be on November 15th. It is not a national holiday, so children may have school and their parents may be working on that day. The families tend to conduct the ceremony earlier, on the nearest Saturday or Sunday.

conduct
とり行う

　いいえ。11 月 15 日でないといけないことはありません。この日は国民の祝日ではないので、子どもは学校があり、親は仕事に行かなくてはならないことがあります。その場合、お祝いを手前の土曜日や日曜日に行うことが多いようです。

お見合い

▶ Track 39

お見合い ▽ ≡

Omiai are arranged meetings between men and women, with the possibility of marriage. They're like arranged marriages, but the two people are free to decide whether or not they want to get married.

　お見合いとは、男性と女性の結婚を目的としてお膳立てされる出会いです。Arranged marriage のようなものですが、結婚したいか否かは、ふたりの自由意志です。

覚えておきましょう

　欧米ではお見合いを arranged marriage と呼びます。当事者の意思を無視した強制結婚と思い込んでいる人も少なくありません。お見合いについて尋ねられたときは、meeting であり、断ることができるものだと明言しておくのがよいかもしれません。

🏛 伝統的なお見合い 🟰

In the old days, the parents asked someone they knew to be the matchmaker*, and that person would look for a suitable partner for the son or daughter. A résumé and photos are often required for traditional *omiai*. It's a lot like a job interview.

*matchmaker = go-between
（仲人、仲介者）

résumé
履歴書

昔からのやり方は、親が知っている人に仲人になってもらうよう依頼し、仲人はふさわしい相手を探します。典型的なお見合いでは、身上書と写真が必要です。就職面接のようですよね。

➕ **Are there arranged marriages in your country?**
あなたの国にもお見合いはありますか？

幸運を呼ぶアイテム

▶ Track 40

🏛 招き猫 🔽 🟰 USE

A *manekineko* is a small cat figurine. It stands on its hind feet and raises a front paw to make an inviting gesture. *Manekineko* symbolize good luck and fortune. It is believed that the right front paw attracts money and the left front paw attracts customers.

hind 後ろの
front paw 前足

招き猫は日本でよく見られる小さなネコの人形です。2本の後ろ足で立ち、片方の前足で招くしぐさをしています。招き猫は幸運と富の象徴です。右前足を上げている猫はお金を招き、左前足を上げているものは客を招くと言われています。

➕ **Do you know where you can find *manekineko* in the city? At the lottery stand!**
街の中で招き猫がいる場所を知っていますか？　宝くじ売り場です！

カエル

In Japanese, the verb "return" and the noun "frog" have the same pronunciation – "*kaeru*." Parents often buy items such as bags, wallets and handkerchiefs with images of frogs for their children. The pun expresses parents' wish that their children always return home safely.

日本語で動詞の return は「かえる」、名詞の frog も「カエル」です。発音は同じです。母親がカエルの絵がついた鞄、財布、ハンカチといった小物を子どもに買え与えることがあります。これは、子どもたちが無事に帰ることを祈る語呂合わせです。

verb 動詞

noun 名詞

pronunciation
発音

pun
語呂合わせ、だじゃれ

だるま

Daruma are round, three-dimensional figures. They are usually red in color, and have no eyeballs. *Daruma* are believed to be the figure of the founder of Zen. People buy *daruma* when making a wish, such as when trying to pass a big examination or win an election. When the wish is granted, the eyeballs are painted in with black ink using a brush.

だるまは丸い 3 次元の像です。通常赤い色をしていて、目の球がありません。だるまは禅の開祖の像だと信じられています。願いごとをするとき、例えば、大きな試験に合格したい、選挙に勝ちたいというとき、だるまを買って祈願をします。願いが叶うと、筆と墨で目玉を描き込みます。

three-dimensional
三次元の、立体感のある

founder
創設者、開祖

election
選挙

grant
（願いを）聞き入れる

マメ知識

招き猫、カエル、だるまのような縁起物を総称して lucky charm と言う。

葬儀 ▶ Track 41

葬儀と宗教 （二）

Today, many funerals are conducted in the Buddhist style in Japan. As the word "funeral Buddhism" indicates, funerals are almost the only occasion we really care about religion. However, in recent years, more funerals are conducted with no religious elements.

indicate
指す、意味する

今日では、日本の多くの葬儀は仏式で行われています。「葬式仏教」という言葉が示すように、葬儀は私たちが宗教を意識するほぼ唯一の機会です。しかし近年は、葬儀を無宗教で行う例が増えています。

通夜と葬式 （USE）

When someone passes away, two events are conducted to send the spirit to heaven – a wake and a funeral. A wake is held the night before the funeral, usually from 6 p.m. to 9 p.m. The funeral is usually conducted during the daytime.

wake
通夜

人が亡くなると、霊を天国に送るためのふたつの儀式を行います。通夜と告別式です。通夜は告別式の前の晩、ふつうは午後6時から9時まで行います。告別式は通常昼間行います。

服装 （USE）

When attending a funeral, all clothes, including shoes, bags and hair accessories, should be black (except men's shirts, which should be white). Shiny or decorative items must not be carried. When attending a wake, dark gray and/or dark blue clothes are acceptable.

shiny
ぴかぴか光った

decorative
装飾的な

告別式に参列する際は、服、靴、バッグ、髪飾りなどすべて黒いものを着用します（例外は男性のシャツでこれは白を着用）。ぴかぴか光るものや飾りのあるものは持っていってはいけません。通夜に参列するときは、濃いグレーや紺の服でもかまいません。

マメ知識

真珠のアクセサリーのみ着用可能。

第五章 ● 昔から今につながる習慣

香典 ▽ USE

Koden is a monetary gift. It should be presented at the reception when attending wakes or funerals. The amount of money is set in accordance with the person's relationship and closeness to the deceased.

monetary
貨幣の

in accordance with…
〜に従って

deceased
故人

香典とは、現金の贈り物です。通夜や告別式に参列するときに、受付で渡します。亡くなった人との関係と親しさによって、金額を決めます。

➕ Do you have customs involving the giving of money or something similar at funerals in your home country?
あなたの国では葬儀で現金またはそれに類するものを渡すような習慣はありますか？

通夜ぶるまい USE 1、2

At *tsuya*, food and alcohol are served in a separate room. Eating and drinking at this event is an act of mourning, so if you are invited, you should not hesitate to attend. You stay for about 20 minutes, finish some food and sake, and leave the room. If you do not have time, you may leave without attending.

通夜では、別室で食事や酒が振る舞われます。この場での飲食は供養を意味するので、もし招待されたならば、遠慮なく参列します。滞在は 20 分程度におさめ、いくらかの料理やお酒に手をつけて退室するのが作法です。時間がない場合は、列席せずに帰っても問題ありません。

清め塩 USE ?

A small packet of salt is handed out to people leaving a wake or funeral. They open the packet of salt before entering their home and sprinkle it over their body. It is also acceptable to ask family members to do this on their behalf. Sprinkling salt is an act of purification.

packet
小包、小さな袋

sprinkle
まく

通夜や告別式の場を去るとき、小さな袋に入った塩が参列者に渡されます。参列者は自宅に入る前、塩の袋を開けて静かに体に振りかけます。家の人に頼んで塩を振りかけてもらうのでもかまいません。塩を振るのは、清める行為です。

➕ Can you think of any purification rituals in your country?
あなたの国で行われている清めの行為を、何か思いつきますか？

結婚式

▶ Track 42

結婚についての考え方 (=) (?) 🖊

The trend in Japan, as well as in many other countries, is for women to pursue their own careers. As a result, fewer women marry, or more women delay marriage. Currently, Japanese men and women marry later in life than before. The option to never marry is more accepted as well.

Traditionally, parents were responsible for ensuring that their children marry. Even as children have had the right to choose their own marriage partner, parental approval has always been quite important. Recently, though, there is growing acceptance that the wishes of the child, and not the parent, should outweigh more. The reluctance towards international marriage is also declining.

Even so, the importance of "remaining part of the family" should not be underestimated. It is essential for children to tell their parents about a potential marriage partner and to arrange for a proper introduction to the family.

outweigh
重要である、価値が上回る

reluctance
抵抗感、気の進まなさ

第五章 ● 昔から今につながる習慣

日本でも諸外国と同様に、女性の社会進出が進むと結婚しなくなる、しづらくなるという傾向があります。男女とも結婚年齢の高齢化はいたし方なく、結婚しないとの選択肢も容認されつつあります。

伝統的に、子どもの結婚は親の責務でした。また子どもが選択権を持てる時代になっても、親の承認無しには結婚に至れないという束縛は普通の現象でした。しかし近年は本人の意志を優先するとの考え方が広まっています。国際結婚に対する抵抗感も、ぐっと薄まりました。

そうは言っても、日本の社会で暮らすのであれば、「個人であっても家族の一員」という意識を軽んじるのは望ましくありません。事前の報告や紹介は必須です。

Ⅲ 結婚式と宗教 (≡)(✎)

Traditionally, Japanese weddings were conducted in the Shinto style or the Buddhist style. Nowadays, the two major styles of wedding are Shinto and Christian. Buddhist weddings have become very rare. Lately, the number of civil weddings, with no connection to any religion, is gradually increasing.

civil
（宗教に対して）俗人の、俗世間の

伝統に従えば、日本の結婚式は、神式もしくは仏式で行われます。最近では、神式かキリスト教式のふたつが主流です。仏式はすっかり珍しいものとなってしまいました。宗教に関係ない人前結婚式も最近は増えてきています。

➕ Are civil weddings popular in your country? I was wondering if it might be only in Japan.
あなたの国では人前結婚式は一般的ですか。日本だけで行われているものかなと思っていまして……。

�Ⅲ 式と披露宴 (USE)(1₂)

There are two events at a wedding; the ceremony and the reception. First, you should check which one you are invited to. In many cases, wedding ceremonies are attended by a small number of relatives. If the invitation does not mention the ceremony, it means you are only invited to the reception.

reception
披露宴

relative
親戚、血縁

婚礼にはふたつの儀式があります。結婚式と披露宴です。招待を受けた際は、まずどちらに招待されたかを確認しましょう。多くの場合、結婚式は少数の親族のみで行われます。受け取った招待状に結婚式について書かれていなければ、披露宴のみに招待されたという意味です。

➕ What is a typical wedding like in your home country? Are home weddings common?
あなたの国の一般的な結婚式はどんなものですか？　家で行う結婚式は一般的ですか？

🏛 女性の服装 ❌ USE

Guests should not wear plain white clothes. Traditionally, black should also be avoided. If you wear black clothes, you should wear decorative or shiny accessories so that it is clear that you are not attending a funeral.

招待客は、白無地の服を着てはいけません。黒も避けるべきであると昔から言われてきました。黒い服を着る場合は、葬儀に参列しているのではないということが明らかになるように、飾りや光るアクセサリーをつけるようにしましょう。

🏛 男性の服装 USE

Men should wear a black suit. The same black suit can be worn at a funeral, but if you wear it with a white tie, it becomes a formal suit for a wedding guest.

男性は黒いスーツを着ます。黒いスーツは葬儀にも着られますが、白いネクタイを締めれば、結婚式の参列者の正式な服装になります。

➕ **Are there any rules about what to wear to weddings in your country?**
あなたの国では結婚式の服装に何か決まりはありますか？

🏛 引き出物 ＝

At the end of the reception, guests are given a gift bag, which is called *hikidemono*. Traditionally, the couple getting married chooses and prepares the gifts. But recently, many couples give gift certificates or gift catalogues, so guests can get whatever they want.

披露宴の最後に、贈り物の入った袋が参列者に渡されます。これは引き出物と呼ばれます。以前は、新郎新婦が贈り物を選んだものでしたが、最近では、新郎新婦は引き出物として商品券あるいはカタログを渡します。参列者はその中から欲しいものを注文します。

お中元とお歳暮 ▶ Track 43

お中元とお歳暮

In Japan, we have a custom of giving gifts twice a year
to thank people for their help and friendship in social and
business situations. The gifts that are given in the
summer are called *ochugen* ("mid-year gift" in English),
and the ones given in the winter are called *oseibo* ("year-
end gift" in English).

mid-year
半年の

　日本では年に2回、社会生活や仕事の上でお世話になったりお付き合いの
ある人たちに対して、感謝の印として贈り物をする習慣があります。夏に贈
るのはお中元、暮れに贈るのはお歳暮と呼びます。

今と昔

Traditionally, the gifts were delivered in person by
visiting the recipients' home. However, in today's
society, they are often delivered by the department store
or individual shop where they were purchased.

in person
本人が直接

　正式には、贈り物は相手方の家に持参するものです。しかし最近では、デ
パートや専門店が直接配達をすることがほとんどです。

Q&A

何を贈ればいいのでしょう？　贈っては失礼になるものはありますか？

Any gift is acceptable! Popular gifts include tea, coffee,
seaweed, sake, wine, beer, soft drinks, flowers, fresh
fruit, meat or fish, towels, gift certificates, and so on.
There are no particular rules for the gifts. You don't
have to worry.

gift certificate
商品券

　何でもいいのです！　人気のある贈り物は、お茶、コーヒー、海苔、日本酒、
ワイン、ビール、ソフトドリンク、花、果物、肉や魚、タオル、商品券な
どなどです。贈り物に特に決まりごとはありません。悩む必要はありません。

お金を贈る習慣

お金を包む [=] [USE]

Giving cash as a gift is indeed very common. It is easier than worrying about what to buy. Wrapping the cash is very important. Whether it is given to congratulate people or express sympathy*, the cash must always be wrapped nicely.

現金を贈るとはごく普通に行われます。何を買って渡したらよいかを心配するより簡単です。贈るお金を包むということが重要です。お祝いするときもお悔やみを表すときも、お金は綺麗に包まなければいけません。

indeed
実に、いかにも

sympathy
お悔やみ

*sympathy =
condolence
（お悔やみ、弔辞）

のし袋 [▽] [=] [USE]

Noshibukuro are decorated envelopes used for monetary gifts – coins or bills. People have to use *noshibukuro* when giving monetary gifts. Breaking this rule is considered extremely rude.

のし袋は、贈答の硬貨やお札を入れるための飾りのついた封筒です。現金を贈る際は、必ずのし袋に入れなければなりません。この決まりを破るのは大変に粗野であるととらえられます。

お年玉 [=]

On or around New Year's Day, people give gifts of cash to their children, young relatives, and/or the children of their close friends. Either coins or bills may be given.

元日や正月には自分の子どもや親戚の子ども、あるいは仲のよい友人の子どもに現金の贈り物をあげます。硬貨でもお札でもかまいません。

マメ知識

お年玉を入れる小ぶりの封筒を「ポチ袋」という。「これっぽっち＝少ないですが」という謙虚な気持ちが表れた表現。

➕ Do you have a custom of giving money on New Year's Day in your country? I used to love this custom when I was a child.

あなたの国には新年にお金をあげる習慣はありますか？　子どものころは大好きな習慣でした。

第五章 ● 昔から今につながる習慣

187

不祝儀（香典）

At funerals or wakes, we give money in an envelope. This is called a *koden*. New, crisp bills should not be used because it gives the impression that you were expecting the person's death.

> 告別式や通夜でもお金を渡します。それは香典です。故人の死を予見していたという印象を与えてはいけないという理由で、新札を用意してはいけません。

crisp
ぱりっとしている

仏前と霊前の違い

When giving *koden*, you must choose the writing on the envelope according to the timing and the religion conducting the funeral. If the *koden* is given during a traditional Buddhist or Shinto-style wake or event, you should write "*goreizen*." If it is given after a traditional Buddhist style funeral, you should write "*gobutsuzen*."

> 香典を渡す際、渡すタイミングと葬儀が行われる宗教によって、封筒に書く文字が違ってきます。伝統的な仏式や神式の葬式や告別式などで渡す際は、「御霊前」と書きます。仏式では葬式の後に渡す場合は「御仏前」と書きます。

➕ Do you have an annual memorial event after the funeral?
お葬式の後に定期的に行う儀式はありますか？

結婚祝い

Cash gifts are given to a married couple at a wedding. Bills should be new and crisp. The amount should start with an odd number – for example, 10,000 yen, 30,000 yen or 50,000 yen. This is because even numbers can be divided in two, and this is considered bad luck for the couple.

> 結婚の際には、現金が贈られます。札は新札でしわのないものでなくてはなりません。額は1万円、3万円、5万円と、必ず奇数にします。2で割れる偶数は不吉と考えられています。

odd number
奇数

even number
偶数

その他習慣 ▶ Track 45

🏮 盛り塩 [USE] [?] 🖊

Salt has been used for purification in the Shinto religion since the old days. People today still use salt for such purposes. One example is how *sumo* wrestlers throw salt into the ring. Another example is *morishio*, which is a small pile of salt on a small plate or a dish left outside shops. The salt is there to repel evil. Some records say that this custom has been around for more than 1,300 years.

repel 追い払う
evil 邪悪、不運

古代より神道では、塩が清めとして使われてきました。現代人もそうします。ひとつの例として、お相撲さんが土俵に塩をまくことが挙げられます。もうひとつの例は、盛り塩です。店の外に小さく塩を盛った皿を置きます。塩は邪気を追い払うと言います。記録によれば、この習慣は 1300 年以上前からあるものだそうです。

> ➕ Do you have any customs for keeping away evil in your home country?
> あなたの国には、悪を追い払うための習慣は何かありますか？

🏮 飲み会 [USE] [?] 🖊

A *nomikai* is a small-scale dinner and drinking party. They offer a chance for people to gather and chat, but many find them stressful because of drinking etiquette and the obligation to entertain superiors. Drinking parties held at home are called *ie-nomi* or *taku-nomi*. When COVID-19 kept bars and restaurants closed, *online-nomi* using video conferencing services like Zoom also began.

所属する集団で開催される、お酒を飲む小規模な食事会を「飲み会」といいます。コミュニケーション手段の一つですが、飲酒を強制されたり目上の人に対する接待を求められたりと、飲み会を苦痛に感じる人も少なくありません。飲み会の中でも、自宅で行うものは「家飲み・宅飲み」といいます。コロナ禍で酒場の営業時間が規制されたことで、Zoom などのビデオ会議アプリを使用した「オンライン飲み」という文化も登場しました。

第五章 ● 昔から今につながる習慣

189

衣替え

Koromo-gae means "wardrobe rotation." This refers to putting away your clothes for the previous season and taking out your clothes for the new season. This custom is said to have started in the Heian period.

put away
片付ける

「衣替え」とは「衣類の入れ替え」という意味です。つまり、それまでの季節の衣類をしまって、これからの季節の衣類を取り出すことです。この習慣は平安時代に始まったと言われています。

Q&A

 子どもの歯が抜けた際は、どのようなことをするのですか？

 USE

According to a Japanese tradition, the child goes out into the yard and stands with their back to the house. If a lower tooth came out, the child throws it backwards, trying to aim at the top of the roof. If an upper tooth came out, the child throws it backwards under the *nokishita*, the space under traditional Japanese houses.

yard
庭（garden より小さいイメージ）

日本の習慣では、子どもは庭に出て家を背にして立ち、抜けたのが下の歯ならば屋根に向かって後ろ向きにその歯を投げます。抜けたのが上の歯ならば日本の伝統的家屋の屋根の下のスペースである軒下に投げます。

覚えておきましょう

　欧米社会には、「歯の妖精：the tooth fairy」がいるとの言い伝えがあります。乳歯が抜けた日の夜、子どもは歯を枕元に置いて寝ます。寝ている間にやってきた妖精が歯を持ち帰るのですが、代わりに小銭を置いていってくれるのです。子どもにとってはうれしい「臨時収入」です。しかしもらえるのはあくまでも小銭であって、お札は期待できません。もし外国人に「日本には歯の妖精がいますか」と質問されたとしたら、この伝説の存在を尋ねられているのだと思い出してください。

日本と四季

文・平田久子

日本人は古代より季節の移り変わりを意識し、その美しさを尊んできました。
その意識は現在でも引き継がれています。テレビのニュース番組では、「今日は立春です、暦の上では春ですが」といったコメントと共に、春の兆しをほのめかす映像が流れます。節句の時期には、飾りをつくる幼稚園児の姿が映し出されたりもします。

現代に引き継がれてきた年中行事のほとんどは、中国から伝わった「二十四節気」(24 solar terms) と「五節句」(24 divisions of the solar year) をもとにしています。

二十四節気では、四季を６つに分けています。
春：立春・雨水・啓蟄・春分・清明・穀雨
夏：立夏・小満・芒種・夏至・小暑・大暑
秋：立秋・処暑・白露・秋分・寒露・霜降
冬：立冬・小雪・大雪・冬至・小寒・大寒

これら十五日ごとの区切りは気象条件の移り変わりを説明しています。農耕を営む上での目安になるため、国全体に広まりました。日付を知らない農民も、二十四節気を追っていれば農耕のスケジュールが適切に組めたのです。

五節句とは、人日・上巳・端午・七夕・重陽の節句を表します。旬の植物から生命力をもらい、邪気を祓うのが、これらの節句の目的と言われています。男女の節句につきものの桃と菖蒲も、古来より魔を祓うものと信じられてきました。

昔も今も、季節を最も実感させるのは食材でしょう。七月末の土用の丑の日 (the day of the ox in midsummer) は、夏バテ防止策として鰻を食す習慣ができました。他にも「正月のご馳走で疲れた胃腸を休めるには七草粥（rice porridge with seven herbs）」、「冬至の日はゆず湯に入り、かぼちゃを食べて風邪を防ぐ」等々、旬の食材を摂り、健康を維持しようとの思いが受け継がれてきました。

季節感を楽しむ行為の裏には、五穀豊穣（the productiveness of grain）と無病息災（state of perfect health）を願う気持ちが込められているのです。

【アメリカ英語 VS イギリス英語　単語の対照表】

●それぞれの使い分けを覚えましょう●

日本語	アメリカ英語	イギリス英語
ごみ	trash	rubbish
ガソリン	gasoline	petrol
（車の）トランク	trunk	boot
薬局	drug store, pharmacy	chemist
地下鉄	subway	(the) underground
駐車場	parking lot	car park
サッカー	soccer	football
アパート／マンション	apartment	flat
エレベーター	elevator	lift
高速道路	freeway	motor way
弁護士	lawyer	solicitor
懐中電灯	flashlight	torch
フライドポテト	french fries	chips
缶	can	tin
クッキー	cookie	biscuit
テイクアウト	take out	take away
幼稚園	kindergarten	nursery school
小学校	elementary school	primary school, lower school
中学校	middle school, junior high school	middle school, secondary school
高校	high school, senior high school	high school, upper school, senior school, college
大学	college, university	university
公立学校	public school	state school
私立学校	private school	independent school, public school（中高一貫の私立）
1階、2階、3階、…	first floor, second floor, third floor, ...	ground floor, first floor, second floor, ...

第六章 ● 価値観・考え方

日本人の価値観

Let's look at some characteristics of Japanese people.

　日本人を象徴する価値観とはどんなものでしょう。「なぜ謙虚が美徳なのか」「敬語は誰に使うものなのか?」など、私たちにとっては当たり前の考え方について質問されることもあるかもしれません。価値観の背景には文化的、歴史的な要素を少しだけ知っておくと便利です。

えへん‼

ご確認をお願いします。

これちょっと見ておいて。

敬語

Is it really the same person? The attitude is so different.
What is *keigo*? Why do people use so much *keigo*?

p.200

時間の感覚

遅延証明書 p.197

A delay certificate? I've never seen one in my country... Where can I get one?

〇〇急行 12:03
電車がまいります・・・

遅延証明書　5 9 15 20 25 30

〇〇鉄道 駅
〇〇〇〇〇

ゴットン
(ゴ――ッ)

電車の到着 p.196

I see. Japanese railways are the most punctual in the world!

～と申します。

頂戴いたします。

名刺交換

Is it good manners to bow when we exchange name cards? *p.202*

お辞儀

お辞儀文化のない国から来た外国人にとって、日本の至るところで目にするお辞儀の多さには驚くでしょう。どんなところでお辞儀を見かけたかを話題にして外国人と話してみるのも面白いかもしれませんね。

電話をかけながらお辞儀 *p.202*

Maybe bowing is automatic. I wonder how they learned it.

どうぞ、よろしくお願いいたします

通帳

ご利用頂き、ありがとうございました。
○○○銀行

ATM

Wow, here is another person bowing! *p.203*

正座して贈り物 *p.204*

Why are they giving me something that's boring?

つまらないものですが……

時間の感覚　▶ Track 46

5分前ルール　□

In Japanese society, being on time* is an absolute requirement. The known rule is to arrive five minutes before the scheduled time. Being late is considered impolite and careless. When you meet someone in a higher social position, you should arrive more than five minutes before the scheduled time.

*on time =
punctual
（時間に正確なこと）

requirement
必要条件

careless
だらしない

日本の社会では、時間に正確であることが強く求められます。よく言われているのは、約束の時間の 5 分前に到着するようにという原則です。遅れることは失礼でだらしないことと考えられています。社会的地位の高い人と会うときは、約束の時間の 5 分前よりももっと早く到着する必要があります。

➕ Sometimes we wonder how this obsession is viewed around the world. It seems that people from outside of Japan have a more generous outlook. What about in your country?

この時間に対するこだわりは、世界の人々からどう思われているのでしょうか。日本以外の国ではもっと寛容な気がします。あなたの国ではどうですか？

obsession
こだわり、（強い）観念

generous
寛大な、寛容な

outlook
ものの見方、あるものに対する

電車の時刻　□

The arrival times of Japanese trains and subways are very reliable. In the morning and evening, during the rush hour, trains arrive every three to five minutes in central urban areas, so usually missing one train is not a big problem.

reliable
信頼できる、（交通機関が）定時性のある

日本の電車や地下鉄の到着時刻は、とても信頼できます。朝と夜のラッシュアワーには、都会の中心部では 3 分から 5 分置きに電車が到着します。1 本乗り損なっても大した問題にはなりません。

遅延証明書 [USE]

In reality, however*, trains and subways sometimes* get delayed. If the delay causes problems, obtain a "certificate of delay" form from the station clerk. You can also download the form from the railroad company's website. However, this only proves that the train was delayed and does not prove that the person who received the form was actually on the train.

*however = though
（そうは言っても）
*sometimes = occasionally
（時々）

とはいえ、ときには電車や地下鉄が遅れることもあります。もし遅れによって問題が生じるような場合は、駅員さんから「延滞証明書」という用紙を入手しましょう。鉄道会社のウェブサイトからのダウンロードも可能です。ただし、これは電車の遅れを証明するもので、もらった人が実際に乗車していたかは証明しません。

➕ Do you think this system would be necessary in your country? In Japan, there are some transport companies that issue delay slips on their website. People can download a slip for about a week after the delay.

あなたの国にもこのシステムは必要なものだと思いますか？　日本では鉄道会社によってはウェブサイトからも遅延証明書を入手できます。1週間くらいの間いつでもダウンロードできます。

集団性　▶ Track 47

集団性とは？ [=]

In Japan, people tend to put more emphasis on collectivism than on individualism. Collectivism can be described as a "sense of unity." It's a core concept that is ingrained in most Japanese people.

collectivism
集団主義

individualism
個人主義

unity
単一性、一貫性

ingrain
浸透した、深く

日本では、個人主義よりも集団主義を重視しがちです。集団主義(collectivism)は一体性と表現されることもあります。これは日本人に染み込んだ価値観です。

➕ In your country, do people think of the group first or the individual first?
あなたの国では集団を優先しますか、それとも個人優先ですか？

ルーツは農耕作業 ❓ 🔖

In my opinion, the reason unity comes first is rooted in ancient social systems. In ancient times, Japan was a farming* country rather than a stock breeding country. Because of this, the basic shared mindset has strong connections to farming.

集団性が重視される理由は、日本の古代の社会制度に起源があると思います。日本は古代より牧畜ではなく農耕が中心の国でした。そのため人々の間にある基本的な考え方は農耕的要素と強い繋がりをもってきたのです。

*farming = agricultural
（農業の）

stock breeding
牧畜（業）

mindset
人の固定された考え方、ものの見方

集団性の形成 🔖

In pre-modern times, harvested rice was collected from each community. Then, this was given to the local leader (*shoya*) as "taxes," called *nengu*. This system made Japanese farmers work as a unit, not individually.

近代以前、収穫された米は集落から集められ、年貢と呼ばれる税金として地域のリーダー（庄屋）に納められました。この制度が、日本の農民たちを個人ではなく集団として労働するようにしたのです。

pre-modern
近代以前の

common saying
よく使う言葉、ことわざ

➕ In Japanese, "It's time to pay the *nengu*" means one has to give up something. Do you have a similar common saying?

日本語で「年貢の納め時だ」と言うと、何かものごとを諦めなくてはならない状況を意味します。あなたの国にもこのような表現はありますか？

近代に見られる集団主義 ＝ 🀄

The Great East Japan Earthquake of March 11, 2011 clearly demonstrated this sense of unity. The news showed people in stricken areas quickly uniting to help one another after the earthquake and tsunami. The fact that people organized so quickly and effectively to help others shows how much importance is placed on group effort and mutual support.

demonstrate
実証する、説明する

mutual
相互の

2011 年 3 月 11 日に起きた東日本大震災は、集団意識がはっきりと現れた例のひとつです。ニュースは巨大地震と津波の後、大勢の人々が助け合う姿を流しました。私たちが迅速に効果的に集結できたことは、日本人が集団での努力をいかに重視しているかを表していると言えます。

Were you in Japan at the time of the March 11 quake?
3.11 の地震のときに日本にいましたか？

（はいと答えた人に）　**Did you think about going back to your country?**
自分の国に帰ろうと思いましたか？
（いいえと答えた人に）**How was it reported on the news in your country?**
あなたの国では地震はどのように報道されましたか？

謙虚の感覚　▶ Track 48

謙虚は美徳

　Modesty is one of the traits that characterize Japanese people's conduct and way of thinking. For example, people don't usually talk about their own abilities or possessions. They also take care to avoid acting arrogant or having a superior attitude. You could say that regarding modesty as a virtue is part of being Japanese.

modesty
謙虚、慎み深さ

trait
（人の性格の）特徴、特質

possession
財産、所有物

virtue
美徳

　謙虚さは、日本人の行いや物の見方を規定する特徴のひとつです。例えば日本人はふつう、自分の特技や財産についてあまり話すことはありません。また、傲慢なふるまいや、人よりも優れていると主張するような態度は控えます。謙虚を美徳と考えるのは日本人であることの一部と言ってよいでしょう。

How is it different from your country?
あなたの国とはどのように違いますか？

敬語 ⚖️ (USE)

The level of politeness we use when speaking to someone in a higher position is called *keigo*. Mastering it takes a lot of practice. As far as I know, respecting someone in a higher position is influenced by Confucianism.

マメ知識

英語で敬語を表す言葉は honorifics。

Confucianism
儒教

自分より身分が上の人に使う言葉のていねいな使い方を敬語と言います。マスターするにはたくさんの練習が必要です。私個人の考えですが、年上の人や社会的地位の高い人を敬うのは、儒教の影響が強くあると思います。

➕ Do you have something like the *keigo* system in your country? If you do, how is it used?

あなたの国には敬語のようなしくみはありますか？　あるとしたらどのように使われていますか？

➕ Do you know what Confucianism is? Sometimes it is regarded as a religion, but it's not really a religion. Confucianism is a philosophical system based on the teachings of Confucius, who lived in China in the 6th century BC.

儒教とは何か知っていますか？　宗教と間違われることがよくありますが、儒教は宗教ではありません。儒教は中国の紀元前6世紀の人、孔子による思想の体系です。

運がよかっただけ 🔊📘

Here is another example. When a person achieves something impressive through hard work, he/she will always say that the result came down to sheer luck, not personal effort.

down to...
完全に

sheer luck
まったくの偶然、運がよかっただけ

もうひとつ例を挙げます。もしある人が一生懸命努力して何か大きな成果を上げると、その人は決まって、自分の努力ではなくまったくの好運でそうなったという言い方をします。

➕ Imagine that today is the day of a big test. Would you tell your friend truthfully how much you studied for that test? In Japan, we usually say "I didn't study at all..." no matter how much we have studied.

今日が大切なテストの日だったとします。あなただったら友だちに自分がどれほどたくさん勉強したか正直に伝えますか？　日本ではたいてい、どんなに自分がたくさん勉強しても「まったく勉強していない」と言います。

つまらないものですが……

When giving gifts to people, Japanese often say a phrase that means "I hope you will accept this unworthy gift." Of course, we hope the person will like the gift. But we don't want to give them the impression that it is very valuable or expensive, because we don't want them to feel that we are in a higher social position. This is one way of showing modesty and consideration.

unworthy
〜に値しない、〜に合わない

人に贈り物をあげるとき、私たちはよく「つまらないものですが、お受け取りください」と言います。その贈り物が価値のあるもの、高価なものという印象を与えないようにします。自分が相手より社会的に上であるとの印象を持たれたくないからです。これは「謙譲の美徳」の例のひとつですね。

➕ But it's a formal phrase, so you don't have to say this to close friends. You can just say that you brought them a small gift.

とは言っても、これは形式張った表現のひとつですので、親しい友人同士でこの表現を使う必要はありません。「ちょっとしたものだけど、どうぞ」というくらいで大丈夫です。

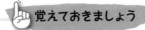

覚えておきましょう

　新渡戸稲造の『武士道』によると「日本人は、どなたかにプレゼントというとき、一所懸命探す。ようやくの思いで品物を探し当ててくるが、いざあなたの前にお持ちしたら、あなたがあまりにも素敵な方だから、あなたの前では私のお持ちしたものがつまらないものに見えてしまいます」という意味で日本人が『つまらないもの』と言ってものをあげると解説しています。

　　　　　　　　出典：『マナーでわかる大人の品格』岩下宣子著（三笠書房）

お辞儀の習慣

▶ Track 49

お辞儀の感覚

Bowing is a part of our life that affects every situation. When we greet, thank or apologize to other people, we usually don't look them in the eye. We lower our head instead.

bow
お辞儀する、頭を下げる

look someone in the eye
（人）の目をまともに見る、（人）の顔をじっと見る

お辞儀は、あらゆる場面に影響を及ぼす、日本人の暮らしの一部です。あいさつをするとき、感謝するとき、謝罪をするとき、日本人は相手の目を見ることはしません。代わりに頭を下げます。

➕ I've seen some other countries that have a bowing custom, too. People in ancient Europe bowed to the king or queen, didn't they? Can you think of any other cases?

私はよその国にもお辞儀文化があることを知っています。昔のヨーロッパでは王様や女王様にお辞儀をしていますよね。ほかにもお辞儀の例はあるでしょうか？

コミュニケーションとしてのお辞儀

At schools, teachers and students exchange bows repeatedly every day. At department stores, the store clerks* bow deeply to customers. In business situations, people often exchange bows repeatedly. Family members bow deeply in front of their ancestors' graves.

store clerk
店員

*store clerk= salesperson

学校では先生と生徒は毎日幾度もお辞儀を交わします。デパートでは店員は客に深くお辞儀をします。ビジネスの場では、お辞儀の交換を何度も繰り返します。家族の成員は先祖の墓の前で深々とお辞儀をします。

モノに対するお辞儀

Some people bow over the phone. Some bow when shaking hands. Many bow to the food in front of them, saying "*itadakimasu*," or even to the empty plates.

電話であいさつをするときお辞儀をする人もいます。握手の際お辞儀をする人もいます。目の前の食べ物に「いただきます」と言ってお辞儀をしたり、空になったお皿にお辞儀をする人はたくさんいます。

人間以外のお辞儀

People are not the only ones who bow. Some signboards at construction areas have images of construction workers bowing. The screens on ATM machines display anime images of bank employees bowing. The guides on GPS screens bow as well.

construction
工事、建造

マメ知識

ATM は automated teller machine、GPS は global positioning system の略。

人間だけがお辞儀をするのではありません。工事現場にある告知版には、お辞儀をする工事担当者が描かれているものがあります。ATM のスクリーンには、お辞儀をする銀行員のアニメ画像が出てきます。カーナビのスクリーン内のガイドも同様にお辞儀をします。

Did you find any other examples of bowing?
このほかにお辞儀するものを見つけましたか？

Q&A

 なんで日本人はそんなにお辞儀をするの？

Many of us probably don't know why we bow, but bowing is part of our life, so we do it automatically. Originally it was not an expression of greeting or respect, but a sign to show other people that we were not the enemy. In one theory, over the years, the meaning of this custom changed to its present meaning of communicating respect.

theory
説、意見、見解

私たちの大部分は、なぜ私たちがお辞儀をするのかを知りません。しかしお辞儀は暮らしの一部であり、無意識のうちにしています。最初はあいさつや敬意を表すものではなく、自分はあなたの敵ではないという意思表示の印でした。長い時間を経てこの習慣が変貌をとげ、敬意を表すという現在の形になったという説もあります。

お礼の感覚

▶ Track 50

お返し　= USE

In Japan, gift giving is a two-way street, in that gifts are "exchanged." In many cases we give return gifts to the gift givers. Giving return gifts is not mandatory, but it's highly encouraged.

two-way street
相互的なもの、相互関係

mandatory
義務的な、強制的な

日本では贈り物は相互的なもので、したがって贈り物は交換されるものです。多くの場合、贈った人にはお返しをします。お返しは義務ではありませんが、強く奨励されるものです。

➕ Don't worry about what to do after you get a return gift. You don't have to give another return gift. It's usually a one-round system.

お返しを受け取っても悩む必要はありません。またお返しをする必要はありません。ふつうは一往復のみです。

お祝い返し　= USE

At celebrations, people are extremely serious about giving return gifts. At wedding receptions, guests are given gifts before they leave. Plans to give return gifts must also be made not long before a baby is born. Giving return gifts in this way is very important because it is believed to express the "sharing of fortune."

お祝いの場では、人々はお返しに対し非常に真剣に気を配ります。結婚披露宴では、招待客は退席前に贈り物をもらいます。出産前には、お返しの計画を立てておきます。お返しは「幸運のお裾分け」なので、大変に重要なのです。

➕ A return gift should be about half the price of the gift you received. There is no strict rule, but it's a kind of unspoken agreement.

お返しは受け取った贈り物のだいたい半額程度のものを贈ると良いでしょう。厳密なルールはありませんが、暗黙の了解のひとつとなっています。

空気を読む

▶ Track 51

場の空気

The Japanese expression *kuki o yomu* literally means "reading the air." It means sensing how other people are feeling in a particular situation. In Japanese culture, people are expected to be aware of the feelings of people around them, and this affects how they behave. In other words, the "air" in this expression means other people's feelings.

日本には「空気を読む」という表現があります。英語に直訳すると reading the air となります。私たちは自然とまわりの人の気持ちをくみ取り、それが自分の決断や行為に影響します。つまり、この表現で言っている「空気」とはほかの人の気持ちを指しています。

➕ You should know the word "KY" too. It's an abbreviation for "*kuki ga yomenai,*" meaning "unable to read the air." It refers to people or actions that disrupt the social atmosphere.

KY という言葉を覚えておいたほうがいいですよ。これは kuki ga yomenai の略語で、「空気が読めない」と言う意味です。その場の雰囲気を壊すようなことをしたり、言ったりする人のことを指します。

ビジネスの場で

Here is an example. At a business meeting with your Japanese client, your client says "It would be difficult" in response to the suggestion you've just made. That's when you have to read the air... I mean read his mind. His answer is probably 90% "No." Japanese people often avoid saying "No," so they use other expressions like "It would be difficult."

I mean...
つまり

ではひとつ例です。あなたはお客さんと仕事の会議をしています。日本人の顧客はあなたの提案に対して「難しいですね」と言いました。ここで、空気を読みます。つまり、彼の本心を読むのです。彼の答えは 90%「No」でしょう。日本人は「No」と答えることを極力避ける傾向があり、その代わりにほかの表現を使うのです。

気を遣う

Here is another common expression — *ki o tsukau*. It literally means "using your mind." This expression implies that one has to use a lot of thought and awareness to guess someone's feelings or understand the atmosphere in a situation. Also, we sometimes use this expression when we want to say that a job is tiring.

imply
(〜を暗に) 意味する、ともなう

もうひとつ日本人に根付いた表現があります。それは「気を遣う」です。これを英語に直訳すると using your mind となります。誰かの気持ちをくみ取ったり、場の雰囲気を察するためには、いろいろと考えたり意識することが求められます。ですから、疲れる仕事ということを伝えるために、ときどき「気を遣う」という表現を用いることがあります。

その他の感覚

▶ Track 52

適当

Tekito can have different meanings depending on the context. One meaning is appropriate and proper. For example, we need to find *tekito* words to complete a sentence. But in a different context, it can be used to describe someone who is irresponsible, random and unreliable. Or it can also mean "do it any way you like." Because this word has opposite meanings, you should be careful!

適当は状況によって異なる意味を持ちます。ひとつは、「適している」「妥当である」という意味です。例えば、ここに当てはまる適当 (tekito) な言葉が欲しい、のように使います。ところが別の状況では、「無責任」、「信用できない」、「でたらめの」と言った意味で使われます。ほかにも「いいからとにかくやって」のようにも使われます。このように、ひとつの言葉ですが異なる意味を持ちますので、気をつけましょう。

Q&A

「適当にお願い」と言われたらどれくらい適当でいいの？

Sometimes *tekito* can be very difficult or confusing. For example, when your boss asks you to staple the documents for the meeting, and he tells you to do it *tekito*. Since he doesn't have time to give you clear instructions, the deep meaning is "think for yourself." So you shouldn't always take the meaning of *tekito* literally—it depends on the situation.

「適当」は時々とてもややこしく、紛らわしい表現です。例えば、あなたが上司にミーティング用の資料のホッチキス留めを頼まれたとしましょう。上司からは特に細かい指示はなく「適当に」と言われたとしても、実はこれは、はっきりとした指示をする時間がなかったからで、「自分で考えてちゃんとやってね」という深い意味があったりします。「適当」という言葉を鵜呑みにしてはいけません。

 微妙

Bimyo can mean "subtle." But nowadays people also use this word when they want to be indirect. For example, "Did you like that dish?" / "Hmmm, *bimyo*....", meaning "Not really, not so much." It is an indirect and fuzzy way of saying no.

「微妙」は、「とらえがたい」という意味です。しかし最近は、直接的または攻撃的になりすぎないようにするためにこの言葉を使います。例えば、「この料理はどうだった？」と聞かれて、「微妙かな」というのは「あんまりおいしくない」という意味です。

subtle
とらえがたい、微妙

direct
直接的な

offensive
攻撃的な

indirect
間接的な

fuzzy
曖昧な

第六章 ● 価値観・考え方

水くさい

Originally, *mizu kusai* referred to liquor or other drinks that had a lot of water mixed in, so the drink didn't have much taste. Later the meaning changed to a weakness in love or sympathy. Nowadays, this word is used when someone is being too formal and polite to someone who is close to them.

sympathy
思いやり、同情

もともと「水くさい」はお酒や飲み物に水分が多くて味気ないという意味で使われていました。後に、愛情や人情が薄いという意味で使われるようになりました。この言葉は親しい人が、遠い知り合いがするようなことをしたときに用います。例えば、あなたの親友が結婚しても何カ月も後まで教えてくれなかったようなときです。

Actually, I didn't know the original meaning of *mizu kusai* before I looked it up. Can you think of any words that might have a different original meaning?
実は私も調べるまで、「水くさい」の本来の意味を知らなかったんですよ。あなたも言葉の由来を知らないけれど使っているような言葉がありますか？

さすが

Sasuga is used as praise. It means "you are great," but not in a surprised way. It shows that the speaker expected that person to do well — for example, if a school's star soccer player has scored a goal.

praise
褒める

「さすが」は褒め言葉として用いられます。これは「あなたはすごい」という意味ですが、驚いて言うのではありません。その人がうまくやるものと期待していたことを表します。例えば学校のサッカーのスター選手がゴールを決めたときなどです。

こまめに

Komame (ni) means little by little or frequently. This phrase refers to actions that should be done continually in small amounts. The TV weather forecast often advises people to drink water *komame ni* when it's very hot outside.

continually
頻繁に

「こまめ（に）」とは、「ちょっとずつ」もしくは「頻繁に」という意味です。一度やって終わりではなく、ちょっとずつ何かを継続的に続けることをさしています。例えば、テレビの天気予報で、非常に暑いときは「こまめに」水分をとるようにとよく勧めています。

⊕ Don't study too hard! You should rest *"komame ni"*—stretch it out!
勉強しすぎないように！ 「こまめに」休憩して、ストレッチしたほうがいいですよ！

⊕ If you are described as a *mame* person, you should be proud. *Mame* has a different meaning than *komame*. It describes people who work diligently or people who are devoted, honest and sincere.
もし、自分のことをまめな人だと言われたら、それは喜んでいいことですよ。「まめ」にはもうひとつ意味があって、何事にも真摯に一生懸命取り組む人のことをさします。

diligently
一生懸命に

devoted
献身的な、熱心な

sincere
誠実な、嘘やごまかしのない

第六章 ● 価値観・考え方

Q&A

 「こまめ」のまめって豆と関係あるの？

Good question. I think many people think *mame* comes from beans — *"mame."* But the truth is it's not related to beans at all. *Komame* is usually written in *hiragana.* When it is written in *kanji,* most Japanese can't read it.

いい質問ですね。日本人でも多くの人が豆の「まめ」に由来していると思っているでしょう。でも、実は豆とはまったく関係ありません。「こまめ」が日本語で書かれるときは普通ひらがなですが、漢字で書かれたものを「こまめ」と読める人はとても少ないでしょう。

「こまめ」を漢字で書くと小忠実。

【地名・時代の伝えかた】

●方向、距離、時間などの共有できる概念を使って説明しましょう。●

　日本特有の時代の名称や場所の名前を外国人にわかりやすく伝えるためには、固有名詞だけでなく、それをさらにかみ砕いた情報を追加してあげましょう。

　例えば外国人に **Where are you from?** と聞かれて、**I'm from Iwate.** と答えたとしましょう。岩手県が日本のどこにあるのかすぐにわかる外国人はあまりいないでしょう。こういうときには以下のように答えることをオススメします。

● I'm from Iwate. It's in the northern part of Honshu.
（岩手県出身です。本州の北のほうです）

また、時代についても同じです。

● Todaiji was built in the Nara period in 8 CE, about 1,400 years ago.
（東大寺は 8 世紀、今から約 1,400 年前の奈良時代に建てられました）

※豆知識①：時代の名前には the がつきます。

※豆知識②：「西暦紀元」を表す CE は Common Era の略。ちなみに「紀元前」は BCE（Before Common Era）。

　この手法は道案内などにも使えます。詳しい道順が言えなくても、時間や距離の情報はとても有益です。

● 質問者： Where is the museum?
（博物館はどちらですか？）

あなた： It's that way. It's about five minutes from here, maybe about 500 meters away.
[行き先を指さしながら]（あちらです。ここから 5 分くらいですね、おそらく 500m ほど先です）

第七章 ● 伝統文化

伝統文化

和太鼓

鼓　*p.235*

Where can I see their performances?

太鼓　*p.235*

When did this drum culture start?

　日本には素晴らしい伝統芸能がたくさんあります。和太鼓、茶の湯、書道、生け花、そのほかにもお正月の遊びである百人一首や福笑いなど……。日本で発祥したものもあれば、大陸から伝わり独自の進化をとげたものもあります。それぞれの文化がどのように生まれたのか説明できると面白いですね。

書道　*p.218*

How do you make the ink?

茶の湯　*p.215*

First, you put in the powdered *matcha*.

Next, pour in hot water and whip it!

Do Japanese still do calligraphy?

剣道
p.231

Is it a kind of Japanese fencing?

What are the sticks made from?

What are they wearing?

柔道
p.229

Why are the belt colors different?

日本の伝統的なスポーツ種目のルーツはほぼ武道にあります。武道は単なるスポーツではなく、精神的な修養を目指すとう点が特徴です。海外でも公式試合が行われるようになり、人気も伸びてきています。国技である相撲についても会話を膨らませるようになりましょう。

How long is the match?

When did sumo start?

相撲
p.226

How do sumo wrestlers get so big?

What do they eat?

華道 ▶ Track 53

生け花

Ikebana is the traditional Japanese art of flower arrangement. It's also called *kado*. It started from early Buddhist flower offerings. By the 15th century, *ikebana* was a popular art form. The traditional style is to arrange flowers, branches and grass in a shallow vase.

生け花は、日本の伝統的な花を生ける芸術です。華道とも呼ばれます。初期の仏教の供花から始まり、15世紀ごろまでに芸術の一形式として広まりました。花や枝、草を浅い花器に飾るのが伝統的なスタイルです。

offerings
神様や仏様へのお供えもの
※ flower offerings で供花

branches
枝

grass
草

生け方

The flowers are not just placed in the vase. They're pushed down firmly onto a metal block called a *kenzan*, which has very sharp needles to hold the flowers and branches in place.

花々はただ花器に入れられているのではありません。剣山と呼ばれる、花や枝を固定する金属製の鋭い針の台にしっかりと刺されています。

firmly
しっかり

剣山

流派

There are about 3,000 *ikebana* schools in Japan. The most famous schools are *Ikenobo*, *Ohararyu*, *Sogetsuryu*, *Koryu*, and *Enshuryu*. The basic concept of flower arrangement is quite similar, but each school's sensibility differs slightly. These differences do not mean one school is better than the others—it depends on each person's individual taste.

school
(芸術などの) 流派

日本には約3000の生け花の流派があります。最も代表的なのは池坊、小原流、草月流、古流、遠州流です。皆、花を生ける際の基本的考え方はほぼ同じですが、感性に多少の違いがあります。その違いは、どの流派がほかより優れていると決めつけるものではありません。個人的な好みでどれが好きか判断すればよいのです。

茶道

🏺 茶の湯

Chanoyu is tea ceremony. It's a traditional way of drinking *matcha*, powdered green tea. The host prepares tea and serves it to the guests. The pleasure of the ceremony is not just drinking tea—it's also looking at the subtle decorations in the tearoom and garden, and appreciating the host's hospitality.

host
主人

subtle
繊細な

> 茶の湯は tea ceremony です。抹茶という粉末の緑茶を味わう伝統的な作法です。主人がお茶を用意して、客に提供します。単にお茶を飲むというだけではなく、茶室や庭の繊細な飾り付け、主人のもてなしを楽しむものです。

> ➕ Is there any traditional drink in your country, like tea in England? Do you have manners you have to follow?
>
> あなたの国にもイギリスの紅茶のような伝統的な飲み物がありますか？ それにはマナーがありますか？

🏺 歴史

The tradition of the tea ceremony started around the 12th century, when tea seeds were brought to Japan from China. In the late 16th century, the tea ceremony master Sen no Rikyu refined the ceremony more to the style we have now.

refine
～を洗練する、～に磨きをかける

> 茶の湯は 12 世紀、茶の種が中国からやってきたころに始まりました。16 世紀末に茶の湯の指導者千利休が、現在見られる形にセレモニーを磨き上げました。

🍵 お茶のたて方 ①₂

Simply put, first you put *matcha* powder into a tea bowl and pour in hot water. Next, you stir untill the tea is foamy. The stirring tool is called a *chasen*. It's made of bamboo and works like a whisk, so it's called a "bamboo whisk" in English. If you have tools for tea making, it's easy to make *matcha* at home.

simply put
簡単に言うと

pour in
注ぐ、注入する

stir
かき混ぜる

foamy
泡立つ

簡単に言うと、最初に茶の粉を茶碗に入れ、お湯を注ぎ入れます。次に茶が泡立つまでかき混ぜます。泡立てる道具は茶せんと呼びます。竹で作られていて、泡だて器（whisk）と同じ働きをするので、英語では bamboo whisk と言います。茶をたてる道具さえあれば、自宅で気軽に抹茶を楽しめます。

マメ知識
泡立て器は whisk のほかに egg beater とも言う。

➕ There are many recipes with *matcha* powder, like *matcha* milk, *matcha* cookies, *matcha* poundcakes, and so on. You should check them on the web.
抹茶の粉を使ったレシピがたくさんあるんですよ。抹茶ミルク、抹茶クッキー、抹茶パウンドケーキなど。インターネットで調べてみてくださいね。

お茶会の基本マナー

▶ Track 55

※ 以下はあくまでも「同席の皆様に失礼にあたらないため」の、最低限を紹介したものです。

1 菓子を食べる

At first, a Japanese sweet is served. You put it on a piece of paper called an *okaishi*, then eat it. You should eat all of it — don't leave anything behind. Keep the *okaishi* to the side.

まず最初に和菓子が振る舞われます。お懐紙と呼ばれる紙の上にそれを載せ、それから食べます。ぜんぶ食べましょう、残してはいけません。お懐紙は脇に置いておきます。

➕ Try this—eat the sweet first, then drink the tea. This will make the taste of the tea better. This type of traditional Japanese sweet is called *wagashi*.
まずお菓子を食べてから抹茶を飲んでみてください。そうするとお茶がおいしく感じられます。このお菓子は和菓子といって、日本の伝統的なお菓子です。

② お茶を飲む

Next, the tea is served. You bow to the server*. Then you accept the tea bowl with your right hand, support the bottom of the bowl with your left hand, bring it near you, and rotate it clockwise twice, about 90 degrees in total. Make sure the picture painted on the bowl is on the side, not in front of you. Finish the tea in a few sips.

次に茶が振る舞われます。茶を出してくれた人にお辞儀をします。それから茶碗を右手に取り、左手を底に添え、自分の正面に近づけます。ゆっくりと右回りに二度、合わせて 90 度になるように茶碗を回します。茶碗の絵柄が正面ではなく、自分から見て横になるようにします。数回にわけてお茶を飲みます。

*__server = host__
（ここでは）お茶を出す人

__rotate__
廻す

__sip__
ひとくち、ひとすすり

③ 飲み終わったら

After you finish drinking, lightly wipe the rim of the bowl where your lips have touched with the tips of your right thumb and index finger. Clean your fingertips with the *okaishi*, the same paper you used for the cake. Rotate the bowl twice, this time counterclockwise, and put it down on the *tatami* in front of you. This time, make sure the picture on the bowl is in front of you.

飲み終えたら、右手の親指と人差し指の先で、くちびるの触れた茶碗のふちを軽く拭きます。菓子を食べるときに使ったお懐紙で指先を拭います。茶碗を左に二度回し、自分の前の畳の上に置きます。今度は絵柄が自分の正面にくるようにしてください。

__wipe__ 拭う
__rim__ ふち、へり
__tip__ 先端
__thumb__ 親指
__index finger__
人差し指

第七章 ● 伝統文化

Q&A

気軽に抹茶を楽しむのってアリですか？

Of course. When you enjoy it in a coffee shop or at home, there is no problem to drink it as you like without worrying about the details. Just relax and enjoy your tea!

もちろんです。喫茶店や家庭で楽しむ場合には、細かいことを気にせず、好きに飲んで問題ありません。リラックスしてお茶を楽しみましょう！

➕ How was the *matcha*? Was it too bitter for you?
抹茶はどうでしたか？　苦すぎましたか？

▶ Track 56

🏆 書道 ⊟ 📷

Shodo is brush and ink writing, usually called calligraphy in English. The tools you need for *shodo* are an ink stone, an ink stick, a brush and paper.

書道とは墨と筆で書くというもので、英語ではふつう calligraphy と呼ばれます。書道に必要な道具は硯（すずり）、墨、筆、それに紙です。

🏆 歴史 🖌 ?

Shodo originally came from ancient China. In the old days, good *shodo* skills were a sign of sophistication. If your handwriting skills were very good, it meant you were trustworthy. Parents expected their children to spend a lot of time on *shodo*.

書道は古代の中国に発しています。昔は、書道の腕前は教養の高さを表していました。達筆であることは信用に足る人物であることを意味しました。親は、子どもが書道の練習に多くの時間を費やすことを期待しました。

sophistication
教養

trustworthy
信用できる、信頼できる

墨

Sumi is ink used for *shodo* (calligraphy) and *suibokuga* or *sumi-e* (ink painting). There are two types of *sumi*. Stick-type *sumi* is soot mixed with gelatin to harden it. Ink is made by grinding the sumi on an ink stone with water. Liquid sumi, also called *bokuju*, is made with soot and chemicals.

墨は書道、また水墨画、つまり墨絵に使われるインクです。墨には2種類あります。棒状の墨は煤（すす）と、それを固めるためのゼラチンを混ぜて作られます。硯（すずり）の上で、水を混ぜてこすりインクを作ります。液体の墨を墨汁と言い、これは煤と化学物質から作られています。

gelatin ゼラチン

soot すす、煤煙

grind
こする、すりつぶす

chemicals
（化学的な）合成物

 Have you ever seen squid ink? It is just like *sumi* ink.
イカ墨を見たことはありますか？　墨インクによく似ています。

 硯

A *suzuri* is a container of *sumi* ink. It's also called an ink stone. A *suzuri* is also used as a part of the ink making process. Specifically, ink is produced by putting a little water on the *suzuri* and rubbing the ink stick on the surface.

硯（すずり）とはインクの入れ物です。ink stone とも呼ばれます。硯はインクを作るための道具でもあります。具体的には、水を入れて硯の平らな部分を棒状の墨でこすとがインクができるのです。

rub こする

 筆

A *fude* is an ink brush. It's made with the hairs of an animal, for example a horse, a sheep or a raccoon dog. Different kinds of animal hair are used for different types of brushes. The hairs are inserted into a bamboo tube, which becomes the handle of the brush.

筆はインク用のブラシです。ウマ、ヒツジやタヌキといった動物の毛で作られています。毛の種類の違いによって、種類の違う筆が作られます。毛は竹の筒に差し込まれ、その筒が筆の柄になります。

raccoon dog
タヌキ

🏆 紙 （二）

The paper used in *shodo* is Japanese *washi* paper.

書道に使う紙は日本の和紙という紙です。

washi
→ *p.233*

🏆 書き初め （二）🈁

Kakizome is a New Year's tradition. On New Year's Day, people write lucky* words in black ink on calligraphy paper. There are local *kakizome* contests, and children's *kakizome* are displayed in public buildings and schools.

*lucky = auspicious
（めでたい、幸先のよい）

書き初めは正月の習慣です。元日に、おめでたい言葉を黒い墨で書道用の紙に書きます。各地で書き初めコンテストが開かれ、子どもたちの作品は公共の建物や学校に飾られます。

➕ What words would you like to write? I can teach you to write them in *kanji*.
何という言葉を書いてみたいですか？　私が漢字を教えてあげますよ。

🏆 水墨画 （二）🈁

Suibokuga, or *sumi-e*, is ink painting done by brushes. Only black ink, the same type that is used for *shodo* calligraphy, is used. The brushes are also the same types that are used in calligraphy. Ink painting was developed in China in the late 9th to 10th centuries. *Suibokuga* came to Japan in the late 12th century, along with Zen.

水墨画または墨絵は筆を使って描かれる墨画です。書道で使われているものと同じ墨のみが使われます。筆も書道と同じものです。この水墨画は9世紀後半から10世紀にかけて、中国で発展しました。日本には12世紀後半に禅とともに伝わりました。

🏆 水墨画の内容 （二）🈁

The early works of *suibokuga* were paintings of Zen monks or Zen teachings. Gradually, *suibokuga* artists added many different types of subjects, such as birds, plants, insects, small animals, and landscapes. Even though only black ink is used in *suibokuga*, the use of different shades of gray and the blank areas of white create a wide variety of combinations and harmonies.

shade
陰影、グラデーション

初期の水墨画は禅僧を描いた絵、あるいは禅の教えを描いた絵でした。それが徐々に、鳥、植物、昆虫、小動物、風景のような、異なった主題のものが加わってきました。墨だけで描かれていますが、さまざまな灰色の陰影と地の白い部分が濃い黒と合わさり、見事な調和を作りだします。

俳句と短歌

▶ Track 57

日本の詩

The oldest poetry book in Japan, titled *Manyoshu*, is over 1,400 years old. The traditional style of poetry combines lines of 5 and 7 syllables.

日本でいちばん古い『万葉集』という詩集は 1400 年以上前のものです。伝統的な詩は 5 音節と 7 音節で構成されています。

俳句

Haiku is a short poem of 17 syllables. These syllables have to be in 5-7-5 format. A *haiku* has to include a word that refers to one of the four seasons.

syllable
音節

俳句は 17 音節の短い詩です。音節が 5・7・5 音の形式です。俳句には季節を表す言葉がひとつ含まれていなければなりません。

歴史

Originally, the 5-7-5 form was the beginning part of a long poem called a *renga*. Then around the late 15th century and early 16th centuries, the 5-7-5 part became an independent poem, called a *haiku*.

5・7・5の形は、もともとは連歌と呼ばれる長い詩の始まりの部分でした。15 世紀の終わりから 16 世紀の初頭にかけ、5・7・5 の部分が詩として独立し、俳句と呼ばれるようになりました。

🏆 短歌 (≡)

Tanka is another form of poetry. The syllable pattern is 5-7-5-7-7. *Tanka* don't have to have a seasonal word.

> 短歌はまた別の詩の形式です。音節のパターンは5・7・5・7・7です。季語は必要ありません。

▶ Track 58

🏆 百人一首 (≡)

Hyakunin Isshu is a card game of 100 *tanka* cards which were written by 100 poets who lived in the 7th to the 13th centuries. At first, they were collected as a poetry book in the 13th century, but now it's known as a card game, and people play it as a New Year's custom.

> 百人一首は、7世紀から13世紀の100人の歌人によって作られた100の短歌を使ったカルタ・ゲームです。もともとは13世紀に作られた和歌集ですが、現在では、カードゲームとして知られていて、お正月にこれをやるのが習慣となっています。

🏆 百人一首の札 (≡)

A set of *Hyakunin Isshu* has 100 letter cards and 100 picture cards. Each picture card has a complete *tanka* poem, as well as the name and picture of the poet who wrote it. Each letter card* has the second half of the poem.

> ひと組の百人一首には100枚の字札と100枚の絵札があります。各絵札には、短歌一首の全部と詩人の名前が書かれ、詩人の絵が付いています。各字札には、短歌の後半部分が書かれています。

*letter card = grabbing card
（取り札）

写真（左）：文字のみが書かれている取り札
写真（右）：読み手が読む絵札

©paylessimages/iStockphoto

©paylessimages/iStockphoto

百人一首の遊び方

▶ Track 59

1 準備

First, the reader is chosen. The reader takes all the picture cards. The other players sit in a circle on the floor and spread the letter cards face up in the center of the circle.

最初に読み手を決めます。読み手は絵札を全部手元に置きます。ほかのプレーヤーは輪になって床に座り、文字の面を上に向けて輪の中に字札を広げます。

2 開始

The reader shuffles the picture cards, takes one, and starts reading the poem out loud. The players look for the letter card that matches the picture card. The first person who finds the matching card shouts "*hai*" and takes it. This is repeated till all 100 cards are read.

読み手は絵札を切り、1枚を取り出し大きな声で詩を読み上げます。取り手は絵札と合致する字札を探します。最初に見つけた人が「はい」と声を上げて、札を取ります。これを100回、全部の札を読み上げるまで繰り返します。

3 勝敗

Needless to say, the player with the most cards is the winner.

言うまでもありませんが、最も多く札を取った人が勝者です。

➕ To get many cards, you have to memorize the 100 poems. We learn about these poems in Japanese classics class. Do you have a card game that uses poems like *Hyakunin Isshu*?

100の短歌を暗記しておかないと、なかなか札は取れません。日本では古典の授業で習います。あなたの国には百人一首のような詩を使った遊びはありますか？

memorize
暗記する

Japanese classics
古典

遊び ▶ Track 60

🏆 将棋 ⊜🍶

Shogi is Japanese chess. It's a board game for two players. The original form of the game was created in India, and traveled to the West, China and then Japan. In the 6th century, *shogi* came to Japan, and the current style was formed in the 16th century.

将棋は日本版チェスです。ふたりで遊ぶボードゲームです。ゲームの原型はインドで作られたもので、その後、西洋や中国、日本に伝わりました。日本には6世紀に伝来し、16世紀に現在の形ができあがりました。

🏆 駒と将棋盤 ⊜📷

Each player has a set of *shogi* pieces that includes 1 king, 1 rook, 1 bishop, 2 golden generals, 2 silver generals, 2 knights, 2 lances, and 9 pawns. The board is rectangular and has a grid of 81 squares. Traditional *shogi* pieces and boards are made of wood, but now there are also plastic ones.

1セットの将棋の駒は王将1、飛車1、角行1、金将2、銀将2、桂馬2、香車2、歩兵9から成っています。将棋盤は長方形をしていて、81の升目になっています。将棋の駒と盤は伝統的に木製ですが、現在はプラスチック製のものもあります。

king 王将

rook 飛車

bishop 角行

golden general 金将

silver general 銀将

knight 桂馬

lance 香車

pawn 歩兵

grid グリッド ※基準となる縦横の線

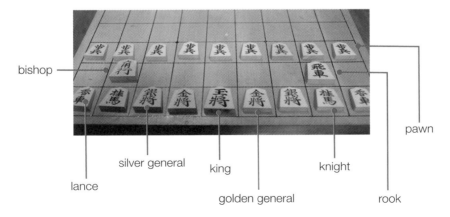

bishop

silver general

lance

king

golden general

knight

rook

pawn

✿ ルール（チェスとの違い）

The rules are similar to chess, but there is one major difference — you can use the pieces that you've captured as your own pieces.

capture
捕える、捕獲する

ルールはチェスと似通っていますが、ひとつ大きな違いがあります。捕獲した相手の駒を自分のものとして使用することができるのです。

> ➕ Today some people play *shogi* over the Internet. You should try it sometime!
> 最近ではインターネット上で将棋を楽しむことができます。お試しあれ！

✿ かるた

Karuta is another card matching game. Children play it often around the New Year. The players take the picture cards while the reader reads the letter cards. The sentences on the cards are old Japanese proverbs or fun pieces of information.

proverb
ことわざ、格言

かるたも札合わせのカードゲームです。子どもたちがよくお正月のころに遊びます。読み手が字札を読み、取り手が絵札を取ります。字札には、日本の古いことわざや面白い情報が書かれています。

✿ 福笑い

Fukuwarai is a face-making game. It is one of the most famous New Year's Day games. Someone with a blindfold on sticks the parts of the face (eyes, eyebrows, nose and mouth) onto a blank piece of paper in the shape of a face. Generally, this is not a game that people win or lose. It's just to make people laugh.

blindfold
目隠し

福笑いとは、顔を作り上げるゲームです。お正月に遊ぶ代表的な遊びのひとつです。目隠しをした人が顔の形をした何も描かれていない紙の上に、顔のパーツ（眉、目、鼻、口）を並べていきます。このゲームはふつう勝敗を決めるものではなく、人を笑わせるために行われるゲームです。

マメ知識

欧米にも福笑いに似た遊び Pin the Tail on the Donkey がある。これは壁にかけられたロバの人形に、目隠しをした人が尻尾をピンで付けるというもの。

相撲

► Track 61

🏆 相撲

Sumo is traditional Japanese wrestling. The origin of sumo is unknown. Japanese mythology says the first sumo match was held between two Shinto gods. The professional sumo league has been popular for hundreds of years. In the Edo period, many *ukiyo-e*, or traditional Japanese woodblock prints, of popular sumo wrestlers were made.

> 相撲は日本の伝統的なレスリングです。歴史があまりにも長いため、はっきりとした起源は不明とされています。日本の神話では、神道の神様ふたりの間で戦われたのが最初の取組と言われています。プロの相撲競技は何百年もの間人気です。江戸時代には人気の関取の浮世絵がたくさん作られていました。

🏆 開催場所と時期

Since ancient times, simple outdoor sumo rings have been built throughout Japan, and people have enjoyed sumo as a pastime sport. Today, the number of sumo rings has decreased in urban areas, but some still remain in rural areas. There are amateur sumo clubs in many areas in which children and adults can participate, and tournaments of various sizes are held. Children who want to take up sumo seriously can go to junior high schools, high schools, and universities that have sumo clubs.

> 古来より日本全国では、野外に簡易な土俵がつくられ、人々は娯楽やスポーツとして、相撲を楽しんできました。現在、都市部では土俵の数は減ってしまいましたが、地方にはまだある程度残っています。子どもから大人まで参加できるアマチュアの相撲クラブが各地にあり、大小様々な規模のトーナメントも開催されます。本格的に相撲を取りたい子どもは、相撲部がある中学・高校・大学に進学します。

マメ知識

『古事記』の神話に相撲が登場する。これが現在確認できる最古の相撲と考えられている。

 Do you like sumo? You can watch it live on NHK. NHK is the only channel that can broadcast it live.

相撲は好きですか？ NHKで生中継が見られますよ。生中継が許可されているのはNHKだけです。

外国人力士

Nowadays, there are many sumo wrestlers who are from foreign countries. The first foreign wrestler who came to Japan in the 1960s was a Hawaiian. Later, four Mongolians, Asashoryu, Hakuho, Harumafuji and Kakuryu, won the grand championship and became yokozuna. Nowadays there are some popular wrestlers from Eastern Europe, too.

現在は大勢の外国出身の力士がいます。最初の外国人力士は 1960 年代にハワイから来ました。その後、朝青龍、白鵬、日馬富士、鶴竜という 4 名のモンゴル力士が横綱になりました。今では東欧出身の人気力士もいます。

取組

To win, a wrestler has to force his opponent out of the ring, or make him touch the floor with a part of his body other than the bottom of his feet. Most matches are very short, often less than 30 seconds.

opponent
（競技の）敵

match
（ここでは）取組

相手を土俵の外に出すか、相手の足の裏以外の体の部分のどこかを土俵に付ければ勝ちです。ほとんどの取組はとても短く、しばしば 30 秒以内で終わります。

まわし

A *mawashi* is the belt, or loincloth, that wrestlers wear. The belts for practice are made of cotton. In tournaments, the senior* wrestlers, called *sekitori*, wear a silk belt. The lower-ranking wrestlers wear a belt made of cotton.

loincloth
ふんどし、腰巻

senior
先輩の、上級の

*senior =
full-fledged
（一人前の）

まわしは力士の試合用の下帯のようなものです。稽古用のものは木綿でできています。本場所では、関取と呼ばれる上級者たちは絹製のまわしを着用します。下位の力士は木綿のものを着用します。

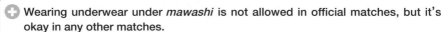

Wearing underwear under *mawashi* is not allowed in official matches, but it's okay in any other matches.

公式試合ではまわしの下には下着をつけてはいけないことになっているのです。でも公式試合以外は（下着の）着用が可能です。

🏆 塩をまく理由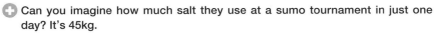

Sumo wrestlers throw salt to purify the ring. The custom is from ancient times, when sumo was a Shinto event.

Shinto
→ *p.253*

力士は土俵を清めるために塩をまきます。塩で清めるのは、相撲が神道の行事だった古代からの習慣です。

➕ Can you imagine how much salt they use at a sumo tournament in just one day? It's 45kg.

大相撲で、1日どのくらい塩を使うか分かりますか？　45kg も使うそうです。

Q&A

お相撲さんはどうやってあんなに大きくなるの？

Traditionally, in the morning, wrestlers practice on an empty stomach. After practice, they eat as much as they can and then take a nap. In the late afternoon, they do chores in the sumo stable, which is called a "*heya*" in Japanese. At night, they eat a big dinner and go to bed. Some say this routine makes them big and strong. If you want to have a body like a sumo wrestler, try this method!

empty stomach
空腹

chore
雑用、決まった仕事

stable
馬小屋、相撲部屋

伝統的には、力士たちは朝早く起きて、空腹のまま稽古をするそうです。稽古の後は食べられるだけ食べ、その後昼寝をします。夕方は「部屋」と呼ばれる所属先の雑用をして過ごします。夜もたくさん食べ、就寝します。この手順によって、力士は大きく強くなると言われています。もしお相撲さんのような体になりたければ、ぜひこの方法をお試しあれ！　最近では、伝統的な手法のみにとらわれず、トレーニングに多様性を持たせている相撲部屋もあります。

ちゃんこ鍋

Chanko-nabe is the famous sumo cuisine. It's a type of stew where a lot of things are put into a pot and cooked together. Chicken broth seasoned with sake and *mirin* is the most basic type of soup used in *chankonabe*. Traditionally, lower-ranking sumo wrestlers are responsible for making *chankonabe* for everyone.

ちゃんこ鍋は有名な相撲料理です。さまざまなものを鍋に入れて煮込むシチューのような食べ物です。基本のスープは鶏がら、酒、みりんで作られます。伝統的に、階級の低い力士が料理することになっています。

▶ Track 62

柔道

Judo is the most popular Japanese martial art. Like kendo and sumo, judo teaches not only fighting techniques, but also mental discipline. From 2012, judo, *kendo*, and sumo became compulsory subjects in junior high schools, so as to encourage more familiarity with Japanese traditions and culture.

柔道は最も人気の高い日本の武術です。剣道や相撲と同様、柔道は戦う技術だけではなく、心の鍛練を教えます。2012年から、柔道、剣道、相撲が中学校で必修科目となりました。日本の伝統と文化に、より一層親しむためです。

martial art
武術

discipline 訓練

so as to…
〜するために

歴史

Judo came from *jujutsu*. *Jujutsu* was considered a necessary martial arts skill in samurai society. After Japan's modernization period, in the mid-19th century, *jujutsu* was developed into a new martial art called judo.

柔道は柔術から発生しました。柔術は侍社会で必須の武術と考えられていたものです。19世紀半ば、日本が近代化した後の時代に、柔術は新しい武術、柔道に発展しました。

第七章 ● 伝統文化

Q&A

柔道着の帯の色の意味を教えてください。

The color of the belt shows the rank. Also, the color of each rank differs between adults and people under age*. Students under 20 start with a white belt. And as they pass each test their belt color changes to yellow, orange, green, purple, brown, and black. For adults, it goes from white to brown, black, red and white, and finally red. When you receive a black belt, you're considered a judo expert.

*under age = minors
(20 歳未満)

帯の色は階級を表します。また、階級の色は少年と成年でも異なります。20 歳未満の少年は白から始め、試験に合格するたびに黄色、オレンジ色、紫、茶、黒と変わっていきます。成年は、白から始まり茶色、黒、赤と白、最後に赤と色が変わります。黒帯を与えられた柔道家は権威と見なされます。

柔道着

The official judo uniform is called *judogi*. *Judoka*—people who do judo—do not hold any objects or wear any protection. Usually they grab each other's collars as a strategy for winning. That's why the collar is made with thicker material.

collar 襟、カラー

柔道の正式なユニフォームは柔道着と言います。柔道をする人——柔道家は道具を持ったり防具を着けたりはしません。相手の襟をつかみ、勝利をねらいます。ですから、襟は厚い生地で作られています。

型

Judo has fixed patterns of movements called *kata*. At first you learn the basic movements, then combine them with actions that are needed at each moment.

柔道には型と呼ばれる決まった動きがあります。最初にまず型を学び、その後、その時々に必要な動きと型を組み合わせることを覚えます。

🏆 勝敗 =

You win a match by throwing the other person to the ground, making them surrender, or by keeping them from moving for a certain period of time. If there is no clear winner when the time runs out, judges decide the winner by counting the total number of movements. This type of judgement is called *yusei-gachi*.

surrender
降参

試合は、相手を床に投げる、降参させる、決まった時間動きを封じることで、勝ちとなります。制限時間内に明確に勝負がつかない場合、審判がそれまでの戦いの内容から勝者を決めます。この判定を優勢勝ちと言います。

➕ Judo became an Olympic event in 1964, when the Olympic Games were held in Tokyo.

東京でオリンピックが開催された1964年に、柔道はオリンピック種目になりました。

剣道

▶ Track 63

🏆 剣道 📹 USE

Kendo is the Japanese version of fencing. People who do kendo are called *kendoka*. *Kendoka* use both hands to hold a bamboo sword, which is called a *shinai*. They wear a helmet, chest protector, and padded gloves.

padded
パッドを入れた

剣道は、日本版フェンシングです。剣道をする人を剣道家と呼びます。剣道家は両手で竹刀と呼ばれる竹製の刀を持ちます。剣道家は面をかぶり、胴（胸を守る防具）を着け、パッドを入れた手袋をつけます。

➕ Kendo and judo are popular activities for children to learn after school in Japan. What is a popular sport among children in your country?

剣道と柔道は学校が終わった後の習い事として人気があります。あなたの国で子どもに人気のスポーツは何ですか？

面
helmet

胴
chest protector

小手
padded gloves

歴史

The history of kendo is very similar to the history of judo. Kendo was originally called *kenjutsu* and practiced by the samurai class. *Kenjutsu* and kendo teach techniques for winning, and also mental discipline. Also like judo, kendo movements are based on *kata*, or fixed patterns of movements.

剣道の歴史は柔道の歴史と似ています。剣道はもともと剣術と呼ばれ、侍階級が学びました。剣術も剣道も勝つための技術と心の鍛練を学びます。また、これも柔道と同様、剣道も型と呼ばれる決まった動きが基礎になります。

折り紙

▶ Track 64

折り紙

Origami is a Japanese paper folding craft. You fold a piece of paper to create a three-dimensional figure like an animal or a flower.

craft
工作

three-dimensional
三次元の、立体感のある

折り紙は紙を折って作る工作です。紙を折って動物や花といった立体の作品を作ります。

➕ It is often said that how you fold the paper shows your personality. Let's see how you do it.
折り紙の折り方には人の性格が表れるとよく言われます。さて、あなたの折り方を見てみましょう。

千羽鶴

"A thousand cranes" is a bundle of a thousand *origami* cranes held together with strings. Usually, the strings are hung from the ceiling.

crane 鶴
bundle 束
ceiling 天井

千羽鶴は、1000羽の折り紙の鶴を糸で結んで束にしたもので、天井から吊るしてかざります。

なぜ千羽鶴を折るのですか？

In Japanese culture, the crane is a symbol of good luck and a long life. People make a thousand cranes to wish for something, for example recovery from an illness, winning an athletic event, or to pray for peace.

　日本の文化では、鶴は幸運と長寿の象徴です。そこで、例えば病気の回復だとか、スポーツ試合での勝利、平和の祈願といった願いごとをする際に、人びとは千羽鶴を折ります。

▶ Track 65

 和紙

Washi is traditional handmade paper. It's usually made from the fibers of plants called *kozo* or *mitsumata*. They are much stronger* than the wood pulp used to make Western paper. That's why documents written over a thousand years ago have lasted till today.

*stronger =
more durable

（耐久性のある、丈夫な）

　和紙は伝統的な手作りの紙です。ふつう、コウゾとミツマタという植物の繊維を使って作ります。これらの植物の繊維は西洋の紙に使われる木材パルプよりずっと強いのです。だから、1000年以上も前に書かれた文書が現在も残っているのです。

第七章 ● 伝統文化

💠 和紙で作られているもの

Washi is very strong, so it's used not just for writing and drawing, but also for making everyday items like *shoji*, fans, and toys. All Japanese bank notes contain *mitsumata* fibers.

note 紙幣

※イギリス英語。アメリカ英語では bill が一般的。

和紙はとても丈夫なので、字や絵を描いたりするのに使われるほか、障子、扇、玩具などの日用品を作るのに使われています。日本の紙幣には、ミツマタの繊維が含まれています。

➕ This is a paper balloon! It's made from *washi* paper, too. Blowing air through the hole makes the balloon puff up.

これが紙風船です！　これも和紙から作られています。穴から空気を吹き込むとふくらみます。

👆 覚えておきましょう

Sadako and the Thousand Paper Cranes (邦題『さだ子と千羽鶴』) という本が、いくつかの言語で出版されています。広島で原爆の被害に遭ったさだ子という少女が、自分の回復を願って千羽鶴を折るという物語です。この本の影響で、外国人の中には「千羽鶴は原爆被害者のためのもの」という誤解をする読者もいるようです。広島平和記念公園にもたくさん飾ってありますし、「千羽鶴イコール放射能被害」という図式は誤解しやすいのかもしれません。

和太鼓

▶ Track 66

🏆 太鼓と鼓 ⊜ USE

The most popular Japanese drums are *taiko* and *tsuzumi*. *Taiko* are drums you hit with sticks, and *tsuzumi* are small drums you hit with your hands.

最も知られている日本のドラムは太鼓と鼓です。太鼓は撥で叩き、鼓は手で叩きます。

🏆 掛け声 ?

In many Japanese drum performances, lead drummers shout cues to the other drummers. In Noh theater, musicians shout in order to share the emotions of the characters in the stories. In cheerful drum pieces, like the music played at local festivals, shouting is encouraged to lift everyone's spirits.

cue 合図

cheerful
楽しい、愉快な

encouraged
奨励される

和太鼓の演奏では、多くの場合、中心となる演奏者が掛け声でほかの演奏者にきっかけの合図をします。能の舞台では、楽器の演奏者は物語の登場人物と感情を共有するために掛け声を発します。地方の祭で行われるような楽しい演奏では、掛け声は人々の気分を高めるという目的で奨励されます。

Q&A

 和太鼓の表面は何の皮でできているのですか？

A *taiko* drum head is made of cowhide. The head of a *tsuzumi* is made of horsehide. The skins are very strong and last a long time.

cowhide
牛革

horsehide
馬革

太鼓の打面は牛革、つまり牛の皮で、鼓の打面は馬革、つまり馬の皮でできています。皮は大変強いので長持ちします。

ひと言に日本の舞台芸能といってもさまざまです。それぞれ似ているようで、歴史も違えば、舞台や小道具、物語の内容も違います。あまり詳しく回答ができなくても、それぞれの特徴や違いなどを簡単に説明できるようにしておくと便利ですね。

能 *p.238*

『石橋　師資十二段之式』
（しゃっきょう　もろすけじゅうにだんのしき）
赤獅子：武田宗典
撮影：前島吉裕

What is Noh?
How did it develop?
What is this character?

落語 *p.243*

See how the fan works.
Are the performers always
sitting?

演者：桂吉坊
撮影：伊東俊介

Why are there no
actresses in *Kabuki*?
Who made the decision?

p.242

「与話情浮名横櫛」
（よわなさけうきなのよこぐし）
与三郎：尾上松也
お富：市川左字郎
撮影：KENTA AMINAKA

上記3枚とも尾上松也
撮影：平田久子

なぜ歌舞伎では男優が女性の役を演じ
るのか、知っていますか？
　　　文楽とは人形劇のことですね。文楽で
はどんな人形が何を演じるのでしょうか？

文楽

p.240

The Japanese
puppet theater

「艶容女舞衣」
（はですがたおんなまいぎぬ）
人形：お園
撮影：Richard Jones

237

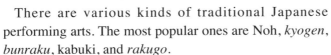

▶ Track67

🔑 日本の舞台芸能

There are various kinds of traditional Japanese performing arts. The most popular ones are Noh, *kyogen*, *bunraku*, kabuki, and *rakugo*.

日本の伝統芸能には、さまざまな種類があります。もっとも人気があるのは、能・狂言・文楽・歌舞伎、落語です。

能

▶ Track 68

🔑 能

Noh is an ancient performing art created about 650 years ago. It's a form of drama with music, chanting, dance, and storytelling. For many years, Noh was supported by aristocrats and samurai lords. The concept behind Noh is quite spiritual and philosophical.

能は650年ほど前に作られた古い舞台芸術です。音楽、詠唱、舞、語りを取り入れた舞踊劇です。長いこと、貴族や大名たちに支持されてきました。能の背後にある思想は、とても霊的で哲学的なものです。

🔑 内容

There are over 250 Noh plays. In most of them, the main character is a spirit. In the plays the spirits talk about religious faith, love, jealousy, war, and remorse. The actions and the lines are highly stylized; they are not realistic at all.

能の作品は250以上あります。その多くは霊魂が主人公です。霊魂は宗教的信条、愛、嫉妬、戦いの話をします。演技や台詞まわしはとても様式化されていて、まったく写実的ではありません。

chant
チャンツ、詠唱する

aristocrat
貴族

samurai lord
大名

philosophical
哲学的

🏆 能の舞台 🟰 USE

The Noh stage is a flat space with a short passageway called a *hashigakari* at stage right. There is a picture of a pine tree at the back of the stage. The setting is very simple — there are no stage sets and only a few stage props — so you have to use a lot of imagination when you see a Noh play.

passageway
通路、廊下

stage right
舞台の下手（しもて）

stage sets 大道具

stage props
小道具

能の舞台は、右手に橋掛りと呼ばれる短い通路のある平面です。舞台の背には松の木が描かれています。大道具はなく、わずかな小道具しかない舞台はとてもシンプルです。ですから、能を見るときは、大いに想像を働かさねばなりません。

➕ Often, Noh performers wear masks with different faces and facial expressions. You should check them out and see what types of emotions they're meant to express.

能の演者は、さまざまな表情の面をつけることがあります。能面がどのような感情を表しているか、気をつけて見てください。

女性の面：
mask of a woman

怨霊の面：
mask of a spirit

☝ 覚えておきましょう

能のお面

　能楽師は舞台化粧をしません。素顔で舞台に立ちますが、面をつけることもあります。

　正式には「おめん」ではなく、「のうめん」もしくは「おもて」と呼びます。英語では mask です。

　能面は、基本的には約 60 種、細かく分ければ約 250 種と言われています。それらは木製で、ひとつひとつ職人の手で彫られます。「鬼神・老人・男・女・霊」の五種類に大別されます。

狂言 ► Track 69

狂言

Kyogen is a type of short play performed in between Noh plays. Even though *kyogen* has always been associated with Noh, the style is very different. Most Noh plays are tragic, and include a lot of dance movements and poetic readings. On the other hand, *kyogen* plays have comical actions and dialogue.

tragic 悲劇の

狂言は、能の作品の合間に演じられます。能とセットでひとくくりにされることが多い狂言ですが、スタイルはかなり違います。ほとんどの能は舞や詩的な語りで演じられる悲劇です。一方、狂言はひょうきんな動きや会話で成り立っています。

狂言の舞台

Like Noh, *kyogen* has no stage sets and limited stage props. The people in the audience are expected to use their imagination as they follow the play.

能同様、狂言も大道具を使わずに限られた小道具で演じられます。観客は想像力を使いながら、物語を追っていきます。

文楽 ► Track 70

文楽

Bunraku is Japanese puppet theater. *Bunraku* puppet plays have been performed for over a thousand years, and the current style was developed in the 17th century. The performance style is a combination of narration, music and puppet manipulation.

puppet 人形

文楽は日本の人形劇です。1000 年以上前からありましたが、現在の形になったのは 17 世紀です。演技は語りと音楽、人形操作の組み合わせで成り立っています。

💠 人形の操作 USE

For important characters, three puppeteers control one puppet. The main puppeteer moves the puppet's head and right arm, the second one moves the left arm, and the third one moves both feet. Their teamwork makes the puppet's movements really lifelike. Less important characters are controlled by one puppeteer.

重要な役の人形は、ひとつの人形を3人の人形遣いが操作します。主となる人形遣いが人形の頭と右手を、2番手が左手を、そして3番手が両足を動かします。3人のチームワークで、人形が生きているかのような動きを作りだすのです。さほど重要ではない役の人形は、ひとりの人形遣いが操作します。

💠 人形遣い ≡

A *bunraku* puppet is between one-half and two-thirds of the size of a person. The puppeteers don't talk. Instead, a narrator called a *tayu* reads the characters' lines. Puppeteers wear black clothing from head to toe, with black hoods over their heads. In some cases the main puppeteers wear black kimono and show their faces.

lines
（ここでは）せりふ

文楽の人形は実際の人間の2分の1から3分の2の大きさです。人形遣いはまったくしゃべりません。大夫と呼ばれる語り手が人形の台詞を語ります。人形遣いは、ふつう頭からつま先まで黒い服を着て、頭には黒いずきんをかぶります。主となる人形遣いは黒い着物を着て顔を見せることもあります。

💠 文楽の内容 ≡ 📖

There are stories about all different types of people — princes and princesses, *Samurai*, farmers, and shop owners. There are also dance pieces. *Bunraku* was created and developed in Osaka, so most of the stories take place in or near Osaka. The narration is done with a strong Osaka accent.

文楽では、王子と王女、侍、農民、店主と、さまざまな人物の物語が繰り広げられます。舞踊の作品もあります。文楽は大阪で作られ発達したので、ほとんどの物語が大阪かその近隣を舞台にしています。語りは強い大阪なまりで語られます。

歌舞伎

▶ Track 70

歌舞伎

Kabuki is a traditional kind of theater that began in the 17th century. Noh and *kyogen* were entertainment for aristocrats and samurai, and kabuki was for commoners. Kabuki has elaborate stage sets, props, and costumes, and the actors wear heavy make-up. All kabuki actors are male, and they play both male and female characters.

commoner
庶民、庶民

elaborate
手の込んだ、入念な

歌舞伎は 17 世紀に誕生した伝統的な演劇です。能と狂言は貴族と侍のもの、歌舞伎は庶民のものでした。歌舞伎は手の込んだ大道具、小道具、衣装を使い、俳優は濃い化粧をします。歌舞伎俳優は全員男性で、男女両方の役を演じます。

歌舞伎の内容

Kabuki explores a wide variety of subjects and characters with stories of commoners, samurai and aristocrats. In recent years, kabuki dramas based on anime and video games have become popular. In all of these productions, the acting and dialogue are stylized rather than realistic.

stylized
様式化された

歌舞伎には多様な主題や登場人物があり、庶民から侍や貴族の話まで、いろいろな物語が繰り広げられます。近年では、アニメやゲームを題材とした作品も上演されるようになりました。どのような作品においても、演技や台詞まわしは写実的ではなく、とても様式化されています。

覚えておきましょう

大向う
（おおむこう）

歌舞伎には、後方席から声を掛ける「大向う：shouters」と呼ばれる観客が、常時数人います。芝居の進行中、俳優が各自持つ屋号（一門ごとのニックネームのようなもの）や、「待ってました！」といった声が掛けられます。初めて歌舞伎を観る人は、「誰が怒っているのだろう」と驚くかもしれません。しかし、大向うはいわば歌舞伎の応援団（cheerleaders）。客席からの掛け声で舞台を盛り上げるというのは、江戸時代から続いている習慣です。

歌舞伎の舞台

A standard kabuki stage is a flat rectangular space. There's a long, narrow passageway called a *hanamichi* at stage right. Most of the action takes place on the main stage, but the *hanamichi* is used a lot — for instance, characters often enter and exit from the *hanamichi*. Instrumental music and singing are added to the action on stage.

rectangular
長方形の

歌舞伎の舞台は長方形の平面です。舞台の右手には花道と呼ばれる細長い通路があります。ほとんどの演技はメインの舞台で行われますが、花道もよく使われます。登場人物はしばしば花道を使って登場したり退出したりします。器楽の演奏や歌が舞台上での演技に花を添えます。

女形の起源

The founder of kabuki was a woman, but women were later banned from kabuki. The government was not happy with actresses who also worked as prostitutes. For kabuki to survive, male actors started playing female roles. These actors were called *onnagata*, meaning female impersonators.

ban 禁止
prostitute
遊女
impersonator
扮装者

歌舞伎の創始者は女性でしたが、後に女性は歌舞伎から閉め出されてしまいました。政府（徳川幕府）が女優たちが遊女でもあるということに不満を抱いていたからです。歌舞伎の存続のため、男優が女性の役を演じるようになったのです。女性の役を演じる俳優は女形と呼ばれました。

マメ知識
歌舞伎にはメイクアップアーティストなる職業は存在しません。役者は皆自分で化粧をします。複雑なものでも、30分程で仕上げます。

▶ Track 71

落語

Rakugo is storytelling. It's performed by one person. The storyteller uses different tones of voice and gestures to portray different characters — small children, elderly people, geisha, samurai, thieves, ghosts, animals, etc.

thief/thieves
泥棒

落語は物語を語るものです。ひとりで演じます。演者は異なった声音や身振りで、幾人もの違った人物、例えば幼い子ども、老人、芸者、侍、泥棒、幽霊、動物などを演じ分けます。

落語の小道具 [USE]

The only props the storyteller uses are a small fan and a cotton towel. The closed fan can represent various objects — a pair of chopsticks or a pipe, for example. The folded towel can be anything flat, like a wallet or a notebook. So it's the combination of the storyteller's skill and the audience members' imagination that makes the performance funny and entertaining.

演者が使う小道具は、小さな扇と木綿の手拭いだけです。閉じたままの扇は、箸になったりキセルになったりと、いろいろなものを表します。たたんだ手拭いは平たいものなら何でも、例えば財布とか手帳といったものになります。演者の話術と観客の想像力が一緒になることで、落語はこっけいで面白いものになるのです。

Q&A

このような芸能はどこで見ることができるのですか？

Noh, *kyogen*, *bunraku*, kabuki and *rakugo* are performed regularly in major cities throughout the year. Most of the *bunraku* and kabuki theaters are equipped with devices called an "earphone guide," which explain the lyrics and the story lines to viewers. Some of the theaters provide the audio in English.

throughout the year
年間を通して

能、狂言、文楽、歌舞伎、落語は大きな都市では一年を通してに上演されています。ほとんどの文楽と歌舞伎の劇場には、歌の歌詞や物語の内容を解説してくれる「イヤホンガイド」が用意されています。英語のイヤホンガイドを用意している劇場もあります。

伝統芸能早わかり

文・平田久子

伝統芸能は難しいと決めつけずに、多少の知識を得ておきましょう。外国の方を案内する際、必要になるのかもしれません。

能楽

発祥は室町時代　物語は武将や公家を巡って展開　テーマは死別した親子や夫婦・恋人の情愛、敗戦の将の自責の念など　江戸時代になって徳川家康は各藩に能楽集団を抱えさせ、一定の地位以上の侍に能を学ばせた　新しく演出に工夫を凝らすことは NG なので、現在の演じ方は侍の時代からほとんど変わっていない

狂言

長く能楽公演において演目と演目の間に挟む形で上演されてきたが、近年では単独でも演じられる　所要時間 15 分程の作品が多く、長くても 40 分程度　登場人物は原則 2 ～ 4 人　内容は武家や庶民のそそっかしさや酒にまつわる失敗がメイン　コミカルな芸能とはいえ、誘うのはくすくす笑いであって爆笑ではない

歌舞伎

江戸時代の幕開けと共に誕生した庶民の娯楽　物語は侍世界を映す硬い内容とは限らず、庶民の喜怒哀楽といったものも含む　封建制度という世情のせいで、庶民の物語にも、家の面子を守るために犯罪を犯す、恋人同士が心中を遂げる、といった苦悩を表す作品が多い　既存の作品に新演出を加えることも、新作を上演することも自由

文楽　別名人形浄瑠璃

発祥は江戸時代中期の大阪　浄瑠璃（義太夫節）を語る太夫、三味線を弾く三味線奏者、人形操作を担う人形遣い、の三つの役割で構成　主要な登場人物を演じる人形は、一体を三人で操作する　言葉（歌詞・台詞）は関西弁　文楽のヒット作品は次々歌舞伎に輸出され、庶民文化大発展の起爆剤となった　既存の作品に新演出を加えることはしないが、新作は時折発表される

伝統芸能の世界は男尊女卑なのか？

文・平田久子

　伝統芸能と呼ばれる芸術は、男性のみによって熟成しました。そして現代でも男性のみが舞台に上がるとの決まりです（日本舞踊は例外）。それは諸外国の人々からみれば、「男尊女卑（male chauvinism）」と呼ばれてしまうのかもしれません。

　侍や貴族階級のものであった能と狂言は、明治維新以降は一般人にも開放されましたが、既存の形式を守ることを尊重しました。女性美を表現する際は、面や布地をまとうといった写実的ではない手法を用いていましたので、女性を取り込む必要はなく、取り込むことで既存の雰囲気が変わるというリスクを歓迎しませんでした。現在では女性の能楽師・狂言師が存在しますが、プロの舞台に登場するのは基本的に男性と限定されています。

■

　文楽の人形は重たいものゆえ、女性が人形遣いになるのは無理と言われています。男性と混ざって義太夫節を語るには男性と同質の声が求められますので、これもほぼ不可能です。義太夫節に限らず、男性だけで占められ発達して来た音楽は、声質が違うとの理由で、女性の舞台進出を敬遠しがちです。

■

　明治の近代化の時代、歌舞伎は女優を取り込みましたが、「歌舞伎は女形がいてこそ面白い」との世間の声に押され、女優は姿を消しました。女形の演技は男性が女っぽく動いてみせるといった単純な真似事ではなく、長い年月をかけ「男から見た理想の女性像」を追求し続けた結果の、「男にしか出せない女性的な魅力」という、芸術性の高い境地に達したものであったゆえ、そのような強い支持を得たのです。

■

　明らかに男性優位ではありますが、最近では女性の落語家が徐々に増えてきました。ひとりの演者が最初から最後まで語り続けるという形式の落語には、性別から生じる違いは問題とはなりにくく、比較的女性が進出しやすいのでしょう。

　伝統芸能は、女性を見下げているわけではありません。さまざまな要素や価値観が枷となり、極めて女性が参入しづらいというのが実情と言うべきでしょう。

第八章 ● 観光地

神社と寺の違いを説明できますか？宗教的なバックグラウンドについてももちろんですが、ほかにも建物としての特徴を外国人に説明してあげることができると、観光地巡りをしている外国人にとっては参考になるでしょう。

神社

本殿　p.255

Is this a house for *kami*?

お賽銭箱　p.255

Will you show me how to pray?

狛犬　p.255

Are these dogs or foxes? What are they for?

手水鉢　p.258

How do I purify myself?

鳥居　p.255

Does this gate have a special meaning?

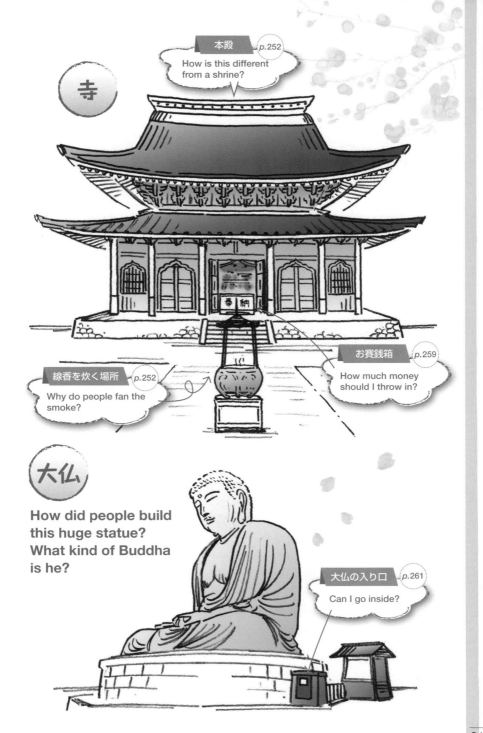

寺 ▶ Track 73

🔲 日本の宗教 ＝ 1₋2

Before you visit a shrine or temple, it's good to understand a little about religion in Japan. There are two main religions—Buddhism and Shinto. Followers of Buddhism worship at temples, and followers of Shinto worship at shrines.

Shinto
→ *p.253*

神社や寺を訪れる前に、日本の宗教について知っておきましょう。代表的な宗教はふたつあります。仏教と神道です。仏教の信者はお寺にお参りし、神道の信者は神社にお参りします。

🔲 仏教 ▽ ✎

Buddhism is one of the main religions in Japan. The Japanese word for Buddhism, *bukkyo*, literally means "the teachings of Buddha." Buddhism came to Japan from China and Korea in the 6th century. It coexists with the Shinto religion. Many Japanese customs are based on a combination of Buddhist and Shinto beliefs.

coexist
共存する

仏教は日本の代表的な宗教です。仏教という日本語は「仏の教え」という意味です。仏教は6世紀に中国や朝鮮を経由して日本に伝来しました。仏教は神道と共存しています。日本の習慣の多くは仏教と神道の信仰が混ざり合ったものに基づいています。

🔲 日本人と仏教 ＝ ？

It is said that about 80% of the population in Japan today is Buddhist. Actually, though, many Japanese don't consciously think about Buddhism very much. Maybe that's because it isn't so closely connected with our daily lives. Some people use the expression "funeral Buddhism," meaning that funerals are the only occasions when they take part in Buddhist rituals.

consciously
意識して、意識的に

今日、日本の人口の約80%が仏教徒だと言われています。しかし、仏教を意識している日本人は多くありません。仏教が私たちの日々の生活にさほど関係がないからでしょう。葬式のときだけ仏教を持ち出すので、「葬式仏教」などと言われることもあります。

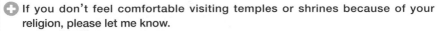

寺

A *tera* is a Buddhist temple. At a temple there are several buildings that contain statues of Buddha and other Buddhist gods and guardians. Many temples have gardens. It is said that there are more than 75,000 temples in Japan today.

guardian
守護神

「寺」とは仏教寺院のことです。仏教寺院には、ブッダや仏教のほかの神々、守護神の像を納めた建築物があります。多くの寺には庭があります。日本には現在、7万5000以上の寺があると言われています。

If you don't feel comfortable visiting temples or shrines because of your religion, please let me know.

もし宗教的な理由で、神社やお寺に行くことが居心地悪いようだったら教えてね。

浅草寺

Sensoji is a famous temple in Asakusa, Tokyo. There's a big gate with a huge red lantern in the middle. There's a long pedestrian street leading from the gate to Sensoji Temple. Along the way, there are many interesting souvenir shops and Japanese specialty food stands on both sides.

lantern
提灯

pedestrian street
歩行者用通路

stand
売店

浅草寺は東京の浅草にある有名なお寺です。入口には赤い巨大な提灯が大きな門につり下げられています。その門からお寺まで長い参道が続いています。道には面白いみやげもの屋や日本固有の食べ物の屋台が並んでいます。

浅草寺の雷門　　　© Katana - Fotolia.com

Would you like to try some sweets? I recommend *ningyoyaki* or *kaminariokoshi*.

お菓子を食べてみますか？　私のオススメは人形焼きか雷おこしです。

📷 金堂（本堂） ＝ USE

The main hall of a temple is called the *kondo* or *hondo*. It's a sacred place where monks recite Buddhist sutras. Buddhist statues are displayed in the main hall.

寺院のメインの建物は金堂もしくは本堂と呼ばれます。お坊さんがお経をあげたりする神聖な場で、そこには仏の像が飾られています。

monk
修道僧

recite
唱える

sutras
（仏教、ヒンドゥー教の）
経典

📷 線香を炊く ？ 1₋2

There may be a large bowl holding burning incense sticks in front of the *hondo*. You can light a new stick and place it in the bowl. Then you fan the smoke towards yourself. The smoke is believed to have healing powers.

healing power
治癒力

本堂へ進む途中、線香が燃やされている大きな鉢があるかもしれません。新しい線香に火をつけて鉢に置いてもかまいません。線香の煙には治癒力があると信じられています。

© heendup/iStockphoto

➕ Let's try fanning. I'll buy a bundle of incense. One bundle has 10 or 20 sticks, so we can share.

煙をかけてみましょう。線香をひと束買いますね。10本か20本くらい入っているので、シェアできますよ。

📷 線香の火の消し方 ？

When you light incense, you should put out the flame by waving your hand. This is because blowing air at the incense is believed to be the same as blowing air at Buddha. So the blowing action is considered rude.

put out
（明りや火を）消す

線香に火をつけたときは、炎を口で吹き消すことはせず、手であおいで消しましょう。線香を口で吹くのは、お釈迦様に息を吹きかけるのと同じであるという理由で、行儀が悪いと考えられています。

📷 三重塔・五重塔

Gojunoto and *sanjunoto* are tiered towers. They developed from traditional Indian buildings called stupa. *Go* means "five" and *san* means "three," so the names came from the number of roofs or stories. The towers store statues, too.

五重塔や三重塔とは層になった塔のことです。インドの stupa（仏舎利塔）から生まれたものです。Go は 5、san は 3 を意味し、階数や屋根の数を表しています。この塔にも仏像が納められています。

📷 鐘 USE

There's usually a building with a big bell hanging from the ceiling. It rings at a certain hour, so it tells you what time it is. On New Year's Eve, temple bells are rung 108 times.

通常、寺には大きな鐘が天井から吊り下げられた建物があります。お寺の鐘の音で時を知ることができます。大晦日には寺の鐘が 108 回鳴らされます。

© mikendo - Fotolia.com

tiered
段（層）になった

stupa
仏舎利塔

story
（建物の高さを表す）階

stupa（仏舎利塔）に由来する塔を正式には pagoda（仏塔）と言う。

108 回は煩悩の数を指す、1年間を指す、四苦八苦（4×9+8×9＝108）を指すなど、さまざまな説がある。

神社

▶ Track 74

📷 神道

Shinto is the ancient religion of Japan. The oldest document mentioning Shinto is from the 8th century. There are many stories about Shinto gods in ancient mythology, just as there are stories about gods in Greek mythology.

神道は日本の古代の宗教です。神道に触れた最古の書物は 8 世紀のものです。古代の神道の神々の物語がたくさん載っていて、ちょうどギリシャ神話のようです。

ancient
古代の

mythology
神話

Greek
ギリシャの

神道について書いてある最古の書物は『古事記』。

第八章 ● 観光地

253

📷 神社 ▣📖🌐

A *jinja* is a Shinto shrine. It is said that there are about 80,000 Shinto shrines in Japan. The size of shrines ranges from very big to very small. Shrines house *kami*, Shinto gods. The shrines are made of wood. Traditionally, a small or medium-sized forest is supposed to be planted next to a shrine – but of course, many shrines in big cities do not have a forest nearby.

神社は神道の聖堂のことです。日本には約 8 万の神社があると言われています。大きな神社もあれば、小さなものもあります。神社は、神道の神 (kami) が祭られています。神社には小さな、あるいは中くらいの森が隣接しているのが通例ですが、大都市には当然ながら近くに森のない神社も多数あります。

📷 代表的な神社 📖🌐

Two of the most famous shrines are Ise Jingu in Mie Prefecture, in the Kansai area, and Izumo Taisha in Shimane Prefecture, in the western part of Honshu. Meiji Jingu is the most famous shrine in Tokyo.

最も有名なふたつの神社は、関西地方の三重県にある伊勢神宮と、本州西部の島根県にある出雲大社です。明治神宮は東京でいちばん有名な神社です。

📷 神社での行事 📖🌐 USE

People visit shrines on holidays like New Year's, and on special days like *Setsubun* and *Shichigosan*. People often take their newborn babies to a shrine, and you can often catch glimpses of wedding ceremonies at shrines, too.

日本人は正月の休みや、節分、七五三といった特別の日に神社を訪れます。生まれたばかりの赤ちゃんを神社に連れていったりしますし、神社での結婚式もよく見かけます。

➕ Everyone can join the *Setsubun* event. It's on February 3rd. Do you want to go?
節分は誰でも参加できるイベントです。2 月 3 日です。行ってみたいですか？

鳥居

A *torii* is a gate at the entrance of a shrine. The gate symbolizes the starting or ending point of a sacred zone.

鳥居は神社の入り口にある門です。その門には「神聖な地域がここで始まる、あるいは終わる」という意味があります。

➕ Do you think the color of a *torii* is red? Technically, it's not red. It's a color called *shu-iro*—it's closer to orange.

鳥居の色は赤だと思いますか？　厳密には赤ではなく、オレンジに近い朱色と呼ばれる色です。

マメ知識

英語では朱色を bright red, Chinese red など と言います。

本殿

The *honden* is the most sacred building at a Shinto shrine. It's only for the *kami*, the god of the shrine*. The *kami* is usually symbolized by a mirror, a stone, a sword, or a piece of wood, not by a statue. You can stand in front of the *honden* and make an offering.

***the god of the shrine**
= enshrined *kami*
（神社の神）

make an offering
お賽銭をあげる、供物を捧げる

本殿は、神社の中で最も神聖な場所です。神だけの建物です。神は通常、鏡、石、剣、木切れといったもので象徴され、像はありません。本殿の前に立ってお賽銭をあげることができます。

狛犬

Komainu are statues of dog-like creatures called *shishi*. You will usually find two of them at the entrance of a shrine. They're guardian dogs. If the statues are foxes instead of dogs, the shrine is an "Inari shrine."

狛犬は獅子と呼ばれるイヌのような生き物の像です。神社の入り口で一対の狛犬を見ることができます。これは守護犬です。もしそれがキツネであれば、それは稲荷神社です。

© Kentaro Ogura - Fotolia.com

第八章 ● 観光地

➕ Have you ever been to Okinawa? You will find many statues that look like *komainu* in Okinawa. But actually they are not dogs or foxes; they are legendary creatures called *shisa*.

沖縄に行ったことはありますか？　沖縄で狛犬のような像をたくさん見かけると思います。ですが、それはイヌでもキツネでもない、シーサーと呼ばれる想像上の生き物です。

稲荷寿司

There is a legend that foxes love *aburaage*. Originally it was not *aburaage* – it was fried mice. In the old days, fried mice used to be offered at Inari shrines, but preparing mice is not easy. So at some point, people started to offer *aburaage* to the foxes instead of mice. That's why *aburaage* stuffed with rice is called *inarizushi*.

油揚げはキツネの好物だという話があります が、実際のところ、好物は油揚げではなくネズ ミです。昔は稲荷神社に油で揚げたネズミがお 供えされていましたが、ネズミを用意するのは 簡単なことではありません。そこでいつしか、ネ ズミの代わりに油揚げがお供えされるようにな りました。これが、油揚げにご飯をつめたお寿 司が稲荷寿司と呼ばれる理由です。

© やすどん - Fotolia.com

Q&A

 稲荷神社とは何ですか？

Inari shrines are a special type of shrine. They are dedicated to Inari, the god of grain. You can recognize them by their fox statues. Foxes are considered to be Inari's messengers. There are thousands of Inari shrines in Japan. The most famous is Fushimi Inari Shrine in Kyoto.

神社の種類にはほかに も、八幡神社、天神神 社、浅間神社などがあ る。

　稲荷神社は特殊な神社です。稲荷という穀物の神を奉納しています。キ ツネの像があるので見分けることができます。キツネは稲荷の使いと考え られています。日本には多数の稲荷神社があります。最も有名なものは京 都の伏見稲荷神社です。

お寺・神社の参拝の仕方

お寺と神社の参拝は、水で手や口を清め、それからお参りをします。まずは清めの手順を見てみましょう。

清めの基本

　参拝は、手水鉢の水で手と口を清めることから始めます。柄杓を右手で持って水を汲み、左手を清めます。柄杓を左手で持ち、同様に右手を清めます。再度柄杓を右手で持って水を汲み、左手のひらで水を受け、口をすすぎます。直接柄杓に口をつけてはいけません。身体を軽く折り曲げ、口の中の水をそっと手水鉢の脇の地面に吐き出します。もう一度左手を水で清めたら、柄杓を元の位置に戻します。

チャレンジ　清めの手順を説明してみましょう。

1　手を洗う　●柄杓を右手で持ち、左手を洗う。次に柄杓を左手で持ち、右手を洗う

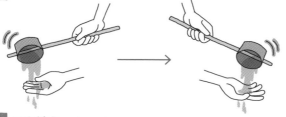

2　口を洗う　●柄杓を右手に持ち、左手で水を受け、口をすすぐ

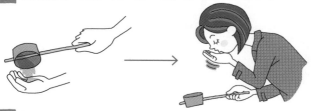

3　柄杓を戻す　●最後に左手をもう一度洗い、柄杓を元に戻す

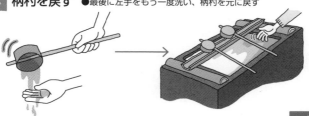

ヒント

basin
たらい、洗面器

ladle
柄杓

purification
清め

switch
交換する

rinse
流水で洗う

pour
注ぐ

palm
手のひら

spit out
吐き出す

回答例は次のページ

清めの仕方回答例　▶ Track 75

1 手を洗う USE 1,2

There's a large basin with ladles. First you pick up a ladle with your right hand. Then you fill it with water and rinse your left hand. Then switch hands and rinse your right hand.

手水鉢のところで、まず柄杓を右手で持ちます。それから水を汲み、左手を清めます。続いて柄杓を左手で持ち、同様に右手を清めます。

2 口を洗う USE 1,2

Hold the ladle with your right hand and pour a little water into your left palm. Then rinse your mouth with the water and spit it out on the ground. Never touch the ladle with your lips — it's considered very rude.

柄杓を右手で持って水を汲み、左手のひらで少しの水を受けます。それから口をすすぎ、水を地面に吐き出します。直接柄杓に口をつけることは無作法な行為と見なされるので、やってはいけません。

3 柄杓を戻す USE 1,2

Finally, hold the ladle with your right hand and rinse your left hand again. Put the ladle back the way it was found. That's the end of the purification ritual.

ritual
儀式

最後に、右手で柄杓を持ってふたたび左手を洗います。前にあったところへ柄杓を戻します。これで清めの儀式はおしまいです。

📷 お参りの方法 [1,2]

In front of the *honden*, you stand up straight, then put an offering of money into the *saisenbako* – the offering box. Then you take hold of the rope and ring the bell two or three times. Next, you straighten your posture again and bow twice. It is better to bow deeply and slowly. After that you put your hands together and clap twice, then pray*. Finally, you bow once again.

offering
賽銭、(神への)奉納

straighten
まっすぐにする

posture
姿勢

clap
手を叩く

*pray =
say a prayer
祈りを捧げる

本殿の前に立ち、まず背筋を伸ばします。それから賽銭箱に賽銭を入れます。縄をつかんで鈴を二三度鳴らします。次に、再度姿勢を正し、2回頭を下げます。深々とゆっくり頭を下げましょう。それから胸の前で手を合わせ二度拍手を打ち、祈りを捧げます。最後にもう一度お辞儀をします。

📷 神社とお寺の見分け方 🔍❌

Check for the *torii* gate. If there's a *torii*, it's a Shinto shrine, and if there's no *torii*, it's a Buddhist temple. Burning incense is only done at Buddhist temples.

鳥居を確認しましょう。鳥居があれば神道の神社ですし、なければ仏教の寺です。線香を炊くのは仏教の寺のみです。

☝ 覚えておきましょう

寺と神社でのお参りの仕方の違い

•寺
　神社との違い。お寺では手を叩かずに参拝します。最近では手を叩く参拝者を結構見かけますが、神仏や周囲に迷惑がかかる行為ではありませんので、とがめられることはありません。

•神社
　神社で黙祷する際は、手を下げたまま行います。手を合わせて祈祷する人が少なくありませんが、これは神式ではなく仏式の祈りのスタイルです。しかし、この間違いも神仏や周囲に迷惑がかかる行為ではありませんので、とがめられることはありません。

寺と神社に行く理由

To be honest, most Japanese people today are not really conscious about religion. Most people go to temples and shrines to experience a feeling of serenity rather than for religious purposes. Of course, we go to shrines for ceremonial occasions, too.

to be honest
正直なところ

conscious
意識している、自覚している

serenity
安らぎ、落ちつき

ceremonial occasions
冠婚葬祭

正直に言うと、現在では日本人の多くは宗教に対してそれほど関心を持っていません。お寺や神社へ行くのは宗教的な理由ではなく、安らぎを感じるためです。もちろん冠婚葬祭のために行くこともあります。

➕ You can buy *omikuji* at both temples and shrines. Do you want to give it a try? It's a lot of fun. It's a paper that tells your fortune. Fortunes are divided into several ranks, from very lucky to unlucky.
神社でも寺でもおみくじが買えます。やってみますか？　楽しいですよ。運命の書かれた紙で、大吉から凶までの間の運勢を教えてくれます。

Q&A

 お賽銭はいくら入れればいいの？

There are no rules about it. You can put in whatever amount you like. Even one yen is OK. Some people say it brings good luck if the amount of money has a sound-alike meaning. For example, "*goen*," which means five yen, can also mean "connection" in Japanese. And "*nijyu goen*," 25 yen, can also mean "double connection." So it's considered lucky to offer these amounts.

決まりはなく、いくらでもおのおの好きな額を入れます。1円でもＯＫです。字にすると意味を持つ額を入れると幸運が訪れるという人もいます。たとえば、5 yen の意味となる *goen* は connection（縁）の意味とも成り得ますし、25 yen は double connection（二重のご縁）と成り得ます。そこで、この金額はラッキーだと考えるのです。

大仏

▶ Track 76

 大仏

Daibutsu literally means "Big Buddha." There's no rule about how large a Buddha statue has to be in order to be called a Big Buddha. Some are standing and some are sitting. Two of the most famous *daibutsu* are the one in Kamakura and the one in Nara. The one in Kamakura is outdoors. The Big Buddha in Nara, in Todaiji temple, is indoors.

大仏は文字通りには「大きい仏様」です。どのくらいの大きさになると大仏と言えるかという点についての決まりはありません。座っているものもあれば立っているものもあります。有名なのは、鎌倉の大仏と奈良の大仏です。鎌倉の大仏は屋外にあり、奈良の東大寺の大仏は屋内にあります。

➕ Are there statues as big as *daibutsu* in your country?
あなたの国には、大仏のような大きな像はありますか？

Q&A

 昔の人々はなぜあのような大きな仏像を作ったのですか？
中はどうなっていますか？

Big Buddhas were built after disasters like epidemics, floods, and droughts, in order to bring people peace of mind. Anyone can go inside the Big Buddha in Kamakura. If you're curious, you should try it — it only costs 20 yen. There's nothing in there — just a dark space.

disaster
災疫

epidemic
流行病の発生

flood
洪水

drought
飢饉

curious
好奇心が強い

大仏は、疫病、洪水、干ばつといった災疫の後に、人々の心の平安のために建設されました。鎌倉の大仏は、誰でも体の中に入ることができます。もし興味があれば入ってみてはいかがでしょうか。入場料は 20 円です。中は空で、ただ暗い空間があるだけです。

仏像

The order of Buddhist images is, from the top to the bottom, *Nyorai*, *Bosatsu*, *Myo'o*, and *Tenbu*. The *Nyorai* and *Bosatsu* have the role of saving people's souls, the *Myo'o*, with his frightening appearance, is a wrathful deity who guides people to the right path, and the *Tenbu* is a bodyguard for the *Nyorai* and *Bosatsu*.

wrathful
激怒した、怒りに満ちた

deity
（多神教の）神

仏像には、上から順に如来、菩薩、明王、天部という序列があります。如来と菩薩は人々の魂を救うという役割を持ち、恐ろしい風貌の明王は人々を正しい道へ導くため叱咤する、天部は如来と菩薩のボディーガードをする、という役割を持っています。

▶ Track 77

温泉旅行

Onsen are hot springs. Going to an *onsen* is more than just taking a bath. It's like a vacation, because people usually spend the night at a hotel or traditional Japanese inn. At an inn, you can enjoy a great dinner with local specialties. The water in an *onsen* has minerals that are supposed to be healing.

温泉とは hot springs のことです。温泉はただお風呂につかるだけではありません。休暇のようなもので、たいがいホテルや伝統的な日本の旅館に泊まります。夕食はその土地のおいしい食材をぜいたくに楽しみます。ミネラルを含んだ温泉のお湯は体を癒してくれます。

 Where do you go for overnight trips in your home country?
あなたの国で 1 泊旅行に行くとしたら何をしますか？

温泉地 🔊❓

There are many *onsen,* or hot springs, in Japan, because there are many volcanoes. There are some famous *onsen* areas around Tokyo, including Hakone, Atami, Yugawara, Izu and Kinugawa. These areas have a lot of inns and hotels.

日本は火山が多いので、温泉も多くあります。東京近辺にも、箱根、熱海、湯河原、伊豆、鬼怒川など有名な温泉地があります。これらの地域には旅館やホテルがたくさんあります。

➕ **What hot springs would you like to go to in Japan?**
日本で行ってみたい温泉はありますか？

温泉の入り方 🔊 1,2

The best way is to copy what Japanese people do. Just remember not to run in the bath area, and don't leave anything in the washing area. Also, if you have long hair, you need to put it up before you go in the bath, to keep it out of the water.

いちばんいいのは、日本人の入浴の仕方をまねすることです。とりあえず、お風呂場で走り回ったり、洗い場にものを置きっぱなしにしないようにしましょう。髪の毛が長い人は、お湯の中に髪の毛が入らないように、湯舟に入る前にまとめて上げておきましょう。

➕ **Be careful not to stay in the bath too long!**
湯舟の中に長くつかりすぎないように気をつけましょう。

家族風呂 🟰📝

Kazokuburo literally means "family bath." It's separated from the public *onsen,* and you can use it only for your family or group. You should reserve it if you want to use it. Also, some guest rooms in hotels have private baths. They're more expensive than other rooms, but privacy is guaranteed.

guaranteed
約束される

文字通りには「家族の風呂」という意味です。公共用の温泉とは別になっていて、家族や少人数のグループのために使えます。家族風呂を使いたいのであれば、予約をしましょう。お風呂付きの部屋というものもあります。お風呂付きの部屋は、なしの部屋に比べて割高ですが、プライバシーが守られます。

露天風呂 (=)(USE)

A *rotenburo* is an outdoor *onsen* bath. Many *ryokan* have *rotenburo*. The women's and men's baths are separate. You can enjoy the scenery while relaxing in the bath. It is especially beautiful during the winter, as you're surrounded by snow.

露天風呂は屋外にある温泉風呂です。多くの旅館が露天風呂を備えています。男風呂と女風呂は分かれています。リラックスしながら景色を楽しむことができます。特に雪に囲まれる冬はとてもきれいです。

➕ Have you ever taken a bath surrounded by snow?
雪の中でお風呂に入ったことはありますか？

有名な場所

▶ Track 78

清水寺本堂と舞台 (=)

The balcony off the southern front of the temple's main hall was often used as a stage. Noh and *Gagaku* (ancient Japanese court music) performances were held here, and even today it is sometimes used for performing arts at important festivals.

© hit1912/stock.adobe.com

The stage is 13 meters high, equivalent to a four-story building. It was built without using a single nail. Many souvenir stores and restaurants surround *Kiyomizu-Dera*, which is always crowded with tourists.

souvenir
お土産

お寺の本堂南正面から迫り出したバルコニーを、舞台と呼びます。実際に能や雅楽が上演されていて、現在でも時折重要な祭事で芸能が奉納されます。舞台の高さは 13m、4 階建てのビルに相当します。釘を一本も使わない工法で建てられています。清水寺周辺にはたくさんのお土産物屋さんと飲食店が並んでいて、いつも大勢の観光客で賑わっています。

📷金閣

Although it is called *Kinkakuji*, the temple's official name is *Rokuonji*. The Golden Pavilion (the temple's annex) was constructed in the late 14th century, destroyed by fire, and rebuilt several times. The present structure was built in 1955. Visitors may only view it from the garden and are not allowed to enter.

annex
別館、分館

金閣寺の名称で通っていますが、実際のお寺の名前は鹿苑寺です。その鹿苑寺の別棟にあたる、金箔で覆われている建造物が金閣です。Golden Pavilion とも呼びます。14 世紀の終わりに建立されましたが、幾度か焼失と再建を繰り返しています。現存のものは 1955 年に建てられました。見学は庭から眺めるのみで、中に入ることはできません。

📷銀閣

The annex to *Jisho-ji* was constructed approximately 100 years after completion of the Golden Pavilion. Although it is called the Silver Pavilion, it has never been covered in silver. Its beauty resides in its refined simplicity, in contrast to the flashy splendor of the Golden Pavilion. Visitors may only view it from the garden and are not allowed to enter.

reside in
〜に存在する、属する

splendor
輝き、豪華さ

金閣建立の約 100 年後に建てられた、慈照寺の別棟です。Silver Temple · Silver Pavilion と呼ばれていますが、銀で覆われたことはありません。豪華絢爛な金閣とは対照的な、しっとりと落ち着いた雰囲気です。見学は庭から眺めるのみで、中に入ることはできません。

第八章 ● 観光地

📷道頓堀周辺

In the Edo period (1603-1867), *Dotonbori* was home to many theaters and was Osaka's version of New York's Broadway. Though there are now fewer theaters, *Dotonbori* has become a lively destination for visitors seeking delicious food and quality souvenirs. In addition, the Glico sign and moving crab sign attract sightseers searching for that perfect photo spot.

© Tupungato/stock.adobe.com

江戸時代、道頓堀には芝居小屋（劇場）がいくつもあり、大阪版ブロードウェイといったところでした。現在劇場の数はかなり減ってしまいましたが、ありとあらゆる美味しい食べ物とお土産物に出会える、大変賑やかな街になりました。グリコの大看板や動くカニの看板は、撮影スポットとして大人気です。

📷 大阪城 ⊟ 🈁 🔖

Osaka Castle, constructed in the late 16th century, was repeatedly burned down and rebuilt. The current castle tower was restored in 1931 using concrete. Fortunately, some of the original structure remains, including the Edo period gates. The castle grounds are mostly barrier-free, with elevators available for visitor convenience. Many of the information boards are written in Japanese, English, Chinese and Korean, to accommodate those from different countries.

16世紀末に建てられた大阪城は、その後幾度も焼失・再建を繰り返しました。現在の天守閣は1931年に建てられたコンクリート製ですが、いくつかの門など、江戸時代の建造物を見ることができます。全域ほぼバリアフリーで、エレベーターも設置されています。案内板の多くは、日本語英語中国語韓国語で表記されています。

📷 富士山 ⊟

Mt. Fuji is the most famous symbol of Japan. It's located in both Shizuoka Prefecture and Yamanashi Prefecture. It's 3,776 meters high — it's the highest mountain in Japan.

© k_river - Fotolia.com

富士山は最も有名な日本の象徴です。静岡県と山梨県にまたがっています。高さは3776メートルで、日本一高い山です。

📷 東京タワー ⊟ USE

Tokyo Tower is the second-tallest structure in Japan. The total height is about 333 meters. It is located in the heart of Tokyo. The tower was completed in 1958, and it is now used for broadcasting and tourism. Tokyo Tower is very pretty when it lights up at night. You should check it out!

© yongyuan/iStockphoto

broadcasting
放送

東京タワーは日本で2番目に高い建造物です。高さは約333メートルです。東京の中心にあります。1958年に建てられ、現在も電波配信を行なっており、観光スポットとしても知られています。夜ライトアップしているととてもきれいなんです。ぜひ行ってみてください！

Q&A

富士山に登るのはいつごろがオススメですか。
登るにはどうしたらいいですか？

The best season is July or August, because it's too cold and dangerous to climb at other times. Actually, facilities on the mountain are open only in summer. Most people want to see the sunrise from the summit, so there are huts along the way. You can go up to the fifth station by car or bus. The fifth station is about halfway up the mountain. From there to the top, you have to walk.

hut
山小屋

fifth station
5合目

　7月か8月がベストです。それ以外の時期の登山は寒く危険です。実際のところ、施設は夏の期間しか営業していません。ほとんどの登山客が山頂からの日の出を見たがるため、道には小屋が用意されています。5合目までは車かバスで行くことができます。5合目は山のほぼ中間の高さにあります。5合目から山頂までは、徒歩で登らなければなりません。

東京スカイツリー

　Tokyo SkyTree is the tallest structure in Japan. The total height is 634 meters. The tower was built to be this height because 634 can be pronounced in Japanese as *mu sa shi*, and Musashi is the old name of the area where the tower is located. Tokyo SkyTree is also used as a broadcast tower. When the weather is clear, you can see the entire Tokyo area and even Mt. Fuji!

© prasit chansarekorn/
iStockphoto

第八章 ● 観光地

　東京スカイツリーは、高さ634メートルの日本でいちばん高い建造物です。このタワーは634メートルで建てられました。634という数字は日本語でmu sa shi（武蔵）と発音することができ、これは東京スカイツリーが建てられている地域の古くからの名称なのです。東京スカイツリーも電波塔として使われています。天気が良い日には、東京全体を展望することができ、富士山も見ることができますよ！

What is the tallest building in your country?
あなたの国でいちばん高い建物は何ですか？

皇居

The *kokyo*, or Imperial Palace, is where the Emperor and Empress live. It's located in the middle of Tokyo. For many years the Imperial Family lived in Kyoto, until the capital was moved from Kyoto to Tokyo in the mid-19th century. The Imperial Family now lives in Tokyo.

the Imperial Family
皇族

皇居は天皇陛下と皇后陛下が住まわれている場所です。東京の真ん中にあります。19世紀半ばに首都が京都から東京へ移るまで、長い間皇族は京都に住んでいました。現在は皇族は東京に住まわれています。

➕ Do you jog? One circuit around the Imperial Palace is a very popular jogging course.
ジョギングはしますか？　皇居を一周するのはとても人気のあるジョギングコースです。

 皇居の広さ

The *kokyo* is huge! Including the grounds, it's 1,150,000 square meters in total — larger than Tokyo Disneyland and DisneySea combined. The site of the *kokyo* is where the castle of the Tokugawa Shogunate used to be.

site
敷地

Shogunate
幕府の将軍

皇居はとても広いです！　全敷地を合わせた面積は115万平方メートルもあり、東京ディズニーランドとディズニーシーを合わせたより広いのです。元は徳川将軍の城が建っていた敷地でした。

© show-m/stock.adobe.com

覚えておきましょう

　天皇陛下の名前は「徳仁（なるひと）」、秋篠宮殿下は「文仁（ふみひと）」です。通常日本にいる日本人は、「天皇陛下」と称号で呼ぶ習慣に慣れきっています。しかし外国では、「エンペラーナルヒト」と名前が表記されるのが普通です。外国人に天皇陛下の名前を尋ねられ、「思い出せません」では困りますね。「ナルヒトハイクツデスカ」と質問され、「それ誰？」では、「自国の象徴の名前を知らないなんて！」と仰天されてしまいます。女性皇族と違い、男性皇族の名前は忘れがちです。恥をかかないために、覚えておきましょう。

皇居付近の観光スポット

Many parts of the Imperial Palace are closed to the public, but people can visit the neighboring* parks — Higashigyoen, Kitanomaru, and Chidorigafuchi. In early April, the cherry blossoms there are absolutely beautiful. There are tours of the *kokyo* which take people to some of the closed areas, but you need to book in advance.

*neighboring = adjacent
（隣接した）

book in advance
事前に予約する

皇居の大部分は一般には非公開ですが、東御苑、北の丸、千鳥ヶ淵といった隣接の公園は公開されています。4月初めごろ、これらの公園では桜の花が見事です。非公開の部分も含めた皇居を巡るツアーがありますが、事前の予約が必要です。

➕ **If I went to your country, where would you recommend I visit?**
もし私があなたの国に行ったら、どこを尋ねるのがおすすめですか？

➕ **What is your favorite place in Japan?**
あなたの日本でお気に入りの場所はどこですか？

Q&A

 皇居の中に予約なしで入る方法はありますか？

Anyone can visit the Imperial Palace on January 2nd, for the New Year, and on the Emperor's birthday. The Imperial Family appears on the balcony of the palace and waves to the people outside. You can find the details on the Imperial Palace website.

正月の2日と天皇誕生日には、誰でも皇居に入ることができます。皇族方が宮殿のバルコニーに登場なさり、集まった人々に手を振られます。詳細は皇居のウェブサイトをチェックしましょう。

日光東照宮

Nikko Toshogu Shrine is one of the most famous shrines in Japan. It's located in Tochigi Prefecture. It was built in 1617. It was dedicated to Tokugawa Ieyasu, the first shogun of the Tokugawa Shogunate. Nikko Toshogu has a number of decorative wooden animal carvings. Most of them are said to be symbols of peace. One of the most famous carvings is the "three wise monkeys."

dedicate
〜を捧げる

decorative
装飾的な

carving
彫刻

three wise monkeys
三猿。「見ざる、聞かざる、言わざる」という3つの叡智を示している。

日光東照宮は日本で最も有名な神社のひとつで、栃木県にあります。1617年に建立されました。徳川幕府の初代将軍、徳川家康のために捧げられました。日光東照宮には装飾的な木彫りの動物の彫り物がたくさんあります。多くは平和の象徴だと言われています。中でも最も有名な彫り物が「三猿」です。

© mura/iStockphoto

➕ Nikko is one of the most popular places for Japanese school trips. Where did you go on a school trip when you were a student?

日光は日本の学校の修学旅行先として有名どころのひとつです。あなたは学生のころ、どこに修学旅行に行きましたか？

➕ The three wise monkeys are famous for their poses—"see no evil, hear no evil, speak no evil." The carving was inspired by a Buddhist teaching which says that people who do not hear, see or speak evil will be spared from evil themselves.

「三猿」は、「見ざる、聞かざる、言わざる」のポーズで有名です。これは、悪事を聞いたり、見たり、話したりしない人は悪事そのものから免れるという仏教の教えから来ています。

📷 富岡製糸場と絹産業遺産群 ⬜ 🔦 USE

Tomioka Silk Mill is the oldest modern silk reeling factory in Japan. It was completed in 1872. It was built to keep Japan competitive in silk production. Silk was Japan's biggest export at the time. The factory was founded with the help of the French, and it continued reeling silk for 115 years. It remained well cared for by the government, and became a World Heritage site in 2014.

silk reeling
製糸

competitive
競争の

富岡製糸場は 1872 年に建てられた、日本で最も古い近代的製糸工場です。当時の日本の最大の輸出産業であった製糸産業の競争力を支えるために建てられました。フランスから（技術的な）助言をもらいながら、115 年間も製糸を続けました。政府による手厚い援助により良好な状態で残っており、2014 年に世界遺産として登録されました。

📷 白川郷 (合掌造り) ⬜ 🔦 🎤

Shirakawago and Gokayama are villages in the Shogawa River Valley, which is in central Japan. They are famous for their traditional *gassho*-style farmhouses, which are made with thatched, sloped roofs to

© LeeYiuTung/iStockphoto

help shed heavy snow. This style of house is very rare, and an important part of Japanese culture. In fact, the villages became a UNESCO World Heritage Site in 1995.

thatched
(屋根の) ふきわら

shed
流す、はじく

第八章 ● 観光地

白川郷と五箇山は庄川流域にある村で、日本のほぼ中央に位置しています。この村は伝統的な造り（合掌造り）の農家が残っていることで有名です。合掌造りとは、茅葺でできた急勾配の屋根で、雪下ろしに適しています。この作りの家はとても珍しく、重要な日本文化です。集落は 1995 年にユネスコの世界遺産として登録されました。

➕ You can also visit a gassho-style house in Sankeien, which is a traditional park in Kanagawa Prefecture. You can go in the house and see the interior.

合掌造りの家は神奈川県にある三渓園という庭園でも見ることができます。中に入って、細部を見ることもできますよ。

📷 原爆ドーム

The Atomic Bomb Dome is a World Heritage site in Hiroshima. The original building was completed in 1915. After the atomic bombing of the city by the United States military in 1945, it was the only building still standing in the area directly under the explosion. The building is part of

© spotty205/stock.adobe.com

a larger complex called the Hiroshima Peace Memorial Park. The complex also contains museums and monuments related to the event.

原爆ドームは広島にある世界遺産です。1915年に建てられた建物で、1945年の米軍による原爆投下の後、爆心地に唯一現存している建物です。原爆ドームは、広島平和記念公園という大きな施設の一部で、ほかには博物館や記念碑も併設されています。

📷 琉球王国

tributary state
属国

invade
侵略する

annex
合併する

essentially
本質的には

The Ryukyu Kingdom ruled the Ryukyu Islands for hundreds of years. It was a tributary state of China. When the kingdom refused Toyotomi Hideyoshi's request for help in conquering Korea, Japan invaded the islands in 1609. After the invasion, they became a tributary state of both Japan and China. They were later annexed by the Japanese Empire, in 1879. Essentially, the islands now make up Okinawa Prefecture.

琉球王国は、数百年もの間琉球諸島を統治していた王国で、中国の属国でした。しかし、豊臣秀吉に要求された韓国征服の援助を拒否したことにより、1609年に日本に侵略されました。侵略後、日本と中国の属国となり、最終的に1879年に日本帝国に併合されました。現在は沖縄県となっています。

📷 首里城　焼失と今後

Shuri Castle, the royal palace of the Ryukyu Dynasty, was almost completely destroyed by fire during the Pacific War. It was reconstructed in 1992 and designated a UNESCO World Heritage site in 2000. In 2019, the main courtyard structures of the castle were again destroyed in a fire. It is currently being rebuilt with the goal of a 2026 completion. A temporary observation deck has been erected in the castle's plaza where visitors can watch the construction in progress.

首里城は、琉球王朝が建てた王城です。太平洋戦争時に大部分が焼けてしまった後、1992 年に復元されました。2000 年に世界遺産に登録されて以降、多くの観光客が訪れていましたが、19 年秋に起きた火災で再度焼失してしまいました。現在、2026 年の再建を目指して工事が進められています。城内の広場には仮設の見学デッキが設けられていて、工事の様子を見ることができます。

➕ If you have time, you should really visit Okinawa. You can experience another kind of Japanese atmosphere there. The musical culture of Okinawa is especially unique. The music really makes you feel like dancing.

もし時間があったら、ぜひ沖縄に行ってみてください。まったく別の日本を体験できるでしょう。特に沖縄の音楽文化は独特で踊りたくなるような感じです。

📷 北海道・東東北の縄文遺跡群の紹介

The Jomon Sites (in Hokkaido and the East Tohoku Region), which were designated in 2021 a UNESCO World Heritage Site, consist of 17 sites: six in Hokkaido, eight in Aomori Prefecture, two in Akita Prefecture, and one in Iwate Prefecture. The Jomon period (15,000 to 2,400 years ago), a time before rice cultivation and agriculture, consisted of hunting, fishing, and gathering to provide for its inhabitants' livelihood. The ruins include not only houses but a cemetery and ritual site, evidence of a spiritual society that revered nature and prayed to its ancestors.

2021 年に世界文化遺産に登録された北海道・東東北の縄文遺跡群は、北海道に 6 ヶ所、青森県に 8 ヶ所、秋田県に 2 ヶ所　岩手県に 1 ヶ所と、17 ヶ所で構成されています。縄文時代（15,000〜2,400 年前）とは、稲作農耕文化誕生以前で、人々は狩りをし、魚を取り、木の実などを採集して生活していた時代です。遺跡には、家だけでなく、墓地や祭事所の跡が残されています。自然を崇める、祖先に祈念する、といった精神性が存在した証です。

© spotty205/stock.adobe.com

奄美大島、徳之島、沖縄島北部、西表島

These areas, which were inscribed as World Natural Heritage sites in 2021, have organisms and ecosystems that differ from those on the mainland due to their geographical proximity to Taiwan and the Philippines. Many plants and animals are threatened with extinction. Getting to these islands takes time and effort, and during typhoon season, there is an increased risk of ship and plane cancellations.

西表島に生息する絶滅危惧種
イリオモテヤマネコ
© yudai/stock.adobe.com

2021年世界自然遺産に登録されたこれらの地域は、台湾やフィリピンにやや近いという地理的所以で、本土とは異なる生物や生態系を有しています。絶滅の恐れがある動植物も多く見られます。これらの島々へ行くには時間と手間がかかり、台風の時期は、船や飛行機の欠航のリスクが高まります。

百舌鳥・古市古墳群

The Mozu Furuichi Tumulus Group is a group of tombs of ancient powerful people built from the late 4th century to the early 6th century. The tombs vary in size from huge to much smaller. None of the tombs can be entered. The nearby Sakai City Museum exhibits replicas of valuable buried artifacts.

© TM/stock.adobe.com

百舌鳥古市古墳群は、四世紀後半から六世紀前半にかけてつくられた、古代の権力者たちの墓群です。巨大なものからうんと小ぶりのものまで、規模は大小様々です。どれも内部に入ることはできません。最寄りの堺市博物館には、貴重な埋蔵品のレプリカが展示されています。

築地場外市場 USE

The fish and produce market in Tsukiji has been relocated to Toyosu, but the area known as the "*jougai shijou*" is still alive and well, with many wholesale and retail food stores and restaurants. Like Toyosu, the stores open early and close by 3:00 at the latest. Tsukiji is within walking distance of Ginza and is always crowded with shoppers and tourists.

築地にあった魚や青果の市場は豊洲に移転しましたが、場外市場と呼ばれるエリアは今も変わらず健在で、卸向けや小売の食材店やレストランがたくさん並んでいます。豊洲同様、店々は早い時間に開き、遅くても3時には閉店してしまいます。築地は銀座から徒歩で行けるので、常時大勢の買い物客や観光客で賑わいます。

©moonrise/stock.adobe.com

日本の世界遺産

文・平田久子

　日本で最初に世界遺産の登録を得たのは、奈良の法隆寺です。1300年以上前に建てられたこの寺は、世界最古の木造建造物（the oldest wooden building in the world）として、国の内外で広く知られています。ほかにも、奈良の正倉院や京都の平等院（十円玉の裏に彫られている建造物）といった木造建築が1000年もしくはそれ以上無事に残されてきたという事実は、石造りの建築文化の人々には信じがたいことのようです。

　白川郷・五箇山の合掌造り集落は、現在でも人々が普通に暮らしています。何百年もの間雨風にさらされて来た合掌造りの家々では、30年から40年に一度、屋根が葺き替えられます。100人以上の男たちが急勾配の屋根に登り、4日間に渡って葺き替え作業を無報酬で行うこの習慣は、今も昔の形式通りに行われます。

　第二次世界大戦中、度重なる空襲によって、日本の大都市の多くは焦土と化しました。あっけなく焼け落ちた建造物の中には、世界遺産の認定を受ける価値があるものも含まれていたに違いありません。しかし、そのような状況の中、奈良や京都の神社仏閣が無傷で残されたのは、私たち日本人だけでなく、世界遺産を尊ぶ世界中の人々にとっても、誠に幸いなことでした。

　現在登録されている日本の世界遺産は、17の文化遺産と4の自然遺産です。

●**文化遺産（Cultural Heritage）**
法隆寺 Horyuji Temple
姫路城 Himeji Castle
古都京都 Ancient Kyoto
白川郷・五箇山の合掌造り集落
Shirakawago and Gokayama Gassho Farmhouses
原爆ドーム Atomic Bomb Dome
厳島神社 Itsukushima Shrine
古都奈良 Ancient Nara
日光 Nikko
琉球王国 Kingdom of Ryukyu
紀伊山地 Kii Mountains
石見銀山 Iwami Ginzan Silver Mine
平泉 Hiraizumi

富士山 Mount Fuji
富岡製糸場と絹産業遺産群 Tomioka Silk Mill and Related Sites
明治日本の産業革命遺産 Sites of Japan's Meiji Industrial Revolution
ル・コルビュジエの建築作品
The Architectural Work of Le Corbusier
長崎の教会群とキリスト教関連遺産
Hidden Christian Sites in the Nagasaki Region

●**自然遺産 (Natural Heritage)**
屋久島 Yakushima
白神山地 Shirakami Mountains
知床 Shiretoko
小笠原諸島 Ogasawara Islands

（2018年7月現在）

（注・リストの表記は日本語英語とも正式名称ではなく、簡略したもの）

おわりに

本書の制作にあたりたくさんの方々にご協力いただきました。
この場を借りてお礼を申し上げます。

【取材協力】
Debra Samuels （料理研究家、フードライター）
Richard Jones
Sonya Marshall
Rebecca Furcron
平田加代子

【アンケート協力】
インターカルト日本語学校
米山陽一
佐々木隼人

（アンケートに回答いただいた生徒の方々）
张 梦
尹 鸿元
金 アルム
王 晓睿
王 文傑
曽 文莉
成 在恩
鄭 牙源
曽 麦多
唐 晓琦
王 雨涵
林 詩佳
俞 之光
ZOLOTUKHINA DARIA
ASCHWANDEN CHRISTOPH
TEE LOO KEONG
LAPLACE MARIANNE ANDREE GENEVIEVE
AYE THEINGI KYAW
GLADYSHEV FEDOR
VOLKOVA EVGENIYA
JACLYN NGAN YI LING

英語にない日本語を伝えるための 9 つのテクニック

増補改訂第 2 版

英語で語るニッポン

2012 年 8 月 10 日　第 1 版第 1 刷　発行
2018 年 8 月 10 日　増補改訂版第 1 刷　発行
2023 年 3 月 10 日　増補改訂第 2 版第 1 刷　発行

コスモピア編集部 編

執筆・取材協力／平田久子

編集協力／田中和也、藤森智世

校正／王身代晴樹、Sonya Marshall、Christopher Belton、Ian Martin、
　　　Daniel L Fishman、Neil Debnam
ナレーション／Jeff Manning、Julia Yamakov
DTP／朝日メディアインターナショナル株式会社

装丁・デザイン／松本田鶴子
本文イラスト／あべゆきこ、中村知史
写真／iStockphoto、fotolia、ゆんフリー写真素材集（https://www.yunphoto.net）、武田宗典、伊東俊介、KENTA AMINAKA、Richard Jones、平田久子、stock.adobe.com

発行人／坂本由子
発行所／コスモピア株式会社
〒 151-0053　東京都渋谷区代々木 4-36-4　MC ビル 2F
営業部　TEL: 03-5302-8378　email: mas@cosmopier.com
編集部　TEL: 03-5302-8379　email: editorial@cosmopier.com
https://www.cosmopier.com　https://www.kikuyomu.com
https://www.cosmopier.net　https://e-st.cosmopier.com

印刷・製本／シナノ印刷株式会社
音声編集／安西一明
録音／株式会社メディアスタイリスト

© 2023 CosmoPier Publishing Company, Inc

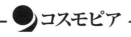

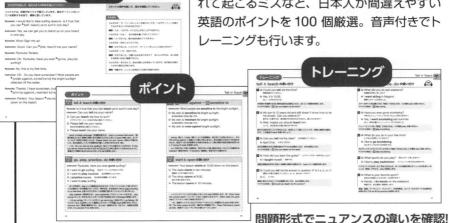